Battered Women's Protective Strategies

Battered Women's Protective Strategies

Stronger Than You Know

SHERRY HAMBY

OXFORD
UNIVERSITY PRESS

Oxford University Press is a department of the University of Oxford.
It furthers the University's objective of excellence in research, scholarship,
and education by publishing worldwide.

Oxford   New York
Auckland   Cape Town   Dar es Salaam   Hong Kong   Karachi
Kuala Lumpur   Madrid   Melbourne   Mexico City   Nairobi
New Delhi   Shanghai   Taipei   Toronto

With offices in
Argentina   Austria   Brazil   Chile   Czech Republic   France   Greece
Guatemala   Hungary   Italy   Japan   Poland   Portugal   Singapore
South Korea   Switzerland   Thailand   Turkey   Ukraine   Vietnam

Oxford is a registered trademark of Oxford University Press
in the UK and certain other countries.

Published in the United States of America by
Oxford University Press
198 Madison Avenue, New York, NY 10016

Library of Congress Cataloging-in-Publication Data
Hamby, Sherry L.
Battered women's protective strategies : stronger than you know /
Sherry Hamby.
pages cm.—(Interpersonal violence series)
Includes bibliographical references and index.
ISBN 978-0-19-987365-4 (alk. paper)
1. Abused women—United States.   2. Abused women—Services
for—United States.   3. Family violence—United States.   I. Title.
HV6626.2.H358 2014
362.82'920973—dc23
2013012788

1 3 5 7 9 8 6 4 2
Printed in the United States of America
on acid-free paper

This book is dedicated to the memory of Eleanor Roehrig. When I think of dedication I think of her, simultaneously one of the gentlest and strongest advocates I have ever known.

CONTENTS

ACKNOWLEDGEMENTS

Perhaps the best part of writing a book is the opportunity it creates to acknowledge all the people who have helped me. First I would like to honor the many front-line advocates I have had the pleasure to know personally. I have learned much from them and I never cease to amaze at the incredible energy and perseverance they bring to this difficult work. I will not be able to name them all, but I would like to particularly mention Cheryl Bushman, Suzanne Darrell, Robert Heflin, Wanda Jackson, Gerry Johnson, Betsy Massey, Fernando Mederos, Michelle Myers, Bobbi Outten, Vern Phillips, and Rose Thompson. I'd like to thank the Ni' Jho'shnii' ("I will help you") advocates from the San Carlos Apache Reservation in Arizona, the Sortir Ensemble et Se Respecter ("Dating with respect") NGO founded in Lausanne, Switzerland, and the Family Wellness Warriors Initiative at the Southcentral Foundation in Anchorage, Alaska. The time I spent with all of you means a great deal to me.

I am very appreciative of Jeffrey Edleson and Claire Renzetti, the editors of this Oxford series on Interpersonal Violence. It was their suggestion that a brief I prepared might become a full-length book. The original brief, developed with input from Andrea Bible, was prepared for VAWnet, the national online resource center on violence against women. I am honored by their support and encouragement. They were a delight to work with throughout the process. I also would like to thank the editorial team at Oxford University Press: Dana Bliss, Agnes Bannigan, Nicholas Liu, Michelle Shu, and the four anonymous reviewers of an earlier draft of the manuscript. The final product is stronger because of their input and careful work.

I owe an especial debt of thanks to Melissa Hurd, who not only read and copyedited an earlier draft of the manuscript in record time but provided invaluable feedback and a fresh perspective. Melissa, you really came through. Thanks also go to the students who assisted me with the literature review: Janie Mejias (especially), Katie DeLucas, Katherine Meyer, Meredith McLean, Deihlia Nye, Galina Podolsky, Aaron Salisbury, and Hayley White. I would also like to thank the students who assisted with coding: Yooson Esther Chi, Sarah Clark, Lauren Croasdaile, and Elisabeth Wharton. Sarah especially was very helpful in thinking about how to use the results of the first VIGOR study to revise the instrument. My other research seminar students, Caroline Dashiell, Elly Ferrell, Cathy Lambert, Laura Logan, Johanna McManus, Caitlin McNaughton, and Matney Rolfe, also helped revise the VIGOR, especially doing a terrific job reading it for language that suggested the tool is only for low-income women, which I hope to have avoided. I would also like to thank the faculty of the Department of Psychology at the University of the South for their collegiality and support. The University of the South also supported the VIGOR studies described in this book with two grants from their University Research and Faculty Development Grant program and I am very appreciative of their support, both tangible and intangible.

I am a much better researcher and scholar than I would have been without the close collaborative relationships that I have been privileged to enjoy over the years. I would particularly like to thank Victoria Banyard, Jacqueline De Puy, David Finkelhor, Bernadette Gray-Little, John Grych, Liza Little, Milling Kinard, Kelly Shaver, David Sugarman, Murray Straus, Heather Turner, and Jean Wilkins. I would also like to thank the longtime staff of the Family Research Laboratory and Crimes Against Children Research Center, who provide all kinds of support, much of it well beyond their official duties: Doreen Cole, Kelly Foster, Toby Ball, and Kaushalia Tailor. I also want to thank those who have been very supportive of me and my work over the years, especially Tammy Russell. For commiserating about mixing writing and academia, thanks to Molly McCaffrey and David Bell. To my sister, Cindy Spruill, for sharing the journey.

To my husband, Al Bardi: Thank you for supporting me while I wrote this book and in so much else. To my children, Lynnaya Bardi Hamby and Julian Hamby Bardi: You mean more to me than I can say. Thanks for our warm family life that inspires me to do this work.

ABOUT THE AUTHOR

Sherry Hamby is Research Professor of Psychology and Director of the Life Paths Research Program at the University of the South.She is also founding editor of the American Psychological Association journal Psychology of Violence. A licensed clinical psychologist, she has worked for more than 20 years on the problem of violence, including front-line crisis intervention for domestic and other violence, involvement in grassroots domestic violence organizations, therapy with trauma survivors, and research on many forms of violence. She is co-investigator on the National Survey of Children's Exposure to Violence, which is the U.S's primary surveillance of youth victimization and the first national effort to measure crimes against children under 12 that are not reported to authorities. She conducted the first reservation-based study of domestic violence among American Indians and collaborated on Sortir Ensemble et Se Respecter, the first Swiss dating violence prevention program. She is a member of the Board of Scientific Counselors at the CDC's National Center for Injury Prevention and Control and was selected in 2013 as a "Woman Making an Impact on Children's Exposure to Violence" by the Safe Start National Resource Center, among other recognitions. She is author or co-author of more than 100 works including *The Web of Violence: Exploring Connections among Different Forms of Interpersonal Violence and Abuse* and *The Conflict Tactics Scales Handbook*. She lives in Tennessee with her husband and two children.

Battered Women's Protective Strategies

Introduction: A Re-Framing of Stereotypes of Battered Women

About 2 years ago during a conference, I ended up at a lunch table next to a woman who works in a victim assistance program in a southern state. Her state, like many, runs victim assistance programs to help all types of crime victims recover from crime. One service they provide is assistance with the costs of repairs for victims of property crime such as household burglary or vandalism. This woman specifically handled cases involving domestic violence. She offered the following example, "So if a batterer kicks the door down of his ex-partner, then we can pay for the cost of the repair to the door." Brief pause. "As long as she has not reunited with him." I asked her why that was a requirement to receive help. She looked mystified. I asked her if there were any relationship status requirements for assisting other crime victims. "No." Did other crime victims get interviewed about the better choices they could be making? Better neighborhood? Better locks? Why can't a woman get help without having to pass some sort of test? She looked—if I was not misreading her expression—astounded and a little annoyed. To her credit, there did seem to be some conflict registered on her face as she pondered, apparently for the first time, why it made sense to treat battered women differently from *every other category of crime victim*. The moment passed, however, and she insisted the situation for battered women was "different" without making any further attempt to specify how.

Assuming that woman is out there somewhere, I would like to say that I understand the powerful indoctrination into the dominant deficit-focused paradigm for victims of domestic violence. As I describe later in this chapter and elsewhere in the book, for many years the dominant deficit-focused paradigm influenced my own work in this field. I spent many years attempting to master this paradigm, not question it. It seemed clear that this young woman had never encountered a contrary viewpoint to the one that she had heard her entire professional life, which is that battered women deserve help only if they do what professionals tell them to do.

It is well known that many victims of domestic violence do not follow the conventional advice of the advocacy community. They do not call the police. They do not go to shelters, or if they do go to shelters, they leave "early" and return to their batterers. The conventional wisdom says that this is an indication that there is something wrong with these women. It is the thesis of this book that there is something wrong with this deficit-focused paradigm. According to conventional wisdom, battered women are typically helpless, passive, and in denial, and it is up to people like me—psychologists, advocates, and other human service providers—to help them do what they cannot or will not do for themselves. It took me a long time to realize it, but all the survivors of violence who I have encountered in emergency rooms, in shelters, in my life, and in the pages of strengths-based scholarship have taught me something important and under-recognized: Battered women are stronger than you know.

Battered women protect themselves in many ways. The stereotypes of battered women as passive and in denial are based on a mistakenly narrow view of battered women's lives. Many people, both professionals and the general public alike, assume that battered women's protective efforts should focus on the risk of further violence. This perspective is limited, however, because the threat of further violence is only one threat created by battering. Battering threatens many domains of a woman's life: her financial well-being, the stability and well-being of her children, her social status and her risk of being stigmatized, her psychological well-being and sense of self-worth, and her hopes and dreams for her future. The threats to these domains can be even greater than the threats of physical injury or pain. Not every woman is alike. Because of cultural, social, and economic differences, among others, these complexities play out differently for different women (Garfield, 2005; Goodmark, 2012). To understand women's protective responses requires a holistic view of their lives.

Victims respond to violence with a variety of protective strategies, but it is important to remember that victims are never responsible for the battering perpetrated against them. Batterers are responsible for their own violence and responsible for controlling their own aggressive impulses, no matter what stresses or frustrations they may face. People must cope with negative events, however, regardless of the cause, including not only accidents and natural disasters but also other people's bad behavior. Likewise, women respond to battering and the numerous threats posed by battering, including but not limited to the threat of bodily harm. Unfortunately, women cannot always protect themselves from all harms simultaneously or even spread harm reduction equally across threatened domains. Rather, acts that protect against one harm can exacerbate others. In particular, the unintended consequences of leaving, especially leaving abruptly in an emergency context, are underacknowledged by many scholars and advocates (for exceptions, see Davies, 2008; Goodman & Epstein, 2008). Escaping the violence as soon as possible may seem like an obvious choice. Reality, however, can be much more complex. Because of the risks of separation violence and a host of other factors, fleeing on an emergency basis does not always represent good coping.

Unfortunately, the focus on crisis responses to domestic violence and the organization of many domestic violence services around emergency shelter has made it difficult to recognize all of the ways in which battered women protect themselves and their loved ones. The goal of this book is to broaden the definition of *what* women are trying to protect and *how* they go about trying to protect it. Although many of these protective strategies are known to advocates and have been previously documented, there is still a gap between women's lived realities and the public stereotypes about battered women and the menu of services offered to support them (Goodmark, 2012). I hope that this book will be a further step in expanding perceptions of battered women and the services offered to women who cope with violence in the home. Although these issues also can apply to battered men, the stereotypes, services, and research are largely focused on battered women. Although some men are battered, most victims of battering are women (Fox & Zawitz, 2010; Hamby, Finkelhor, Turner, & Ormrod, 2011; Truman, 2011) and they are the focus of this book (*see* Chapter 3 for more discussion of gender and violence).

WHEN PARADIGMS BECOME BLINDERS

I am a clinical psychologist and I am also a scientist. I believe in the power of science and that the world is a better place because of the scientific method. One of scientists' most important activities is noticing when a paradigm is not fitting all observations. The deficit-focused paradigm that has created a stereotype of all (or virtually all) battered women as passive and in denial does not accurately describe many battered women. An alternative to this deficit-focused paradigm is offered—one that focuses on women's protective strategies and takes a holistic approach to understanding women's lives. Battered women are making a careful calculus and considering the myriad factors that ought to go into any decision to make a major life change. They are not "compromised," to use the word of an indignant listener responding to a presentation (Hamby & Clark, 2011) about victimized women having "strengths," "options," and "ideas." Battered women are in difficult, stressful, and sometimes frightening situations and doing their best to figure out how to deal with them.

I have made a concerted effort to find as much data as possible to document battered women's protective efforts. Science requires accurate description of phenomena. However, survivor's strengths are greatly understudied. In 2012, a search in PsycInfo, the major reference database for psychologists, produces more than 40,000 results for publications including the terms "domestic violence," "partner violence" or "battering" (and variants). Searching just for "domestic violence" alone produces more than half a million hits in Google Scholar, an even larger database of scholarly materials. Yet, for some protective strategies in this book, I have struggled to find more than one or two data sources. By looking only for evidence that confirms stereotypes and fits within the bounds of the dominant deficit-focused paradigm, we have missed the opportunity to tell another story about survivors of domestic violence. Despite the relative inattention to battered women's protective efforts, I do believe that momentum is building for a positive re-framing of women who have experienced battering. A number of scholars have made important contributions to this re-framing, including Jill Davies, Ed Gondolf, Lisa Goodman, and Beth Richie (Davies, Lyon, & Monti-Catania, 1998; Gondolf & Fisher, 1988; Goodman & Epstein, 2008; Richie, 1996). Many authors cited in this book have helped raise awareness of battered women's efforts to protect themselves and their loved ones. By creating a framework for understanding protective strategies, identifying the full range of risks these strategies are designed to counter, and gathering evidence of battered women's protective strategies, I hope to add to this momentum.

As a clinical psychologist—and a person—I understand that there are many, many aspects of life and of relationships that are barely touched on by the methods of contemporary social science. I have tried to bring that insight to bear on the points in this book as well. I have tried to relate existing data to the real-world concerns of victims, advocates, and other front-line professionals. I have wrestled with the challenges of bringing these two sources of knowledge together. My goal is to offer both informed and nuanced insights about the lives of those who have experienced domestic violence. I am certain that there is room for improvement in the result, but I hope that at least some of what appears here will be useful to others.

It has taken me a long time to come to the views I present here and a long time to learn to approach the research literature with a strengths-based focus. I was trained in the dominant domestic violence paradigm and I was at one time immersed in it.

Thinking back now, I realize that disconfirming evidence was apparent from my first experiences in the field of domestic violence, but it took me a long time to realize this. The first time I went to a battered women's shelter was as a research assistant, when I was a student. Most of my work on the project involved administering questionnaires to a "control" group of women who had not experienced violence. Surprisingly, the control group was the hardest to recruit, because it turned out that approximately three-fourths of the community women had a history of domestic violence, although few considered themselves to be victims because of mostly minor incidents that occurred long ago (Drown, 1986). We were expecting sharp lines between "victims" and "nonvictims," because the paradigm says battered women are unlike other people. Rather, we found a continuum.

In the years following, I spent many hours, including some in the wee hours of the morning in an emergency room, counseling battered women with the standard safety planning and standard advice. I recommended leaving. I predicted that other options were not viable and that there was little, if any, hope the batterer would change. I used the commonly available tools for dangerousness assessment and safety planning. I told more than a few that they were in danger for their lives, in part because I gave insufficient consideration to the very high rates of false-positives in dangerousness assessment tools (more on that in Chapter 2). I seldom looked beyond the violence to make a more comprehensive and nuanced assessment of risk.

Back in those days, when I was doing a lot of crisis counseling with battered women, I did not have children myself. Now I have two: a daughter and a son (12 and 9 years old, respectively, at the time of this writing). My perspective has changed dramatically since having children of my own. Back then, there were numerous instances when I called every shelter within a 200-mile radius and found none that had room for children or would take adolescent sons. It was even hard to find a shelter who would take a boy older than age 6 years because the boys were perceived to be potential threats to other residents. In my experience, shelters are completely inflexible about these rules, regardless of the situation or the particular boys in question. So—and it is difficult to admit—I would suggest to women that they leave without their children. Often I would suggest first that perhaps the children could stay with the woman's mother or even her mother-in-law, although the practicality of that seldom worked out. Some women do not have the sort of parents or in-laws who are suitable to leave children with. Perhaps even more importantly, these women knew that even if they did manage to drop their children off with relatives, most relatives would have little personal and no legal recourse if the perpetrator showed up at the doorstep to claim them. In reality, these steps are no more protection than leaving children with the perpetrator.

I suggested just that plenty of times too. I can still picture some of their faces, morphing from disbelief to guardedness in a flash. They were unfailingly polite, almost all of them. "Thank you for the suggestion, but I don't think that would work out." That response did not deter me. I felt it was my duty to press for "safety"—their safety. I would encourage them to re-think, assure them that it would just be temporary. By "temporary" I usually meant no more than the 30 to 60 days one might be able to stay in a shelter until something else could be worked out. A couple of times regarding adolescent boys I even raised the possibility of a homeless shelter as an alternative living arrangement. The mother and her female children could go to the shelter for battered women while her teenage boys stayed in the closest homeless shelter. This plan would get everyone away from the batterer. No one ever took me up on that, perhaps recognizing better than I did that exposing a teen to a stay in a homeless shelter could be dangerous and traumatizing. There was also the suggestion to let the children stay with their father. They were already living with him anyway, so in that respect it would not really be different, and often they were not a target of violence themselves, or so I told many women—and myself.

As a mother now, the main thing that impresses me about all of those encounters is the unfailing politeness. I wish someone had been less polite and spelled out the limitations of these plans. I look at my son and I can hardly conceive of being away from him for 60 days, much less leaving him for 2 *months* or with people I do not know or trust. I have never done that and I hope I never have to. I would gladly give up my own personal safety if I thought it would minimize the chances that my son or daughter would be left undefended with a dangerous person, and so would all of the mothers I know. I have made this statement at a number of conferences and there is always widespread nodding and murmurs of agreement among the other mothers in the room. It is my view now that it ought to be illegal for any federally or state-funded service agency, including any shelter that gets any public money, to refuse to serve minor children. A solution that does not involve looking after the children is no solution at all. The foster care solution, so widespread now in some jurisdictions for families in which domestic violence has occurred, also has far more adverse consequences for children than are generally acknowledged—adverse consequences above and beyond those created by the initial disadvantage leading to placement (Viner & Taylor, 2005). I do not like to endorse identity politics, but there is almost nothing about helping battered mothers that I do not view differently now that I have children of my own. There are many other lessons I have learned from battered women—lessons about realistic timelines for starting over and lessons about the possibility of achieving change from within a relationship. It took a long time, but I finally recognized that the standard paradigm needs a critical examination.

LOOKING BEYOND "WHY DO WOMEN STAY?"

The question "Why do women stay?" still drives a lot of the discourse around battered women (for recent examples, *see* Kim & Gray, 2008; Koepsell, Kernic, & Holt, 2006; Lacey, 2010), and practitioners, researchers, and the media still often focus on the perceived deficits of victimized women. This arises from a narrow definition of the problem and unfortunately contributes to a victim-blaming orientation. A person is not inherently a "victim" (Leisenring, 2011). This is not some essential quality of a person; victimhood is a socially negotiated status. At any given time, virtually every so-called "battered woman" could also be described with multiple other identity labels, not only family-related identities such as mother, daughter, and wife but also other social identities such as employee, volunteer, or athlete. There are also the personal identities associated with their residence (New Yorker, Southerner, Londoner), their religion, their sexual orientation, their race, and other characteristics. These different identities, each with different degrees of privilege and oppression, intersect in ways that affect women's responses to violence (Crenshaw, 1991). When we call someone a "victim," we are singling out that aspect of their life and centralizing it. To understand women's decisions, including their decisions to remain in or terminate a relationship, requires recognizing the other aspects of their lives.

THE NEGATIVE FILTER IN SERVICES
FOR BATTERED WOMEN

More than 40 years after domestic violence began to be widely recognized as a social problem, providers and advocates of all types still routinely apply treatment plans that amount to little more than "You should leave right now." I have seen women pressured and even berated in the emergency room at 3:00 A.M., bleeding and bruised, asked to not just figure out what to do that very night and cope with the emergency but to make a long-term commitment to stay at the shelter "for the whole program" and decide then and there "that they are never going back." I have a personal policy of avoiding major life decisions at 3:00 in the morning, to say nothing of making them while bleeding. No one else in the emergency room is being asked to make major life changes. The man in the next bed hacking up his lungs from 50 years of smoking is not being belittled because he will not commit to quitting cold turkey then and there. Diabetics receiving emergency insulin are not threatened with lack of further medical care if they do not stop eating cake. Moreover, these people are directly contributing to their medical condition—presuming that no one is making them smoke or deviate from their recommended diet.

THE NEGATIVE FILTER IN RESEARCH
ON BATTERED WOMEN

The deficit-focused paradigm permeates the research literature, too. There are numerous ways that battered women are disparaged in the research literature. It is so common that an entire book could be written on that topic. A few are highlighted here to help flesh out how the dominant deficit-focused paradigm manifests in contemporary research. The research field still has a way to progress.

Name-calling and insults in the published "scholarship" on battered women. Although we might like to think that scholarship on victimized women no longer includes openly disparaging comments such as labeling victimized women "compliant zombies" (Mills, 1985) and "Downtrodden Dorothy" (Gayford, 1976), this still occurs. Authors have described battered women with phrases such as "intentional game players" (MacEachen, 2003). MacEachen (2003) even suggested that women with a history of child sexual abuse often "provoke rape and battery in order to satisfy [their] needs..." (p. 127). Battered women are said to have "masochistic self-states" (Stein, 2012). The learned helplessness model compares women to shocked, caged dogs (Walker, 1979, 1984, 1993). Similar models also rely on conceptualizations of victimized women's cognitions and behaviors as distorted, irrational, and pathological (Dutton, 1995; Graham, Rawlings, & Rigsby, 1994). A psychiatric diagnosis was invented specifically for battered women (Walker, 1984, 1993), again suggesting that there is something unique about battering even in relation to other traumatic, life-threatening events. It is suggested that their problem is insufficient motivation to change in a burgeoning literature on the "stages of change" (Burke, Mahoney, Gielen, McDonnell, & O'Campo, 2009; Burkitt & Larkin, 2008; Chang et al., 2010). In a recent critique of the positive psychology literature, battered women are used multiple times as exemplars of people for whom forgiveness and other normally positive thoughts and gestures should be viewed negatively and discouraged (McNulty & Fincham, 2012). The stubborn persistence of negative and even disparaging attitudes and the implicit professional acceptance of them as indicated by their publication in peer-reviewed journals and scholarly books are telling evidence of the adverse effects of the dominant paradigm about battered women. It is wrong to talk about other human beings this way. It would even be wrong to talk about perpetrators this way, but it is especially unfathomable to talk about victims of violence this way.

The problem with "stages of change" applied to victimized women. One example, important because research in this area appears to be increasing, is the problematic application of motivational theory to battered women. It is far from clear that it is appropriate or helpful to extend the transtheoretical model (TTM) to victimizations. The TTM model, including its best known component, the stages of change, was developed for addictions, particularly smoking cessation (Prochaska & DiClemente, 1983). The five stages begin with *precontemplation*, which is characterized by denial and reluctance to make changes and move progressively until individuals get to seriously addressing a problem over the long term, called *maintenance*. Although the stages of change have been used for many problematic behaviors, it is questionable whether the model is appropriate for coping with *someone else's* behavior. Addictions are very different from the situations faced by victims of violence. Presumably there is no one threatening the smoker or the alcoholic with bodily harm or financial ruin if they do not take another smoke or drink. Some researchers gloss over the distinction between being unmotivated and unable to change, but there is a world of difference between those circumstances. The "decisional balance" between the pros and cons of responses to victimization are seldom a matter of motivation; these decisions frequently involve avoiding even greater personal danger, homelessness, and threats to loved ones. Given the long and unfortunate history of attributing women's victimization to their own masochism, there surely can be no reason to use a model associated with addictions.

This is all the more true given that TTM is, at best, modestly effective for smoking, substance abuse, diabetes management, and other conditions for which it has been studied extensively (Sutton, 2001; West, 2005). TTM has been the focus of several very cogent critiques that raise serious questions about whether it is a helpful model even for individuals' own problematic behaviors (Adams & White, 2005; Riemsma et al., 2003; Sutton, 2001; West, 2005). Further, studies that applied this model to victimized women nonetheless found considerable evidence for protective strategies. For example, one study found women in all "stages" were engaging in active pro-safety behaviors, which is especially impressive given that more than three in four said they needed help with housing, food, and other basic needs (Burke, et al., 2009). There is little evidence that motivational issues are primary in coping with victimization, and given the lack of evidence, it is more important to avoid needlessly victim-blaming or personality-based approaches to working with victimized women.

Should battered women forgive? A more nuanced approach to character traits, as recently recommended in a critique of positive psychology (McNulty & Fincham, 2012), would doubtless be good for the field of psychology. The question of whether battered women are in some wholly unique circumstance that makes positive characteristics especially problematic for them is, not, however, an accurate reflection of common life experiences. These authors have suggested: "Rather than thinking and behaving so charitably, such women [those experiencing domestic violence] may benefit from (a) attributing their partner's abuse to his dispositional qualities rather than external sources, (b) expecting the abuse to continue, (c) not forgiving the abuse, (d) remembering the abuse, and (e) being less committed to the relationship. In other words, so-called positive processes can sometimes be harmful for well-being, whereas processes thought to be negative can sometimes be beneficial for well-being. Of course, most people do not face severe interpersonal abuse, leaving it possible that these and other so-called positive psychological processes are beneficial for most people." (McNulty & Fincham, 2012, p. 102)

Experiencing interpersonal violence, however, is actually a very common experience across the lifespan. Estimates suggest more than one in three women will experience domestic violence, rape, or stalking by an intimate partner (Black et al., 2011). More broadly, the National Survey of Children's Exposure to Violence shows that 1 in 10 children experience injurious violence *every year* and 1 in 3 have experienced injurious violence by late adolescence (Finkelhor, Turner, Ormrod, & Hamby, 2009). In these cases, too, most perpetrators are known to the victim; many are family members. It is simply not true that severe interpersonal violence is rare. Would that it were so.

Setting some parameters for what should be forgiven and when is certainly a good idea, but their analysis seems to suggest that forgiveness (and also kindness, optimism, and other positive traits) are only good ideas when confronting minor or acute problems. Surely the suggestion that there is no role for forgiveness or other character strengths when dealing with serious problems or chronic stressors cannot be accurate. At the very least, it is a substantial departure from ethical principles that have been in place for centuries. Far more extreme violence than battering has been forgiven, and this is often perceived as one of the highest expressions of human goodness. For example, one well-known story of forgiveness is the Truth and Reconciliation Commission (TRC) in South Africa, which was designed to help the people of South Africa forgive after the horrors of apartheid and to work to reintegrate perpetrators and victims alike into a single society (Tutu, 1999). Tutu and Mandela have been honored around the world for what is often recognized as an extraordinary achievement. A more plausible alternative hypothesis is that serious problems and the character strengths we use when coping with serious problems are complex processes that are not well captured with group differences on simple self-report measures. Qualitative research has shown that forgiveness can be an important part of the healing process for some victimized women (Yick, 2008). A more nuanced approach is needed in more quantitative research too (*see* Chapter 13 for further discussion about research directions).

When trying hard is bad. Surprisingly, some authors have suggested that using multiple means of coping with the complex problem of intimate partner violence might be maladaptive. As one main premise of this book is that multiple protective strategies are good, this view is worth examining. Women's coping should not be called maladaptive without evidence that their coping strategies are inappropriate to their individual situations, just as forgiveness should not be deemed inappropriate without considering the particulars of a given situation. One study compared abused to nonabused women without specifying the nature or severity of the nonabused women's problems. One important alternative hypothesis is that domestic violence is more complex than many life problems, and thus it should not be surprising that abused women had higher scores than nonabused women for most coping strategies. One would think that more coping efforts would be perceived as good. However, these authors conclude that every type of coping that was more common by victimized women was an inappropriate response to domestic violence. Confrontive coping "may place a woman at risk for more abuse" (Mitchell et al., 2006, p. 1514). Distancing "does little to empower the woman to gain more control in the relationship" (p. 1515). But self-control is not good either, because "women may experience more abuse and not have a support system because she relied solely on herself" (p. 1515). Accepting responsibility will "evoke negative thoughts about themselves" (p. 1515). But escape avoidance can lead to feeling a "loss of control" and even illicit drug use (p. 1515). One could just as easily present these findings in a positive light and conclude that high rates of most coping strategies indicate that victimized women are mobilizing more resources to address the complex problem of domestic violence. These authors are correct that multiple strategies are the norm. Without the negative filter of the dominant paradigm, this would be seen as a good thing.

Understanding what we know and don't know. As these few examples suggest, there is a lot we do not know about coping with domestic violence. Existing research has by far the most to say on strategies women use to protect themselves and their children against physical violence, to the extent that data on pro-active, protective behaviors are offered at all. The lack of research on other strategies by no means implies they are less frequent or less important —just less studied. In some cases the strengths-based framework used in this book leads to a different interpretation of data than that offered by the original authors. Behaviors that are sometimes interpreted as dysfunctional or passive may be protective of other goals or needs. For example, as discussed in more detail on Chapter 8, choosing not to disclose abuse is often deemed to be denial or some other cognitive distortion. Concealing abuse or other strategies to dis-identify with victimization, however, can just as easily be seen as impression management strategies that are efforts to minimize the social stigma of being publicly identified as a victim or to minimize the shame that would come to the family for revealing a family secret. Such impression management strategies are common among those with potentially concealable stigmatizing conditions (Goffman, 1963; Herek & Capitanio, 1996).

A STRENGTHS-BASED APPROACH TO UNDERSTANDING AND WORKING WITH BATTERED WOMEN

It is easy to critique research and practice in the social sciences. There is no such thing as a perfect study or a perfect intervention. Thus, I have tried to limit my critique of the existing deficit-focused paradigm to the essentials that are needed to understand how a focus on protective strategies is different. My main goal is to develop a viable alternative to this paradigm that improves on deficit-focused views of battered women. I also hope to describe a strengths-focused paradigm in such a way that it will also be relevant for the many victimized women who do not seek services and for friends and family members who are trying to support them. I have drawn from my experience not only conducting research and providing services in the area of domestic violence but also my broader experience with all types of violence and other health and mental health problems. Chapter 2 describes the framework for a strengths-focused paradigm.

A FEW COMMENTS ABOUT TERMINOLOGY

Terminology is an important element of science, intervention, and policy (Dragiewicz, 2011; Hamby & Grych, 2013). I would like to offer a few thoughts about the terms

I have used. In the domestic violence advocacy field, people who focus on strengths often use the word "survivor." I use this word too, but it is not the only term I use for several reasons. In my experience, "survivor" is an insider word. Some feminists and advocates use it, but few others do. "Survivor" is meant to be more positive and empowering, but it is also more distancing—it dilutes the reference to the violence. Also, "survivor" is almost exclusively applied to women who have left their batterers, and I do not want to imply that "surviving" only applies to women who leave. Finally, "survivor" is not much of an improvement over "victim." As I discuss in detail later in the book, all of these terms make violence a person's "master status" (in Goffman's terminology) and I do not think experiencing a victimization is the most important feature of anyone. I also want to acknowledge that there are other important characteristics of "batterers" as well as "victims." None of us should be defined solely by the worst incidents in our lives. Personally, I like "women who have been victimized" or "women who have experienced domestic violence," similarly to the way that "AIDS patient" was redefined to "person with AIDS" by the gay community in the 1980s. Put the person first and their experience or condition second. So I have used those phrases some, but they are lengthy and I have stopped short of creating an acronym like PWA, again because that seems like inside baseball and I am not sure it ends up being more humanizing than the alternatives.

Creating endless new terms for the same phenomena is an obstacle to communication and an obstacle to science, as John Grych and I have written elsewhere (Hamby & Grych, 2013). The field of domestic violence (or intimate partner violence or spouse abuse or wife-beating or woman abuse.....) is particularly problematic in this regard. As Dragiewicz has pointed out (2011), no term is perfect. My subject is violence and I need reasonably brief, effective ways to refer to the people who have become embroiled in violence. Some colleagues have recently helped me understand these issues better. They let me know that their organization has a policy of always referring to "Alaska Native people," never just "Alaska Natives." In the majority culture, we refer to "American Indians" or "Latinos" far more than we say "Whites" or even "European Americans." It is a subtle but effective way of conveying race privilege. I realized, looking at an earlier draft of this book, that sometimes I referred to "female victims" and subordinated their gender to their victimization status. I have chosen to reverse this, even recognizing that some individuals may not identify as "women" or may reject binary definitions of gender (for a similar approach, see Bible, 2011). Thus, "victimized women" and "battered women" are the main phrases I use, because these are brief phrases that make "women" the primary characteristic and use terms for their experience of violence that will be familiar to a wide audience. I hope the result is a balanced approach.

CHALLENGES TO RECOGNIZING BATTERED WOMEN'S PROTECTIVE STRATEGIES

Any paradigm shift faces institutional pressures to maintain the status quo. Although there are many such pressures, a few of particular note are described here.

The need to look in the mirror. This book is intended to prompt people to examine the "usual standard of care," as they say in medicine, and give that standard a critical re-evaluation, even when that means reflecting critically on one's own work in the field.

I know from my own experience looking back on my work that this can be uncomfortable. A few colleagues, after either reading an earlier draft of this book or hearing a presentation I have made on these topics, have responded with varying levels of dismay that I am questioning some of the conventional wisdom about domestic violence. It is easy to use a phrase such as "conventional wisdom"—a distancing phrase that does not really connote that many people spend a great deal of their lives and devote considerable resources to learning the conventional wisdom. Their social status in their profession and in their communities has been tied to their use of standard practices. This is true for me, and it has not been easy to choose to write about it. I can hardly be surprised when people's initial reactions are insistence that these women are impaired and that their years of viewing them and treating them as impaired do not need re-evaluating. I do not doubt people's good intentions in their past work with victimized women.

I honor the courage and the sacrifices of many advocates, researchers, and other professionals who work with victimized women. However, research and intervention skills should never be seen as completed accomplishments (Hamby & Grych, 2013). Knowledge is a constantly moving target. Any advocate, scholar, or provider who has not recently re-assessed what they are doing and why they are doing it is not performing best practices. Science is about change and progress. We know much more about violence and the ways people cope with violence than we did when domestic violence first came to widespread attention in the 1970s. No one uses computers from the 1970s, and most people would be horrified to find their hospital was not offering the latest surgical techniques and the most up-to-date medications. We value the first computers, the first antibiotics, and many other conceptual and technological firsts for the role they played in getting us to the capabilities we have today. In this way, I hope to honor the early approaches to addressing domestic violence, including the shelter movement and the first efforts to create dangerousness assessments and safety planning, while at the same time suggesting possibilities for improving them.

The horror story approach. Similarly to other efforts to ameliorate social problems that rely heavily on charitable contributions and other uneven sources of revenue, the battered women's advocacy movement is strongly invested in depicting the problem as an ongoing crisis (Hamby & Gray-Little, 2007). Although a crisis mentality is typical of the approach to many social problems, it does have costs (Wang, 1992, 1998). One cost is the suppression of good news. It is rare to hear a story about a man who hit his partner, but the couple worked on the problem and he learned to control his angry impulses, although treatment outcome studies indicate this can occur (O'Leary, Heyman, & Neidig, 1999; Stith & McCollum, 2011) and numerous anecdotal reports indicate men can learn to be nonviolent. Indeed, in the latter case, some of these men go on to become advocates for nonviolence (Paymar, 2000). Although I recognize that the crisis mentality has political benefits, it also has costs. People can tire of efforts to address a problem that never seems to get better. Alternatives need to be explored. Making progress on a problem and having effective solutions can also be arguments for continued financial support. For example, the Centers for Disease Control has recently started a "winnable battles" campaign for many public health problems (http://www.cdc.gov/winnablebattles/). Domestic violence can be a winnable battle. Otherwise we risk eventually burning out and discouraging people from allocating dollars for the important problem of domestic violence.

A lightly trained workforce. I know many advocates who I consider heroes. Their bravery and their stamina are truly awe-inspiring. Many of them are born "natural helpers" who have acquired formidable gifts in being an authentic advisor and guide from their own life experience. At conferences, congressional hearings, and other national venues, it is largely those advocates who are present. The reality is, however, that services for battered women are so woefully underfunded that most advocacy positions are filled by paraprofessionals who often have as little as 1 week of training before being thrust in the field. Salaries are so low that many advocates have no background or education in counseling or health care at all. Many are also young and in their first jobs. Turnover among advocates and volunteers is often high (Logan, Stevenson, Evans, & Leukefeld, 2004), and many of them serve as the lone advocate on-call during nights, weekends, or holidays, despite having little experience.

The result is that there are many advocates out there who understand little about the counseling role and the challenges that role entails. Knowing how to recognize and control your own emotional response to the occasionally frustrating actions of clients is a difficult but essential clinical skill that does not get mastered (or often even covered) in a 40-hour training session. With specific regard to recognizing protective strategies, one main tenet of feminist therapy is that you should not place yourself above the client. As Laura Brown has stated, "What is inherent in feminist therapy is the radical notion that silenced voices of marginalized people are considered to be the sources of greatest wisdom" (Brown, 2010, p. 2). Looking down on your clients as passive or "compromised" is not a therapeutic position.

"White savior syndrome" (helping those seemingly less fortunate to elevate your own self-esteem) is a similar phenomenon that is observed across the charitable world but is never a good thing (Cammarota, 2011). These are not problems with individual advocates. These are systemic problems. Advocates need more training and agencies need more staff. The chronic underfunding of this important public health issue is a major obstacle to progress. Regarding the need for a strengths-based approach, a lightly trained workforce is problematic because brief trainings cannot possibly present everything that is needed to understand the full context of women's lives and the full range of their coping strategies. Brief trainings can only present the most minimal information on local resources and policies, dangerousness assessment, and safety planning without a thorough and contextualized approach to understanding women's lives.

Serious psychological difficulties of some victimized women. I recognize that there are some battered women with serious mental health issues. Psychological problems, even serious psychological problems, are not that rare, and in any sufficiently large group of people, some will have experienced clinical levels of psychological distress. There are literally millions of battered and formerly battered women, and any group this large will always include people with the most serious psychological problems, including psychotic disorders such as schizophrenia and bipolar disorder, major developmental problems including autism spectrum disorders and mental retardation, and personality disorders. As is well documented, many of these victimized women also suffer from symptoms of post-traumatic stress. However, the women with the greatest psychological difficulties should not be used as exemplars for the whole group. It is unscientific to pick the most psychologically impaired victimized women to represent the whole group of people who have sustained violence in a close relationship. We do not use the lowest functioning members of a group to represent those who have been through other extreme events. We manage to recognize that many soldiers need help for post-traumatic stress without painting all soldiers as helpless. We acknowledge that many survivors of 9/11 or Hurricane Katrina wrestle with enormous losses incurred during those tragedies without suggesting they are weak or passive. It is not logical to paint a group that numbers in the millions with a single brush of denial and passivity and helplessness. Many women exhibit extraordinary strength and resilience when confronted with a violent partner. All battered women, including those with the greatest psychological difficulties, could benefit if we better understood how these resilient women dealt with their victimization.

A strengths-based approach can help with these and other issues by providing a fresh take on the problem of battered women and guidance on what changes need to be made. The advantages of a strengths-based approach that focuses on protective strategies outweigh the disadvantages. The field has stagnated somewhat, and in recent years there have been relatively few innovations in services or research, but a shift to a strengths-based approach suggests numerous possibilities for positive change. It is my hope that the material highlighted in this book can serve as a foundation for future progress.

THE LAYOUT OF THE BOOK

Chapter 2, A Holistic Approach, will make the case for taking a broader view of coping strategies as well as risks. It proposes a holistic coping framework using a process known as multiple-criteria decision making. In many ways, battering is similar to a wide array of other bad things that can happen, and one disservice to battered women is treating domestic violence as a problem that is somehow completely unlike any other. However, like many bad events, ranging from relationship-specific ones such as serial infidelity to other adverse events including conventional crime, the best way to deal with the situation often involves multiple strategies. Further, these strategies might differ quite substantially from one person to the next, depending on the broader context in which each person finds herself. A framework for approaching complex problems and the multiple risks they present leads to recognizing more protective actions.

Although the book will primarily focus on the coping efforts of women in violent relationships, understanding coping requires appreciating all of the challenges victimized women face. Chapters 3, 4, and 5 present the full risk picture. As with protective strategies, it has taken a long time for professionals to realize that it is not just about the violence. Although financial dependence has probably received the most attention of these, there are many others, and comprehensive overviews are hard to find. The risks will be broken down into five broad types: (1) what batterers do to keep victimized women from leaving; (2) money and other financial problems that make it hard to cope; (3) institutional obstacles to leaving violent relationships; (4) social and practical problems that interfere with coping; and (5) personal values that complicate women's choices. Focusing on batterer behavior can raise questions about gender differences, and I make a few points about gender differences in violence in Chapter 3. Some risks disproportionately affect members of politically disadvantaged groups or those with unique needs. Women whose race, ethnic identity, sexual orientation, or country of origin places them in the minority in their current communities often encounter unique risks not faced by more privileged women. Women with physical disabilities and whose age is not that of the typical victim stereotype—too old or too young—also often have trouble getting useful help. These issues are also addressed in the material on risks.

Chapters 6 through 11 each focus on protective strategies, organized into broad general categories shown in Figure 1.1. Chapter 6 describes immediate situational strategies. Protective strategies can begin as soon as the violence is initiated. Examples include many types of self-defensive moves, including fleeing the house, calling for help, and luring the perpetrator away from rooms with guns and knives. Chapter 7 focuses on protecting children, family, friends, and pets. As shown in Chapter 3, many batterers' most serious threats are aimed at children and other loved ones, not at their partners. Many women prioritize protecting their children or other loved ones and take numerous steps to make sure they are not harmed. The topic of Chapter 8 is reaching out for social support and managing the challenges of the risks of stigma when disclosing negative information about oneself. Chapter 9 discusses the importance of spiritual and religious resources in many women's coping strategies. One of the great disservices of much coping literature is defining prayer as a "passive" (poor) response. Although most social services are appropriately secular, sometimes this secularity comes at a cost of failing to recognize the importance of faith and spirituality to many people—all the more so as they deal with personal crises. This chapter will reframe prayer and other expressions of spirituality as positive coping. Chapter 10 addresses the use of formal services, including legal remedies and services, such as shelters, specifically designed for people who have sustained domestic violence. Chapter 10 also includes the use of traditional health, mental health, and social services. Many women overcome the stigma of help-seeking and financial obstacles to access many health, mental health, and legal services when coping with violence. This will be another opportunity to reframe common perceptions, because sometimes it is assumed that all victimized women should seek formal services and that those who do not are acting

Figure 1.1. The Array of Battered Women's Protective Strategies.

passively or are in denial. Compared to many problems, however, rates of help-seeking among victimized women are similar or higher. Chapter 11 describes "invisible" protective strategies. Research can be a surprisingly conservative enterprise, and despite more than 40 years of scholarship on domestic violence, there are many ways that women cope with violence for which we have little data. For example, saving money is an important step that opens the door to many other coping options, but we know little about it. Other aspects of coping, such as heterogeneity in approaches to coping, have also received little attention. This chapter will encourage providers, support networks, and victimized women themselves to think creatively about both coming up with such strategies and recognizing them when they do occur.

Although the book's primary emphasis will be raising awareness of all the myriad self-protective strategies in which most women engage to cope with the complex risks posed by domestic violence, this framework has important implications for risk assessment, safety planning, and other interventions for battered women. This is addressed in Chapter 12. The form of many of these interventions has changed little in more than 20 years. Beyond recognizing the many protective strategies, this volume will suggest some new directions to take to put together a balanced portfolio of safety planning steps that are woman-centered and cover multiple risks. Finally, Chapter 13, the conclusion, provides a few final thoughts on battered women's protective strategies. The conclusion will summarize the arguments for a reframing of the way that professionals who deal with violence and the general public view battered women. Several suggestions for systemic reform are also presented. Some of the material discussed here boils down to whether you see the proverbial glass as half-empty or half-full. This is an unabashedly half-full book. We will not question why every single woman does not go to the police or seek shelter—rather we will marvel that significant numbers of women do seek such services, often in the face of formidable odds and less-than-ideal service responses. I hope to illuminate the enduring strengths of women who have experienced violence.

A Holistic Approach to the Complex Problem of Battering

The Mohawks of Akwesasne have a reservation near the U.S.-Canadian border on the St. Lawrence River. The remote location and hydroelectric power provided by the river have unfortunately made this area attractive to industry. As a result, the tribe is located near several large manufacturing plants that process large amounts of aluminum and other metals (Arquette et al., 2002). According to local scientists, these plants have for many years produced byproducts that have contaminated much of the land and ground water in a widespread area, including reservation land and the surrounding region, which includes parts of upstate New York and the provinces of Ontario and Québec in Canada.

Mary Arquette and her colleagues tell an insightful story about an outsider, non-Indian, majority-culture toxicologist who came to the reservation and commended an audience of tribal members for the decline in their consumption of native fish, animals, and herbs (Arquette et al., 2002). From this person's dualistic, non-Indian perspective on the problem, the logic was simple: No local foods = No toxin exposure = No adverse health effects. The members of the Mohawk community saw the situation very differently, however. They saw the losses of traditional hunting and fishing practices that were an integral part of their culture. They saw the loss of traditional medicines that play an important role in both physical and spiritual healing.

Mohawk community members also did not see anything so wonderful about the modern majority-culture American diet. The contemporary American diet is high in fat and calories and low in vitamins and nutrients. Many Mohawk people have indeed adopted this diet and this dietary shift has been accompanied by a seemingly endless cascade of adverse health effects including diabetes, heart disease, stroke, high blood pressure, and obesity, many of which are now at epidemic proportions in the Mohawk and many other North American communities, native and non-native alike (Arquette et al., 2002).

This story exemplifies the importance of a holistic understanding of any problem and provides an analogy for the problem of battering. Few problems exist in isolation. Making a change in one area will almost inevitably affect other areas, including many areas that are equally or even more important. This is true about the problem of battering. For the problem of battering, it is important to understand that it simply does not work—that it is impossible—to focus only on the issue of physical danger, out of context from the rest of a woman's life circumstances. Women's lives cannot be taken apart like a machine and only apparently "faulty" elements replaced. Simplistic formulations might hold some appeal but do not represent complex realities. No relationship ≠ no violence. No relationship ≠ no adverse consequences. A woman's relationship with her partner is typically woven into every aspect of her life, from her childrearing to her living situation to her budget to her work circumstances to her relationships with family, friends, and the community in which they reside. Although women, victims and nonvictims alike, can and do make changes in these relationships all the time, they do so in consideration of all the rippling effects such changes will have throughout their lives and those of their children and other loved ones.

COPING WITH VIOLENCE IS LIKE COPING WITH ANY SERIOUS PROBLEM

One disservice to battered women is treating violence as a problem that is somehow completely unlike any other. Although this may not seem particularly damaging in and of itself, it opens the door to negative portrayals of victimized women as being particularly helpless or passive. In many ways, battering is similar to a wide array of other bad things that can happen. Battering shares many features with other major relationship problems such as serial infidelity and involvement with a partner with an addiction to drugs or gambling. In all of these cases, the key problem is with the partner's behavior. It is because of the intimate relationship that another person's problem resonates through the relationship and the family. Battering also shares features with natural disasters that often have effects that permeate across multiple life domains. Battering shares features with the environmental contamination created by industrialization. Battering shares features with institutional and societal oppression, including racism and sexism, and the ways that prejudice creates chronic stresses and imposes limits that also have long-term adverse consequences for health and well-being. It shares features with conventional crime and the way that a mugging or a burglary can cause acute and unpredictable harm. The best way to deal with almost all adverse situations involves multiple strategies. For most adverse situations, the standard recommendations are to be planful and calm. I am not sure how fleeing in the middle of the night became the most esteemed coping strategy for dealing with violence. It very seldom seems to be particularly advantageous (although outcome data are, as with many other standard interventions for domestic violence, surprisingly lacking). However, built into the idea that emergency fleeing is best are many assumptions about battering that are not supported by existing evidence. Principle among these is a remarkably narrow definition of the problem.

THE LIMITS OF CURRENT APPROACHES TO SAFETY PLANNING & DANGEROUSNESS ASSESSMENT

We need a substantial broadening of the ways we typically think about two core aspects of advocacy: dangerousness assessment and safety planning. The main purpose of this book is to develop a positive, holistic, strengths-focused framework for viewing women's coping with domestic violence. One of the major premises of the book, however, is also that such a positive framework is still largely lacking in the field, despite some movement in a more positive and respectful direction in recent years.

To understand how a holistic approach differs from current standards of practice, it is necessary to have some background in current standards of practice. I recognize that many advocates go well beyond the tools described here and assess victim's coping across many domains of their lives. Nonetheless, despite the existence of best practices by many providers, these best practices are often hard-won perspectives developed from years of field experience, not what is taught in graduate schools or advocacy training. The formal, published tools that have been passed around shelters and the advocacy community for years, the material that is widely available on the Internet, and the questionnaires that dominate in research on domestic violence have a surprisingly narrow range and considerable uniformity of content. That content focuses almost exclusively on the risk of physical assault.

Consider dangerousness assessment. Reviews of several widely used tools (Laing, 2004; Websdale, 2000), including the three best-known and most widely used questionnaires (Campbell, 2005; Hart, 1990; Kropp, Hart, Webster, & Eaves, 1995), have shown that the questions focus narrowly on predictors of severe physical violence, such as substance abuse problems, criminal history, serious mental illness, and access to weapons. Many experts in dangerousness assessment point to the need to account for the context of a woman's situation (Campbell, 2001). However, existing tools do not provide explicit guidance, in the form of structured questions, for doing so. Going back to the point in Chapter 1 about a lightly trained workforce, the result is that many times dangerousness assessment, to the extent it occurs at all, tends to stick to the questions available in published tools. Originally, some of this research was designed even more narrowly to predict lethal violence, not just dangerousness. Because this also colors the perceptions about dangerousness assessment in the field, the challenges of lethality assessment need to be more widely appreciated.

Although the desire to predict homicide is certainly understandable, for statistical reasons, accurately predicting lethality is not mathematically feasible. This results from several factors. Although even one homicide is one too many, in comparison to the size of the population or even to the number of victimized women, intimate partner homicide is quite rare and it is very difficult to predict rare events (the proverbial needle in a haystack). Further, all of the known predictors are relatively common in the population. The vast majority of alcoholics, drug addicts, and criminals will never commit a murder. On the other hand, some people who do commit murder have none of these problems. Taken together, these factors mean domestic violence homicides are unlikely to ever be predicted accurately (Hamby & Cook, 2011). The negative effects of inaccurate prediction include making some women more fearful than they need to be and some women less fearful than they need to be.

Why is this bad? Because inaccurate risk assessment turns into poor safety planning and risk management. In my experience, poor risk assessment creates problems in the advocate–client relationship. Many of the women seeking help have partners who look high risk on these assessment tools. Nonetheless, when you tell them that they are in danger for their lives, they look at you like you don't know what you are talking about. I used to think, like so many others seem to, that this was because these women were in denial. Yet, those women are still alive. My assessment of their risk was wrong—in statistical language, they are false–positives. Some advocates seem to think that it is always a good thing to tell women that they may be killed. The day I wrote this section, in January 2013, someone forwarded me an online magazine article entitled, "Leave Before He Kills You."

There are, however, under-recognized downsides to overestimating risk. On the victim side, this is one of the reasons that many advocates and providers think all victimized women need to flee in the middle of the night and sacrifice all of their belongings and their way of life and even perhaps custody of their children. However, for many women, a slower, more planful approach would be reasonable because they are not, in fact, in imminent danger for their lives. On the perpetrator side, overestimating risk leads to people potentially getting punished more harshly than they deserve. I know that many people think domestic violence perpetrators are punished too lightly, not too severely, but the latter can happen and it is not fair for people to be treated like would-be murderers when they are not would-be murderers. In the domestic violence field, this is one reason that people think couples therapy is problematic but not all people with a history of perpetrating assault are at risk for escalating to homicide.

Other downsides stem from the original goal of predicting lethality as well. The wish to identify potential homicides still influences what issues are considered salient on dangerousness assessments. Some authors explicitly equate "risk" solely with physical danger (Roehl & Guertin, 2000). Physical danger, however, is only one of many significant risks most victimized women face. Although it is certainly possible for individual advocates to ask about other areas, the fact that formal assessment tools focus on the risk of physical danger ends up giving pride of place to that issue and implicitly sends the message that physical danger to women is more important than physical danger to children, losing custody of children, losing one's home, and other important risks. Although this is the case for some women, it does not describe the situation of every woman who has experienced domestic violence or even the situation of every woman who has experienced severe domestic violence.

The situation is much the same for safety planning. The National Coalition for Domestic Violence, for example, has a high profile website on domestic violence (http://www.ncadv.org/) that serves as a resource for state coalitions and other organizations throughout the country. The National Coalition's safety plan focuses on avoiding weapons, getting ready to flee from imminent danger, and hiding from further attacks once you do flee. The only item that is not directly related to avoiding physical danger is the last one: taking documents to file for benefits or legal action. Which benefits should be applied for and which legal actions to take are not specified, although a list of suggested documents is provided.

The National Coalition for Domestic Violence safety plan is extremely similar to others that are widely available or easily accessed through the Internet, such as those on the websites of the National Domestic Violence Hotline and many state domestic violence coalitions. Most of them are adapted from the safety plan widely disseminated by a well-known advocate, Barbara Hart (Hart & Stuehling, 1992). Although this was innovative at the time and helped to draw attention to some important aspects of domestic assaults, her safety plan remains widely copied but largely untested. Some organizations have added a few global suggestions to "acquire job skills" or to stop using drugs and alcohol (again, the specifics on how to accomplish these goals are not provided). Sometimes finances are at least mentioned, but in many cases they are not. The American Bar Association (http://apps.americanbar.org/tips/public-service/safetipseng.html) at least mentions several types of legal actions a victim can take. None provide any guidance on how to choose among the options and few offer specifics on any strategies that are not directly related to physical safety. Many safety plans devote more space to rope ladders and padlocks than to providing guidance on dealing with the financial, legal, and social risks faced by virtually all battered women. Happily, a few alternatives are finally being developed. These are discussed in more detail in Chapter 12. Although some have improved over what is still, at the time of this writing, the usual standard of care, they stop short of offering a new theoretical framework to support and guide new approaches to intervention. One such framework is offered here. This framework has three main components: recognizing multiple risks, recognizing multiple coping responses, and using a method for addressing battering that is adapted from research on other kinds of complex problems.

A HOLISTIC APPROACH FOR THE COMPLEX PROBLEM OF DOMESTIC VIOLENCE

A Broader View of Risks

A broader view of risks opens the door for recognizing the broader array of protective strategies in which many victimized women commonly engage. Rethinking terminology is the first step toward a more holistic, protection-centered approach. "Risk assessment" is a far better term than "dangerousness assessment." "Dangerousness assessment" already narrows the field of interest to a focus that is too compartmentalized and fragmented. "Risk assessment" is broader and is used for many complex problems. There are several categories of risk that most victimized women face and that should be automatically considered by all advocates, providers, and researchers seeking to understand domestic violence. These risks will be discussed in detail in Chapters 3, 4, and 5. A brief overview is presented here. Understanding the range of risks is essential for developing a comprehensive framework. In this book, I use the term "risk" broadly. A risk is anything that might produce a loss. Risks can encompass factors that are sometimes referred to as barriers or obstacles— for example, financial risks can include the high costs of accessing many services (such as divorce lawyers). The risk of encountering racism or prejudice is another way of describing what is sometimes called the barrier of limited access to culturally sensitive services. Risks can also, of course, refer to different types of physical danger. Integrating these under a single rubric of risks helps to show how they combine to create the unique situations each woman must face and helps to illustrate similarities that are often not appreciated in the field.

Separation Violence

> *"Even if I leave my husband he will still be a threat."*

Personal physical risks, as in classic dangerousness assessment, certainly belong on the list. The well-documented and well-known phenomenon of separation violence, however, has not been fully integrated into typical dangerousness assessment practices. The entire shelter and advocacy system is largely set up around victimized women fleeing abuse, but it can sometimes be more dangerous to leave than to stay (Mahoney, 1991). In one study, more than half of attempted homicides of intimate partners were precipitated by leaving (Farr, 2002). The National Violence Against Women Survey

(Tjaden & Thoennes, 2000b) also showed that physical violence often persisted after the end of a relationship; almost one in four women (22%) said the violence continued after the relationship ended. Not only did it often persist, but in a few cases (4%) the relationship *only became* physically violent after the victim attempted to leave. The pattern for stalking was even more dramatic—57% of stalking victims were stalked only *after* terminating a relationship (Tjaden & Thoennes, 1998). A longitudinal study of more severely victimized women also found that terminating the relationship did not always end violence. In that study, among women who had been completely apart from their partner the entire 12 months of the study, 6% had still been physically assaulted, 30% psychologically abused, and 17% stalked (Bell, Goodman, & Dutton, 2007). (Further, as discussed elsewhere, not all of the women who did have contact continued to be assaulted or abused.) Yes, personal physical risk should be considered but in a more nuanced way than often occurs. Although separation violence is a well-known phenomenon, the coping literature seldom acknowledges that terminating a relationship is not always a successful protective strategy. No major safety planning tool even mentions the risk of separation violence.

Other Risks Posed By the Batterer

Many women are more concerned about physical risks posed to others than they are about their own endangerment. Batterers often threaten children, parents, and friends who offer support or assistance or sometimes almost anyone in the victim's orbit. Pets are threatened. Legal threats to fight for custody or to accuse the victim of aggression herself are also common. Many times threats to others are also only made when a woman suggests leaving.

Financial Risks

Financial dependence is one of the most common reasons that victimized women remain with their partners. More and more data show that divorce has lifelong financial consequences, and one of the strongest predictors of financial well-being is being in an intact marriage (Grinstein-Weiss, Hun Yeo, Zhan, & Charles, 2008; Hanson, McLanahan, & Thomson, 1998). Married couple households have, on average, nearly four times the assets as female-headed households (Ozawa & Lee, 2006). The effects of divorce are worst for women and children (Hanson, et al., 1998). Many people scoff at the idea that concerns about one's standard of living would get in the way of exiting an abusive relationship, but financial status is just as important as physical safety to one's long-term well-being. If a victim must move from a nice house in a good neighborhood to low-income housing in an area riddled with crime and violence, then she may not, significantly lower her exposure to violence. Other life-threatening financial risks may confront women with disabilities or chronic health problems, who may not be able to take the risk of losing health insurance or be able to live alone.

Explicit financial planning should be part of every risk assessment and part of every safety plan—or risk management plan, a more comprehensive term. Fleeing is not a particularly useful thing to do if you have to return 30 days later and ask to be taken back into the batterer's home. Moving out is expensive and so is obtaining a legal divorce for those who are married. Too often we avoid directly addressing just exactly how expensive these actions are in the twenty-first century. These costs are outlined in more detail in Chapter 4. Altogether, in most parts of the United States they will add up to a few thousand dollars, maybe more. In many other parts of the world they will also be the equivalent of a few months' salary for many people.

Institutional and Legal Risks

Institutional and legal risks are a heterogeneous group, which includes a range of obstacles such as lack of space in shelters, being arrested oneself if one calls the police, being reported to child protective services (CPS) if one discloses being a victim of abuse, and ending up with an enormously unfair custody decision, divorce settlement, or visitation plan. If she's religious, then her religious leader may berate her for not taking the covenant of marriage seriously enough. Some victimized women face specific institutional risks, such as the risk of deportation, which can affect both documented and undocumented immigrants (Perilla, 1999; Villalon, 2010). In the United States and elsewhere, members of minority and other oppressed groups face unfair treatment and implicit messages that services are not really intended or designed for them.

Social and Personal Risks

Another enormously important area is social risks. These frequently represent the main reasons for the coping choices that women make. Everything that we typically ask victimized women to do involves "spoiling" their public identity (to use Goffman's terminology, 1963). As long as the public still believes they are in a happy relationship, women can claim the desirable social statuses of "married," "romantically involved," "happy family," and so forth. They are also still entitled to perceptions that they are competent and desirable. To disclose abuse, end a relationship, file for divorce—these may eventually lead to a better life, but in the short term they involve accepting the spoiled identities of "victim," "divorced," "single mother," "failed marriage," and the like (Goetting, 1999; Hamby & Gray-Little, 2007). If they flee or even if they simply tell others about the battering, then women risk losing at least some social support. They may lose tangible forms of support, such as babysitting that their in-laws provide after school. Victimized women may struggle with personal values to commit to marriage "for better or worse" or fear loneliness. In some cultural, ethnic, and religious communities, women who choose relationship termination may face lifelong dishonor.

A Broader View of Coping

> "...battered women are the strongest women. And nobody will ever change my mind with that. We've had to learn to how to survive."(Davis, 2002, p.1254)

"Good" coping has traditionally been narrowly defined as leaving the relationship and typically extended only to steps in direct support of leaving, such as filing for an order of protection (e.g., Katz, Tirone, & Schukrafft, 2012; Rhatigan, Street, & Axsom, 2006). A holistic analysis of risks indicates that women can be protective through actions intended to address any of the risks faced in the context of battering. A protective strategy is any step that is designed to minimize the possibility of incurring a loss. Battering is usually a complex problem, and coping with it usually will require multiple strategies. Thus, just as "risk assessment" is a more comprehensive term than "dangerousness assessment," "risk management" is much preferred over "safety planning." Coping is not just about safety, it is about making an integrated plan to maximize outcomes for a woman and all of her family. There have been a few people who have recognized for a long time that women respond in complex ways to violence by their partner and that the situation is more complex than staying versus leaving (Campbell, Rose, Kub, & Nedd, 1998; Cavanagh, 2003; Davies, 2008), but this needs broader recognition in the field.

LEAVING IS NOT THE ONLY PROTECTIVE STRATEGY

The discourse on battering is dominated by a focus on leaving, but leaving is not the only way to deal with violence (Hamby & Gray-Little, 2007). Too many stories of women who have gone from victimization to empowerment focus only on women who have left (e.g., Goetting, 1999). Some women view coping with battering as more about "achieving nonviolence" than about leaving the relationship (Campbell et al., 1998). Some people manage to address the problem of violence from within the relationship. In stark contrast to the conventional wisdom on the topic, battering does not always prove to be a never-ending cycle that can only be interrupted by relationship termination. There are data on this from community samples (Jasinski, 2001), military samples (Rabenhorst et al., 2012), and also from research on couples therapy, at least for those who do not experience the most severe abuse (O'Leary et al., 1999; Stith & McCollum, 2011). There is even evidence of this from help-seeking women recruited from shelters and courts (Bell, et al., 2007). In Bell and colleagues' study, after 12 months, many of the women who had spent the entire period with their partner were not experiencing violence at the 12-month point. Indeed, the majority (84%) were no longer reporting physical assault, although only 45% also reported that they were no longer experiencing psychological abuse. About three-fourths (77%) were not being stalked. Although of course that means that troubling numbers of women were still experiencing these forms of abuse, it also clearly indicates that some relationships improved while they remained intact. This was not even particularly rare. Another study of couples who had been excluded from a clinical trial because of frequent and/or severe male-on-female violence found that approximately one in four couples (25%) were no longer experiencing violence when re-contacted 2 years later (DeBoer, Rowe, Frousakis, Dimidjian, & Christensen, 2012). Although this certainly suggests a high level of risk, this study likewise suggests that it is not particularly rare or unheard of for couples to find a way to end the violence while maintaining a relationship. It is especially notable in DeBoer and colleagues' study that improvement was found even among individuals from the most violent subgroup identified in their evaluation.

In one of the first studies I conducted on domestic violence, a few women described similar patterns:

> "He was drunk. I hid the car keys and wouldn't give them to him. Therefore, he shoved me around, then hit me with his fist. Then I bit him and he stopped and took the keys and left….The above instances [description of fight was earlier in the questionnaire] happened in the first 6 or 7 years of my marriage [she estimated a total of 6 to 10 incidents, with the one described here being the worst]. I have now been married 15 years, the abuse is gone, and I feel closer to my husband than I did when we were first married."

"One light slap because he thought I was hysterical and "that's what they do on TV."
Married less than 6 months. It was 25 years ago. I was in school, lots of pressure, prob-
ably crying a lot. All-in-all our relationship has been pretty even keel."

"I threw his dinner plate on [the] floor. He broke my radio. This was very early in
marriage, we were having adjustment problems....Married 20 years, both of us dif-
ferent in many ways. Mutual respect for each other even though not as close as we used
to be."

"This [arguing, yelling, 1 slap] was a one-time incident; never occurred again; both
remorseful; both of us shared some blame." [Woman in 15-year long relationship]

"We tend to have "heated verbal disagreements" and in 10 years only one incidence
of a violent argument with some pushing (I was pushed)."

"[Husband] hit wall, threw chair. I feel that we have grown a lot over the years, he
is very different from 7 years ago."

We have had evidence that solutions are possible both in and out of relationships for some time. Like most, I have been slow to recognize the importance of this evidence, because it does not fit the dominant, deficit-focused paradigm. We have known about the risk of separation violence for years, decades even, and yet our services still take little to no formal acknowledgement that leaving may not stop the violence and might even make it worse. It is time for this to change. Leaving is not the solution for every woman, every time.

MANY WOMEN USE MULTIPLE COPING STRATEGIES

Women use an impressive range of protective strategies to cope with violence, which are described in detail in Chapters 6 through 11. Although discussing each strategy individually has the benefit of appreciating each strategy's specific features and how those can contribute to a comprehensive approach, one feature of women's coping that can get lost is that most women are engaging in multiple strategies. Most protective strategies can be used in combination with other protective efforts. Further, these strategies might differ quite dramatically from one person to the next, depending on the broader context that each person finds herself in. This is another element of women's coping with violence that has been somewhat lost in the traditional approach to understanding domestic violence. Hamby and Gray-Little (1997) found in their community sample that the average number of protective strategies increased as the level of violence progressed from minor to more severe. Another study found that women who had been both sexually and physically assaulted used more help than those only physically assaulted (Cattaneo, DeLoveh, & Zweig, 2008). One study found that once women did access a service, they tended to access that service at least two or three times for formal services and three to five times for informal sources of help (Brabeck & Guzmán, 2008). Altogether, more than three-fourths (77%) of the Mexican-origin women in Brabeck and Guzman's study had accessed more than one type of formal service, with an average of between three and four formal help-seeking efforts in a 6-month period. In the VIGOR study (described in more detail at the end of this chapter), the average number of options identified by women was more than 7 and the range extended up to 19 different protective strategies (Hamby, 2013b). Another study found victimized women had already tried an average of 5 of 9 safety-seeking steps (Glass, Eden, Bloom, & Perrin, 2010). We need to learn much more about how many different ways victimized women typically try to address the problem of violence and other forms of abuse.

MULTIPLE CRITERIA DECISION MAKING

Fortunately for victimized women, battering is not the only complex problem, and there have been many efforts in many fields to improve decision making for complex problems. One of the most well-established approaches for addressing complex problems is called Multiple Criteria Decision Making (MCDM) (Hajkowicz, 2008). As will be described in more detail both here and in Chapter 12, the principles of MCDM can be used to conduct more holistic risk assessment and risk management for battering. The main purpose of MCDM is to improve decision making for complex problems. MCDM was not specifically designed for battering or violence of any kind. In fact, it is more commonly used in fields such as engineering, environmental science, and other areas where problems are often complex and simple, one-step solutions are seldom available (Hajkowicz, 2008). It can, however, be adapted to the circumstance of battering. MCDM offers a useful heuristic framework for understanding battered women's protective strategies. It is incredibly important to realize that battering is, in fact, *like many other problems*. Yes, it has unique aspects, but it is also true that there are all kinds of major adversities that people deal with all the time. Sometimes these are individual adversities, such as unemployment or addiction, and sometimes they are systemic ones, such as natural disasters. Battered women are not the only ones who have ever faced a complex problem, and they can benefit from some of the solutions that others have discovered.

Multiple criteria decision making has been used to address a wide array of problems. For example, it has been used for selecting routes for nuclear waste transport (Chen, Wang, & Lin, 2008), promoting recycling (Gomes, Nunes, Helena Xavier, Cardoso, & Valle, 2008), understanding stock trading (Albadvi, Chaharsooghi, & Esfahanipour, 2007), deciding the best locations for ambulances and other emergency vehicles (Araz, Selim, & Ozkarahan, 2007), and understanding "medical tourism" (people going outside their country of residence to obtain medical treatment) (Bies & Zacharia, 2007). It is especially popular for problems in very complex systems such as environmental sciences, engineering, agriculture, and finance (Hajkowicz, 2008).

What do these problems have in common with battering? Just a few moments consideration will reveal many similarities. There are multiple facets to all of these problems. Even more importantly, "success" at dealing with these problems can be evaluated on multiple criteria. Even more specifically, MCDM was developed partly out of recognition that not all criteria are easily evaluated with dollars or some other uniform metric. Many complex problems in fields such as engineering or finance are addressed using cost–benefit analysis. "Cost" is another way to express loss or risk. Cost–benefit analysis is useful if all of the pros and cons of a problem can be well-represented by their monetary value. However, people have realized that not all issues are easily converted to dollars and cents. For example, in environmental science, it might be hard to put a cash value on maintaining a pristine natural environment, although that may be one of the most valuable assets to consider in a decision-making process. So MCDM allows for many types of value judgments about the risks of potential losses posed by a particular complex problem. Finally, to use MCDM, you need to have multiple options from which to choose. These options will usually vary in how well they meet different criteria.

In its applications in environmental science, engineering, and other areas, MCDM can be rather complicated, with flow charts, algorithms, statistical weights, and various ranking options. The basic principles, however, can be illustrated with a simple example. Take the case of trying to select routes for nuclear waste transport that Chen et al. considered. There are several values or criteria that immediately come to mind. For example, one criterion would be to transport the material as quickly as possible, so it is on the road for a shorter period of time. On the other hand, keeping nuclear waste away from major population centers is a priority too, so that if there was an accident, there would be fewer casualties. So a short route that went through a major city might be less preferable than an itinerary through less populated areas. However, because a faster emergency response will also help minimize casualties and reduce environmental contamination, it might also be best not to get too far away from help if an accident does occur. So that might caution against taking the most remote routes. The "best" route (if one is going to transport nuclear waste, which is another issue) will be one that takes into consideration all of these criteria. In MCDM analysis, there is even a way to give more importance to (or "weight" in statistical terms) some criteria more than others. Hopefully this example helps to illustrate how the principles of MCDM can readily be applied to the problem of battering. A concrete example of forms that can be used with people who have experienced domestic violence is provided in Chapter 12.

DERIVATIVE LOSSES

The broader fields of risk management and MCDM have some wonderful concepts that can be extended to the problem of battering. *Derivative losses* refer to negative outcomes that stem from the interconnectedness and interdependence of complex systems (Jiang & Haimes, 2004). The concept is similar in some respects to the term "collateral damage" that has been popularized in military applications, although the term "derivative losses" is not a euphemism for loss of life or intended to minimize the extent of such losses. On the contrary, the concept is intended to draw attention to all sorts of potential harms that may not be immediately apparent in the moment of crisis. Derivative losses are common after many types of adverse events, such as terrorist attacks, wars, or natural disasters. For example, in the case of a natural disaster such as flooding or hurricane, derivative losses can refer to subsequent events such as the looting and vandalism that sometimes occurs afterward.

CASCADING EFFECTS

Derivative losses are well known to sometimes have a *cascading effect*, "which may be far greater than the initial loss inflicted by the direct disturbance" (Jiang & Haimes, 2004, p. 1215). As Jiang and Haimes point out, the derivative losses and cascading effects result from the interconnectedness of many large systems. For example, looting and vandalism after a natural disaster can progress to violence and further lawlessness and can directly impede the recovery from the initial damage caused by the storm. The spread of crime can make local businesses reluctant to re-invest in a community, further slowing recovery. Although these ideas were developed for large systems such as communities, there are many parallels to the family system. Many women have said that the bruises are not the most harmful part of the battering experience (Follingstad, Rutledge, Berg, Hause, & Polek, 1990). Battering is a very apt example of a phenomenon that has derivative losses and cascading effects, such as when a woman loses a job or friendships because of the batterer's behavior, and this creates further economic dependence and social isolation, which make it harder to respond to the violence. The recognition of interconnectedness and the derivative risks and losses that can be created by battering need to become part of our paradigm for understanding battering.

DECISION MAKING IN CASES OF "STRICT DOMINANCE"

In MCDM, an option is considered to have "strict dominance" if it is better than others at addressing some risks and at least as good as other options for all risks. It is good news when such an option is identified, but many complex problems will not have an option that is so clearly better than all other choices. Strict dominance is a useful concept to understanding how leaving the relationship is viewed by the field. In MCDM language, relationship termination is treated as though that option has strict dominance over all other possible strategies for all victimized women in all circumstances. Of course, in reality, most battered women are not facing circumstances so easily solved. For battering and many other types of complex problems, it is important to identify the best available option or combination of options given all available information about a problem. In practice, this is what many domestic violence agencies are instinctively doing when they recommend multiple options such as seeking orders of protection and staying in shelter and getting job training. A more explicit recognition of this complexity could help improve these services even more, especially if that recognition avoided simplistic statements about relationship termination.

THE MULTIPLE CRITERIA DECISION-MAKING PROCESS

This section describes the conceptual framework underlying MCDM. For a risk assessment and risk management tool that explicitly applies MCDM to battering and can be used with survivors of violence, *see* Chapter 12. The first step in MCDM is to structure the problem by identifying goals and criteria. The general goal, as with most approaches to problem solving, is to maximize benefits and minimize risks. This process has "multiple criteria" in the name to explicitly recognize that there is no single benchmark that signals success or failure for many complex problems. Maximizing personal safety/minimizing personal danger can be one criterion but in the MCDM process it does not have to be the only criterion. Other goals and other risks can also be identified. All of the risk categories that we have been discussing can be included: other people's safety, financial, institutional, legal, social, and psychological.

Some sort of prioritizing of all of these goals and risks is required in the MCDM process. In many applications, this can involve complicated weighting, scoring, or rank ordering. Although computers are making their way into many clinical settings, they are still not widely available, especially for client use, in a variety of shelter, emergency department, law enforcement, and other service settings. Although there is some loss of complexity and sophistication when more complicated weighting formulas are not applied, in essence this is a conceptually simple process that does not require complex calculations. In its most simple form that almost anyone can use in any setting, it is only necessary to identify the most important goals a woman is trying to maximize or risks she is trying to minimize. For practical purposes, it is easier to limit this to three or four of the highest priority issues, but this can be expanded if desired. These then become the "multiple criteria" part of the MCDM process.

In traditional MCDM, it is possible to move directly to identifying options. In many systems, identifying viable options implicitly includes recognizing resources and abilities. For the situation of battering, however, and because of the pervasive effects of the dominant, deficit-focused paradigm, I have found it helpful to separate these processes and have women first identify their strengths and resources. Options can then be identified in a third step. MCDM options for battering can certainly include "traditional" advocacy services such as shelters, orders of protection, and support groups. Newer services such as couples counseling and less violence-focused options such as job training are examples that go beyond these traditional ones. We need to expand our toolkit. A better appreciation of risks will help focus on other needs and options—financial planning, job training, coping with a stigmatized identity, talking with family members or clergy.

The last step is the key to the MCDM process. In conventional MCDM analyses, each option is rated on how it performs relative to each criterion. As described above, in the best case scenario, one option will emerge that has "strict dominance." When strict dominance is lacking, then the option or options are chosen that help the most overall, taking all of the different criteria into consideration, even if it is not the number one best choice for some of them. In some cases, it may be possible to implement more than one option and thus further improve the final outcome. This, of course, is often the case in situations of battering, where one can certainly seek both housing and social support, for example, at the same time. The idea is to develop a package of steps that will combine to produce the best outcome in the shortest timeframe. Timeframes need not be immediate. Longer time horizons and realistic implementation plans are also common elements of MCDM solutions. The result is a personalized plan that links coping responses to specific prioritized risks, rather than a generic, one-size-fits-all checklist of safety precautions. MCDM also explicitly allows for the fact that these priorities may vary across individuals or even over time for the same individuals and that the same priorities (such as preserving pristine environments) may not be selected by everyone in similar situations.

One important outcome of an MCDM approach is that it can potentially improve the field's response to the most disadvantaged women as we try to help them address multiple needs. Perhaps even more importantly, it offers a way to reframe what may look like poor coping or denial through the recognition that some victimized women may be prioritizing other goals and risks in addition to or more highly than their own personal safety. Additionally, it is no secret that most domestic violence programs are, intentionally or not, aimed at the most disadvantaged women. MCDM, unlike shelters and many other domestic violence services, is just as appropriate for women with considerable resources as it is for women with few resources. Currently, we are neglecting all of the accountants, teachers, health-care professionals, professors, and others who also experience domestic violence and may feel that shelter-based services are not meant for them. Advocacy should not just be about free shelter and we need to work to make the broader population aware that the domestic violence field has more to offer than free short-term housing.

THE VIGOR STUDIES

I have conducted two studies asking victimized women to talk about risks, options, and plans (Hamby, 2013b). One of the main project goals was to refine the Victim Inventory of Goals, Options, and Risks (VIGOR), an alternative approach to safety planning that is based on MCDM (the tool itself is described in more detail in Chapter 12). Data from these studies can help inform many of the issues addressed in this book. The first VIGOR study included 101 women who had all sought help from one of two domestic violence organizations in two different southern U.S. states. This was an ethnically and racially diverse sample who were 54% African American, 26% European American, 11% Latina, 8% American Indian and 1% other race. They were mostly low-income women who reported incomes under $18,000 per year (71%). They were asked to describe their risks, resources, and options in a semi-structured format that allows women to use their own words on a written risk assessment and risk management tool. These questionnaires were later coded by two students. This type of coding can include the viewpoints of many more victimized women than can typically be included in qualitative research. One of the students who worked on the coding, Sarah Clark, also worked with me to revise the VIGOR. The second VIGOR study used a new version of the form that was revised following the results of the first VIGOR study. The second study included 98 women with histories of domestic violence who were recruited from domestic violence agencies and local contacts of two advocates in the same southern U.S. states. The sample was also ethnically and racially diverse, including 29% African-American, 29% Latina/o, 26% European American, 14% American Indian, 1% Asian, and 1% other. It was a very low-income sample, with most women reporting income below $18,000 per year. Some of the results of these studies and quotes from some of the women are included throughout the book. Either with or without the use of the VIGOR assessment tool, the VIGOR framework can provide a conceptual tool for understanding how victimized women cope with battering.

CONCLUSION

Battering is a complex problem and we need more sophisticated and nuanced approaches to coping with it. Our existing efforts place too much emphasis on the crisis response and not enough on systematic planning to minimize all types of risks. The field's continuing emphasis on leaving as the most important, if not the only, coping strategy fails to recognize the existence of risks other than immediate physical danger and the threats of separation violence. There is much that we can learn from research on addressing other types of complex problems. A well-established method for addressing complex problems, MCDM, offers particular promise for a conceptual framework and a guide to intervention. The conceptual framework involves recognizing multiple risks, recognizing multiple possible strategies for addressing those risks, and carefully balancing and weighing the best combination of strategies. There are as many ways of acting protectively as there are women coping with violence. Despite the limitations of the research, there is substantial evidence that women engage in all kinds of protective strategies and seek many types of help as they attempt to improve their situations. We will not be able to describe all of them but perhaps we can start to appreciate the wide array of strategies that are used. Often times even with limited resources and limited support, women are persistent and energetic copers.

Protective Strategies in the Context of Battered Women's True Risk Burden: The Multitude of Risks Batterers Can Create

Why include information about risks in a book about protective strategies? Protective strategies cannot be fully appreciated without an accurate awareness of the many potential losses that victimized women confront. Understanding the full range of risks is part of accurately defining the complex problem of battering and generating the multiple criteria that any woman must balance as she attempts to protect herself from all of the harms caused by a violent partner. Although there are many more services and legal protections available to victimized women today than there were 30 or 40 years ago, most women still face substantial risks or losses in accessing services or using other protective strategies (Davies et al., 1998; Justice & Courage Oversight Panel, 2008). These risks can be organized into five categories: batterers' behavior, financial risks, institutional risks, social risks, and the dilemmas that arise from personal values that complicate women's choices. In this chapter we focus on risks that are directly posed by the batterer. Although most research on battered women and domestic violence emphasizes the physical violence itself, with some emphasis on psychological and sexual aggression, this limited picture of risks does not begin to fully describe the situations many victimized women face. One of the best existing summaries of all of the risks and obstacles experienced by victimized women was prepared by the lawyer Sarah Buel (1999). Most of these factors create very high costs (financial and social) for many coping choices, but they can particularly make it difficult to end the relationship. It is critical to understand that contrary to the widespread assumption in service provision that leaving is the best way to increase safety, there is ample evidence that much inter-relationship violence is initiated or worsens after separation as the batterer redoubles efforts to maintain control (Farr, 2002; Mahoney, 1991; Tjaden & Thoennes, 1998, 2000a). Although this chapter goes beyond the usual narrow focus on direct forms of violence and abuse, even this is not an exhaustive review of all of the risks a batterer can present.

To truly see all of the protective steps that women take requires recognizing all of the losses they face. Thus, in Chapters 4 and 5 we will address derivative losses and cascading effects. Chapter 4 covers financial and institutional obstacles and Chapter 5 takes up common social and personal risks. The literature on battering often presents these challenges in global terms such as "batterer's threats" or "limited financial resources." However, it is in the details that these problems really come to life. It is also the details that make it easier to see how many of the problems battered women face are the same problems that many have of us have experienced, such as trouble making ends meet or conflict with in-laws. Violence does not happen in a vacuum. It is part of the ebb and flow of life's challenges.

Data are available for most but not all of these risks. Just because there is no data for some, however, does not mean they are not substantial issues. Domestic violence research, like much social science research, develops habits and patterns that can be hard to break. Thus, there are hundreds and hundreds of studies on how many times women have been hit by their partners, but few explicating all of the ways that women get threatened. Dozens of researchers have explored post-traumatic stress symptoms in women who have sustained violence, but few have studied resilience. Chapter 11 is entirely devoted to protective strategies that have been largely invisible to research. Here, I have drawn on the available scholarship and also on the experiences of hundreds of women I have worked with or known to bring these obstacles to light. In cases where research data are limited or lacking, I hope that identifying these issues will inspire researchers to cast a wider net in their study of abuse.

GENDER AND THE REALITY OF BATTERING

Getting into the details of batterer behavior will immediately raise questions about gender for some. Claims that women are equally as violent as men are incorrect. Can women be violent? Sure, sometimes. Sometimes women do horrific things. One morning in 2001, Andrea Yates drowned all five of her children. Some people, including a few women, commit horrific atrocities that are hard to understand even for those of us who have spent our entire adult lives trying to understand violence. I have known a few cases of women who acted violently in intimate relationships. It is a significant issue, and I have written extensively on gender differences in domestic violence elsewhere (Hamby, 2005, 2009a; Hamby, Finkelhor, & Turner, in press; Hamby, Finkelhor et al., 2011; Hamby & Turner, in press).

There are a great many important things that can be said about gender and domestic violence, but the most important one related to the topic of this book is that the research suggesting gender parity is ignoring many important aspects of domestic violence because of an overly narrow definition of the problem. Most studies on domestic violence ignore sexual violence, for example. Getting pushed by someone who has raped you is not like getting pushed by anybody else. One reason sexual violence is understudied is because it is easier to get approval to study physical than sexual violence at many universities. However, this is no excuse. Researchers should not use proxy measures for domestic violence that distort what is actually going on. That is not science.

I am a co-author of a widely used questionnaire to measure domestic violence, the Revised Conflict Tactics Scales (CTS2) (Straus, Hamby, Boney-McCoy, & Sugarman, 1996). That measure improved on its predecessors by adding items on sexual assault and injury. It was a sincere effort at the time to create a better tool for measuring domestic violence. Still, that measure also falls short of an adequate self-report proxy for the phenomenon of domestic violence. The CTS2 is now 17 years old. The original is 40 years old. Science is about progress. You would not want a 40-year-old—or even a 17-year-old—cancer treatment, and social scientists should stop settling for outdated technology. If you had a screening test that consistently gave a different result than all of the other tests for a medical condition, then you would question the screening test, not the condition. All of our other indicators for domestic violence—including arrests, police reports (even when they do not lead to arrest), homicides, help-seeking, witness reports, and other survey formats—do not show gender parity and comprise far more data points than the mostly small convenience studies using questionnaires like the CTS2 and others very similar to it. Many people nonetheless conclude the quick screening measures are correct and not these other sources of data, although many of these other sources represent more contextualized and detailed assessments of domestic violence than can a few items on a questionnaire (Hamby, 2009). It is a scandal that we are little better at measuring domestic violence than when we first started studying the problem in the 1970s.

It is also a scandal that many people in psychology and social work are so little informed about the major criminological and public health databases on domestic violence and often get away with treating small studies on college students more seriously than these important nationally representative surveillance tools. For example, it is not widely understood that the only reason the Archer meta-analysis (2000) found gender "parity" is because he selectively eliminated the criminological and public health databases and data on sexual violence. If he had included even one of the criminological or public health databases in a sample-size weighted analysis, then his results would have been different, because these databases are several times the size of most studies published in psychology (the smallest has "only" 16,000 participants). A phrase that I see often in my role as journal editor, that "most data" on domestic violence show gender parity, is not accurate. The National Criminal Victimization Survey (NCVS) interviews 70,000 or so people every year and has never found gender parity or anything close to it (Truman, 2011). Just a single year's worth of NCVS data adds up to more interviews than all of the gender parity studies combined, and this has been repeated every year for 20 years. Ignorance of data across scientific disciplines is another adverse consequence of the hyperspecialization of violence research about which my colleagues and I have written elsewhere (Finkelhor et al., 2009; Hamby, 2011; Hamby & Grych, 2013). Hyperspecialization hampers us in our ability to make informed scientific critiques.

Another important problem with research on gender differences in domestic violence is that it mostly ignores the types of threats covered in this and the following chapters (Goetting, 1999). As far as I am aware, there are few studies on risks and obstacles that include female perpetrators or male victims (of heterosexual violence—a few studies on same-sex relationships have been done). Clinically, however, I have never heard of a single instance when a woman lashed out at her partner or tried to keep him from leaving by threatening to kill her own children or her mother-in-law or her partner's boss. I have never known of a case where a woman kidnapped her partner or called in a false report to the police in a remote area so that it would take them longer to respond to her house and she would have more time to beat up her partner. These and other extreme acts are regularly perpetrated by men. This is the stuff of battering. It seems likely that some women out there somewhere have done things like these, because it is a big planet and a lot of bizarre things happen. But I am confident there is no "gender parity" in these behaviors. Based on my clinical experience, good guesses about which of the threats discussed in this book might be relatively common among female perpetrators are the threat of suicide and the threat or act of destroying a partner's valuables (such as damaging a partner's car). Even these examples—of self-directed aggression and property-directed aggression—suggest some of the important differences between male and female aggression.

Women and men are not "similarly situated," to use the legal term (MacKinnon, 2005). This is still not true in the stable, wealthy democracies of the world that have largely embraced egalitarian values, if not yet fully put them into practice. It is certainly not true in many other less advantaged countries. When it comes to making threats, women may never be similarly situated, because we are smaller and less muscular than men (McDowell, Fryar, Ogden, & Flegal, 2008; Powers & Howley, 1997). Beyond physiological differences, we are still far from similarly socially situated also, as will become more apparent in Chapters 4 and 5. I can empathize with some men's desires to not always be portrayed as the "bad guys" in domestic violence and perhaps see the situation of domestic violence as a chance to take the heat off of all of the other ways that men and boys are more violent than women and girls (FBI, 2011; Hamby et al., in press; Truman, 2011). I also can empathize with the desires of some women to act as if women are now similarly situated with men and that we can "give as good as we get." The traction these wishes are getting in the field (by authors such as Mills, 2003) is certainly one sign of their power. I think these are normal, understandable responses, just like it is a normal, understandable response to get angry and frustrated with a client who is not following your treatment plan. But it is the job of professionals to be conscious of these responses and to take responsibility for not letting wishes and emotional reactions get in the way of science, policy, and intervention. A feminist response to violence is not about reifying victimhood. A feminist response to violence is a nuanced, holistic, and contextualized response to the full spectrum of individual, social, and cultural factors that are at play in any case of domestic violence.

Some people who self-identify as feminist seem to think that the path to a better future lies with claims that women are as violent as men and at least as equally dysfunctional (e.g., Mills, 2003). There are a lot of feminisms. That is not, however, my feminist vision. My vision is not about achieving equal levels of violence and dysfunction. My feminist vision of an egalitarian future is one of mutual respect and includes an abiding faith in men's and women's capacities to be nonviolent. It has long been my impression that is the best description of what might be called "mainstream feminism." As far as I have ever been able to tell, it is the vision of all of the feminists with whom I am personally acquainted. The path to this future lies in an analysis of violence that is informed by the ways that individuals are situated in gender, race, class, and other social and political characteristics (Crenshaw, 1991). As outlined in Chapter 2, domestic violence is a complex problem and requires a sophisticated analysis of all of the ways that domestic violence touches lives and all of the ways in which victimized people actively engage in protective strategies. To adequately understand the reality of battering requires incorporating these complexities. To the extent that an underappreciation of women's strengths and protective strategies has become typical of the field is the extent to which, in my mind, the field has strayed from a coherent, scientifically based feminist analysis. Intervention, policy, and future science need to be informed by an understanding of these complexities. A scientific feminism will readily show that women are, as I have said in this book, stronger than you know.

THE RISKS POSED BY BATTERERS' THREATS AND BEHAVIORS

The risks posed by batterers are listed in Table 3.1 and described in detail in the following sections.

BATTERER THREATENS TO KILL HIS PARTNER

"If I can't have her, nobody can." This is such a common sentiment among batterers that it has become cliché. Although many people assume that leaving an abuser will make a victim safer, the time following a separation can be the most dangerous (Farr, 2002; Tjaden & Thoennes, 2000a). In the VIGOR 1 study, approximately

Table 3.1 Protective Strategies in Context: Understanding Everything Batterers Can Do That Influence Women's Protective Strategies

Batterer threatens to kill his partner
Batterer threatens to kill or harm children or other people close to the victim
Batterer threatens pets
Batterer threatens to commit suicide if she leaves
Batterer threatens to kidnap children
Batterer threatens a contested divorce or custody battle
Work interference, school interference, and economic abuse
Separation violence
Batterer stalks victim when she tries to leave or spend time away from partner
Batterer engages in cyberstalking or cyber-harassment
Batterer promises to change
Batterer begins treatment for violence and/or substance abuse
Batterer minimizes or denies violence
Batterer blames the victim for violence
Batterer hides violence from family, friends, police, and courts
Batterer isolates victim
Batterer makes distorted claims about partner
Batterer threatens to destroy partner's belongings
Batterer does not provide child support

Note: The emphasis in this table is on recognizing risks created by batterers that go beyond direct physical and sexual violence. To understand how survivors cope with violent partners requires recognizing all the risks they face and all the considerations they must balance. Tables 4.1 and 5.1 present additional risks that should be incorporated into any risk management plan.

one in six women (17%) reported in this open-ended format that one major risk they faced was fear that their partner would kill them. Many batterers attempt to keep a victim near them by making a variety of threats. Most women who have been assaulted by their male partners (55%) report being threatened before the actual attack, according to data from the National Criminal Victimization Survey (NCVS), the largest U.S. survey on crime (Felson & Messner, 2000). Threatening behavior is more common prior to male-on-female partner assault than for any other victim–offender relationship (Felson & Messner, 2000). Threatening to kill her is one of the most dangerous and unfortunately one of the most common threats made by batterers. Women are at increased risk of death or serious injury after they leave or announce their intentions to leave. In one study of attempted intimate partner homicide, most of the victims (60%), all women, had either left their relationship (47%) or told their partner that they were going to leave (13%) (Farr, 2002). For the women who had left, 93% said the reason for the attack was the fact that they had left the perpetrator.

The ease with which guns can be acquired in the United States creates danger for battered women. In a survey of battered women, 71% of victimized women who lived in a house with a gun reported that the gun had been used to threaten to shoot or kill her (Sorenson & Wiebe, 2004). Guns can also contribute to a general climate of fear. Almost half (41%) of one group of shelter residents said that when guns were in the home, the guns were routinely kept unlocked and either loaded or stored next to ammunition (Sorenson & Wiebe, 2004). Homicide rates are far higher in the United States than they are in other stable, wealthy democracies and gun availability is one key reason why some women are especially vulnerable to these threats (Hemenway, Shinoda-Tagawa, & Miller, 2002).

BATTERER THREATENS TO KILL OR HARM CHILDREN OR OTHER PEOPLE CLOSE TO THE VICTIM

Many victimized women are willing to risk separation violence and other threats directed at themselves. It is much more difficult to risk the safety or well-being of their children. Many batterers take advantage of the fact that many, if not most, mothers will place their children's safety above their own. Threats to harm children, and sometimes other loved ones, if a woman tries to end a relationship or engage in other coping strategies can limit many women's options. It is important to distinguish between two types of danger to children. One type is threats to children *if* a woman leaves, gets a job, or makes other changes the batterer does not want. The second is increased danger to children when they are in the home with the perpetrator. Women respond differently to these threats. The second can make a woman more likely to leave. The first can have the opposite effect. Some women are in terrible catch 22's when both are true. One large study in Colorado found that one in six (16%) women said that the batterer had threatened to kill or harm their children (Pearson, Thoennes, & Griswold, 1999) and another found that one in four had experienced similar threats (Anderson et al., 2003). More broadly, almost half (47%) of the women in the VIGOR study reported concern about their children's well-being, including threats to harm. For those women who do experience such threats, fear for others' safety is one of the strongest predictors of coping strategies (Amanor-Boadu et al., 2012).

Batterers will also threaten parents, siblings, relatives, and friends. Sometimes their threats are targeted at people who they perceive to be advocating for the victim and her safety. Other times, they threaten loved ones because they know that many victimized women will try to protect others, even at risk to their own personal safety. In one study, almost half (47%) of help-seeking survivors reported that their partner had threatened to harm their family or other loved ones and one in seven (13%) said their family members had actually been harmed (Anderson et al., 2003). Batterers do not just threaten loved ones. Sometimes coworkers or other acquaintances who may not have even known about the abuse are threatened. These are often dual threats to shame and publicly humiliate women as well as try to control them by threatening others. Some batterers are so consumed by jealousy that they will threaten any man who speaks to the victim, no matter how brief or impersonal the contact. Batterers know most people (not just victimized ones) would have trouble living with the guilt if any harm came to others, even when they are not legally responsible for the violence.

BATTERER THREATENS PETS

Pets are important life companions for many people but can be especially important to survivors of abuse, who are often socially isolated and traumatized by the batterer. Pets are important sources of emotional support for many people (Friedmann, Thomas, & Son, 2011). In one study a majority (73%) of pet owners said the comfort of pets helped them deal with the abuse (Flynn, 2000). Pet ownership is also common. In studies of shelter residents, between 40% and 82% owned pets (Ascione, 1998; Carlisle-Frank, Frank, & Nielsen, 2004; Faver & Strand, 2003; Flynn, 2000; McIntosh, 2004). Some people would rather place themselves in danger than feel partly responsible for harm to their dogs, cats, and other pets. Although any harm to pets is clearly the responsibility of the batterer and not the victim, some survivors feel they may be able to limit the harm to pets and others if they stay with the batterer.

Although some shelters can arrange care for a woman's pets, many women must leave their pets behind when they go to a shelter for domestic violence. Even if they do find pet care during their shelter stay, rental apartments and other likely post-shelter living situations seldom allow pets. Thus, leaving an abuser can also mean leaving behind beloved animal companions. Shockingly, almost half of pet-owning victimized women report that they have had pets harmed, threatened, or killed (Ascione, 1998; Ascione, Weber, & Wood, 1997b; Carlisle-Frank et al., 2004; Faver & Strand, 2003; Flynn, 2000; McIntosh, 2004). This is an underserved issue. Despite the widespread occurrence of pet abuse as part of the pattern of violence and control, few shelters make any efforts to respond to the needs of battered pet owners. In a survey of the largest shelters in each U.S. state, only 27% reported that shelter intake interviews included questions about pet abuse, although 85% indicated that women had reported abuse of their pets to shelter staff (Ascione, Weber, & Wood, 1997a). As of 2012, the largest national survey on domestic violence agency services conducted by the National Network to End Domestic Violence did not ask about services for pets (*see* http://nnedv.org/ for detailed information on this survey).

Threats and assaults against pets delay some women's decisions to leave their abusers. This ranged from 18% to 48% in the studies cited above (with a pooled average of 26% across six studies). In one study, for women who did delay seeking help, the delay was longer than 2 months for 63% of women (Flynn, 2000). In one study (Faver & Strand, 2003), women whose pets had been threatened were seven times more likely to factor in their pets' welfare when deciding to leave. It is well known that many women return to their abusers after a shelter stay, and one study (Carlisle-Frank et al., 2004) asked victimized women about the role of pets in past attempts to leave. They found that almost half (48%) had considered returning to the batterer because of concern for their pets. Many of these women (25%) said they had gone back to their batterer because of concerns for their pets, a figure which jumped to 35% when limited to women who had seen their pets previously abused. Given all of the many factors that contribute to coping decisions and the wide variation in women's personal situations, it is notable that such a large percentage of women are heavily weighting concern for pets. Unfortunately, existing analyses are not detailed enough to know if certain subgroups, such as women with no children, may be more likely to emphasize concern for pets in their decision making.

BATTERER THREATENS TO COMMIT SUICIDE IF SHE LEAVES

When the topic of batterers' suicidal threats comes up, I have heard more than one advocate (with varying degrees of sarcasm) say, "And the problem with that would be...?" But few people would be totally immune from feelings of guilt or second-guessing their actions if someone close to them did commit suicide. Certainly those of us in health care or public safety often go to great lengths to keep people, even known perpetrators, from killing themselves. Imagine if the suicidal person was your partner or the father of your children. You might be willing to sacrifice a lot to avoid being involved in his untimely death, no matter how innocently. Among individuals arrested for domestic violence, approximately 1 in 7 (14%) males and 1 in 11 (9%) females have threatened suicide (Feder & Henning, 2005). Some samples of battered women report fairly low levels of this threat—for example, only 4% of women in one shelter survey reported that their partner had threatened suicide (Sorenson & Wiebe, 2004), but it can be a major constraint when it does occur.

BATTERER THREATENS TO KIDNAP CHILDREN

Sometimes batterers who stop short of threatening to murder their children will still threaten to take them away from their mother and hide them where she cannot find them. Many victimized women are fearful of leaving their children at school, daycare, or other places where their father may abduct them, with the possibility of her not discovering what has happened for hours. In the National Survey of Children's Exposure to Violence, fully 72% of the cases of custodial interference occurred in homes where children had been exposed to violence between their parents (Hamby, Finkelhor, Turner, & Ormrod, 2010). Although some of these cases appeared to be women fleeing with their children, many incidents involved perpetrators interfering with custody arrangements. In shelter samples, this problem is very common. In one study, approximately one in three women (32%) said their partner had threatened that they would never see their children again, and almost one in five (18%) reported that their partner had taken their children without their okay at least once (Anderson et al., 2003).

BATTERER THREATENS A CONTESTED DIVORCE OR CUSTODY BATTLE

Not all threats are criminal. Other common threats are nasty divorce battles—especially to contest custody of the children (Bryan, 1999). In the VIGOR 1 study, 27% of women reported fear of losing custody as an important risk they were facing (Hamby, 2013b). Contested divorces are enormously expensive—often running into the tens of thousands of dollars. Not only low-income women but also many middle and even upper middle income women lack the financial resources to retain a lawyer. More than 10 years ago, Sarah Buel recounted her experience of being told there was a 3-year wait for a divorce through a legal aid office and that all the private attorneys she contacted wanted an initial cash retainer of at least $10,000 (Buel, 1999). In my experience these are still common obstacles. Even women who can access such resources are still at risk—custody decisions, amazingly enough, often give little weight to past violence, and many batterers are able to gain full or partial custody of their children (Bryan, 1999). Many women choose to remain with their spouse rather than risk losing custodial care of their children.

WORK INTERFERENCE, SCHOOL INTERFERENCE, AND ECONOMIC ABUSE

On-the-job harassment is a common experience for women who are being battered. A recent review of this literature indicates that 35% to 56% of victimized women reported being harassed at work, 55% to 85% reported being made late or missing work because of violence, and 24% to 52% reported losing their job because of violence (Postmus, 2010). Many women (16%–59%) report that their partner discouraged or prevented them from working (Postmus, 2010). Employers are often not supportive, and 44% to 60% of victimized women, across studies, reported being reprimanded at work for problems stemming from victimization (Postmus, 2010). Recent studies have found even higher rates. In one, two of three women (68%) reported that their partner tried to keep them from going to their job, more than half (59%) said their partner demanded that they quit, and nearly one in three (32%) said they had been beaten up for talking about needing to get a job for themselves (Postmus, Plummer, McMahon, Murshid, & Kim, 2012). Another study found that 85% of victimized women experienced at least one type of work interference by their batterer and provided some details on the range of forms this abuse can take (Swanberg, Macke, & Logan, 2006). Stealing car keys or transportation money was reported by two in five women. Interference during the workday was common too, such as harassing women on the phone or in person. In this study, more than one in five (21%) women experiencing battering had lost their job because of work-related harassment by the batterer, and most of them (63%) reported problems such as inability to perform their job to the best of their ability. One in four had also had problems with their partner not showing up as agreed to take care of the children. The partners of 15% of the women had lied about their children's health and safety to get the woman to quit work (Swanberg et al., 2006). Although work interference has been more commonly studied, school interference was reported by almost one in four women (23%) in one study (Anderson et al., 2003).

A recent study of shelter clients provides some of the most detailed available evidence on other types of economic abuse that can occur in addition to work and school interference (Postmus et al., 2012). Almost all of the women in this sample had experienced some form of economic abuse. Some of the more common controlling behaviors included the batterer demanding to know how money was spent (88%) and making important financial decisions without consulting the victim (83%). More extreme behaviors such as demanding receipts and change from "permitted" spending were reported by the majority of women (73%) also. Batterers' spending rent or bill money on other purchases was reported by two of three victimized women (69%) and more than half reported that batterers intentionally built up debt in their partner's name (59%). This study is also notable because Postmus et al. also established that women with less education were more vulnerable to economic abuse than other women.

SEPARATION VIOLENCE

As mentioned in Chapter 2, separation violence is a serious and significant problem. Many femicides take place after the woman has separated from her partner and moved into different housing (Farr, 2002). Nonfatal assaults also continue or worsen during this time for many victimized women. As noted earlier, The National Violence Against Women Survey (Tjaden & Thoennes, 2000b) showed that physical violence often persisted after the end of a relationship, with almost one in four women (22%) reporting the violence continued after the relationship ended. Walking away in safety is not an option for many victimized women.

BATTERER STALKS VICTIM WHEN SHE TRIES TO LEAVE OR SPEND TIME AWAY FROM PARTNER

As described above, batterers frequently continue to pursue victimized women even after they leave (Tjaden & Thoennes, 2000a). Stalking represents a wide variety of harassing and threatening behavior, including following the victim around town, showing up at the victim's house or work, sending frequent unwanted messages or packages, and even making threats. Although restraining orders typically prohibit all of these forms of contact, some batterers are so obsessed with their partners that they continue to stalk despite the risk of arrest. Approximately one in four women reported that their partner had violated their restraining order in one study (Shannon, Logan, & Cole, 2007). Even more surprisingly, the mean number of violations was more than nine—clearly indicating that for some men, restraining orders are minimal barriers to repeatedly approaching their partner. Less surprisingly, more than half of the women reported feeling unsafe, despite having separated (Shannon et al., 2007). Many women feel forced into a choice of quitting their jobs, ending their friendships, and moving to other cities. Even this does not solve the problem of stalking for some victimized women—some have been pursued thousands of miles cross-country. Some victimized women continue to be stalked even after such extreme measures as changing their legal names and social security numbers.

BATTERER ENGAGES IN CYBERSTALKING OR CYBER-HARASSMENT

There is no question that computer technology has been a boon to stalkers and technology has made stalking more severe for many women. As technology advances, stalking continues to get easier and easier. Many men use instant messaging or other programs to repeatedly contact their partners and ex-partners. Some batterers also stalk their partners by hacking into personal e-mail accounts or secretly installing keystroke monitors so that they keep track of everything a woman does on her computer. There are "apps" such as "Creepy," which uses information embedded in Flickr and Twitter online posts (Kakavas, 2010). Geographic data (GPS) are routinely collected by most phone and mobile devices and are retained in numerous places, including material that gets posted on various websites (Maass & Rajagopalan, 2012). A Creepy user can access this location information just with a person's Flickr or Twitter id. No password is required. Not only is the person's location provided but also the date and time that the person was at that location.

Other apps that can be used by stalkers include Spousespy (also known as "ephone Tracker"; Retina Software Private Limited, 2006) and Family Tracker (LogSat Software LLC, 2011). These and other similar apps require that the program be installed on a device before the spying and tracking can take place. As the program names suggest, this makes them most useful for people to stalk people who either live with them, used to live with them, or others who could get access to someone's mobile device. Foursquare is an app for mobile phones that encourages people to post their whereabouts voluntarily (Crowley & Selvadurai, 2009). Unlike Facebook and Twitter, this information typically goes to anyone using the Foursquare app in the person's vicinity, not just "friends" or even "friends of friends." The author of Creepy says that his intent was "not to help stalkers or promote/endorse stalking" (Kakavas, 2012) but, rather, to show how easily such information is obtained. The Spouse Spy makers are less concerned with such distinctions and suggest that it "feels harsh but failing to see the signs of infidelity in your partner can lead you to a break up. So don't ever ignore the importance of knowing what is happening in your partner's life. And it's literally easy to keep tabs on what's going on in their life." Regardless of the programmers' intentions, they have made stalking accessible to many people who would not otherwise have the technical know-how to track people with this degree of precision. Even seemingly more innocuous programs such as Facebook help stalkers by allowing them to see regular status updates about a partner or ex-partner.

Cyberstalking and cyber-abuse by intimate partners was commonly reported in a qualitative study of forms of cyber harassment (Hamby et al., 2011). This finding led me to include questions on cyber-abuse in the second VIGOR study (Hamby, 2013a). Cyber-abuse was reported by 65% of the VIGOR 2 sample. Sending frequent unwanted messages, reading the victim's e-mail without permission, and sending angry text messages were the most common forms, reported by 57% to 59% of the sample. Each of the nine forms assessed were reported by at least 35% of the sample. Cyber-abuse, when it occurred, was a more frequent form of abuse than physical or sexual violence (although correlated with both). There were no differences in frequency of cyber-abuse between women who were still with their partner or who had ended the relationship. This suggests the common stereotype that these forms of abuse only happen after relationship termination is inaccurate. These data also show, once again, that relationship termination does not ensure an end to abuse.

BATTERER PROMISES TO CHANGE

Less extreme behaviors can also make it harder for victimized women to leave or make other changes. Especially after the first violent incidents, a batterer's promises to change can be very compelling and persuasive. Divorces and separations are unpleasant, difficult processes that nearly always result in loss of financial well-being, loss of two parents for the children, and/or other upheavals. Everyone knows that all relationships face difficulties. After the first assault, especially if it was non-injurious and/or occurred during a period of unusually high stress, many partners may hope to work things out so that the violence does not occur again. Indeed, for many relationships, this does occur—more frequently than is recognized by some (Jasinski, 2001; O'Leary et al., 1999; Rabenhorst et al., 2012; Stith, Rosen, McCollum, & Thomsen, 2004). The line between a problem that can be handled within the relationship and a level of violence and control that can only be escaped by leaving is fuzzy and gray—not sharp and clear. Batterer's promises are very common. In one study of why women withdrew protection orders, more than one in four women (26%) said that their partner had promised to change (Roberts, Wolfer, & Mele, 2008). In one of the earliest studies of factors that promoted staying with a partner, Strube and Barbour (1983) found that 51% of the women in their sample said their partner promised to change if they stayed in the relationship.

BATTERER BEGINS TREATMENT FOR VIOLENCE
AND/OR SUBSTANCE ABUSE

Batterers agreeing to undergo treatment can create a Catch-22 for victimized women. Many victimized women have encouraged their partners to get help for years, and when they finally do, either on their own or because of court order, treatment can hold out the promise of change and improvement. Some programs for batterers and substance abusers promise the potential for dramatic results for anyone willing to dedicate themselves to the program. The court system, either implicitly or explicitly, endorses these interventions when they order them. If a judge and the district attorney think that this is what needs to happen, then should not a victim expect real change on the horizon? Many victimized women would like to salvage their marriage or relationship, if only the violence would stop (Campbell et al., 1998). Thus, when partners enter treatment, victimized women are often more likely to stay. In a study of women who petitioned to withdraw protective orders, 29% said that they were withdrawing the petition because their partner had started some type of counseling or rehabilitation

(Roberts et al., 2008). A slightly higher number (35%) said they were no longer afraid of the batterer, suggesting that there may be other interventions that are changing their views of the situation. Unfortunately, the effects of interventions for batterers are modest at best and near zero when victim reports are used to assess outcome (Feder & Wilson, 2005; Gondolf, 2012). Many others drop out of treatment, and the legal response to that varies widely from jurisdiction to jurisdiction. Many courts do not follow through on whether batterers complete treatment, but the majority of dropouts appear to persist in violence.

BATTERER MINIMIZES OR DENIES VIOLENCE

"Minimization, denial, and blame" are cornerstones of batterer behavior. Most interventions for batterers focus on these cognitive distortions in an attempt to get batterers to take responsibility for their behavior (Cavanagh, Dobash, Dobash, & Lewis, 2001; Dragiewicz, 2011; Pence & Paymar, 1993). Unfortunately, most batterers do not accept personal responsibility for what they have done and are experts in the fine arts of victim blaming and externalization. Minimizing the severity of the violence is one key tactic. They use phrases like "only once," "hardly touched her," and "never was serious about hurting her," to make it sound like the violence is no big deal.

A step beyond minimization is outright denial—"I never laid a hand on her," "I didn't mean to hit her with it," "I don't know who slashed your tires but it certainly wasn't me." Many times these denials are made for the benefit of police or others who might judge the batterer, but sometimes events are so chaotic that a batterer will feel able to deny all or part of what happened even in conversations with the victim. "You were so upset you didn't realize I was only trying to keep you from leaving. I would never intentionally hurt you. I love you." If his image of himself is that he is basically a good person, then he simply refuses to acknowledge that he, "a good person," could act violently. In one study, most (76%) survivors reported that their partner had denied incidents of abuse (Anderson et al., 2003). It is well established that batterers under-report violence compared to their partners' reports of violence, providing another kind of evidence that denial is common. Further, one study found that batterers who denied violence was a problem for them or that they needed to change under-reported their violence to an even greater degree than other batterers (Alexander & Morris, 2008).

BATTERER BLAMES THE VICTIM FOR VIOLENCE

The last element of the batterer's triumvirate is victim blaming. "You drove me to it" can be expressed in an apparently infinite number of ways, all of which somehow twist a situation around so that the violent person's behavior seems more like the responsibility of the victim than the perpetrator. Unfortunately, this kind of externalizing is common in many cultures—for example, "The kids are driving me crazy" or "My boss is making me nuts." Even inanimate objects are sometimes blamed—how many of us have fumed in frustration when a home repair has not gone smoothly or railed against the system when we get caught up in red tape? The provocation is often minor, even trivial—dinner wasn't ready on time, an errand was forgotten—but batterers are engaging in a culturally common practice of blaming others for their own emotional states. It is no wonder that victimized women can find this confusing and respond by wondering how they might do better. One of the main goals of batterers' intervention and marital therapy is often to get a person to accept responsibility for their own emotional reactions. After all, many things one person finds annoying will not bother someone else. It is a choice to get angry, not a necessary response to provocation. Unfortunately, that is not the message most victimized women hear. As shown in one study, they hear that their partners' problems are their fault (83%), that the batterers' violent behavior is their fault (71%), and that no one else would ever want them (61%) (Anderson et al., 2003). Heard often enough, there are few of us who would not at least question what we may be doing wrong.

BATTERER HIDES VIOLENCE FROM FAMILY, FRIENDS, POLICE, AND COURTS

Although a lot of minimization, denial, and blame are directed at the victim, batterers also use these and other strategies in an attempt to hide the violence from anyone who might intervene to help the victim. Some batterers intentionally assault women where it will not show in public, so that bruises are hidden. Sexual assaults are particularly seldom visible. Collecting physical evidence of a sexual assault is, at best, an awkward and difficult experience. Batterers also use strategies such as identifying the victim as the aggressor and blaming her for any physical damage in the house (Leisenring, 2011). They also accuse their partners of lying. Sometimes it boils down to who can tell the better story, and an emotionally distraught victim can be less convincing than a calm perpetrator (Leisenring, 2011). Some men have even resorted to self-inflicted wounds or will turn the tables to their advantage by calling the police first to claim victim status (Leisenring, 2011). One especially potent lie is to accuse victimized women of being motivated by greed when they seek divorce. Courts are still often very punishing of victimized women in the divorce process (Bryan, 1999).

BATTERER ISOLATES VICTIM

Minimization, denial, and blame are made infinitely more effective by socially isolating the victim. Most of us rely on others for feedback and a sense of perspective. People often offer support and sometimes advice to each other for romantic relationships, the challenges of child-rearing, the demands of extended family, the politics of career choices, and even for small matters such as the best places to shop and what outfit would look best for a particular occasion. Batterers do not take the risk of being contradicted by loved ones. They find ways to systematically cut off family and friends and progressively narrow a victim's social network (Lanier & Maume, 2009). Most try to control who their partners speak to or see (Anderson et al., 2003).

Batterers also have means of limiting transportation. Although I have not seen a lot of data on this, I have come across it clinically numerous times. For example, some batterers keep track of the mileage on their partner's car or mark their tires with chalk so that they know if the victim has gone anywhere unexpected. Thus, arranging transportation for any kind of help-seeking can even be considered dangerous. Further, some batterers keep everything in their name, including cars, house, or other property. Thus, at any time a woman could technically be accused of grand theft auto whenever she uses the family car. Although it might be unlikely that she would be convicted, many batterers engage in that type of harassment and sometimes find law enforcement personnel who, wittingly or not, take part in the harassment. Some batterers intentionally live in remote areas where their partners have little access to public services. When the only available perspective is the batterer's perspective, it is much harder to see through the minimization, denial, and blame and to generate all possible coping responses.

BATTERER MAKES DISTORTED CLAIMS ABOUT PARTNER

Batterers can be veritable propaganda machines. Not all of their distorted messages are specific to violence. Some violent men also criticize and humiliate their partner and frequently tell her that she will never be able to support herself and live independently (Anderson et al., 2003; Merritt-Gray & Wuest, 1995). Many battered women experience a loss of self-esteem in a battering relationship, sometimes leading to depression and other more serious psychological symptoms. The lies and propaganda may continue after a woman has left. Batterers will often do everything they can to discredit the victim. Batterers are often experts at presenting themselves as the "true" victim in the relationship. Infidelity is a common obsession among batterers. They often accuse their partners of affairs on the flimsiest of evidence—even a brief, public conversation with a sales clerk can provoke suspicion and rage. Accusations not only help to justify their behavior but also stigmatize the woman, who may suddenly seem primarily responsible for the end of the relationship. Claiming a woman is crazy is another common tactic (Anderson et al., 2003).

BATTERER THREATENS TO DESTROY PARTNER'S BELONGINGS

Almost all women will face a drop, sometimes a precipitous drop, in their standard of living if they leave a violent partner (Ozawa & Lee, 2006). Batterers often punish their partners further by destroying their belongings. Often they focus on objects of sentimental value that are irreplaceable. Other times they will cut up all of the nicest clothes a woman owns to make it difficult for her to return to work. These tangible property losses need to be considered in a holistic risk analysis as well. More than 7 in 10 victimized women had experienced this in one study (Anderson et al., 2003).

BATTERER DOES NOT PROVIDE CHILD SUPPORT

Efforts to secure the victim's return can persist for months and even years after a separation. One way that batterers continue to make it difficult for survivors is by avoiding child support payments. Some are more than happy to sacrifice the well-being of their children to place their partner in financial straits or even just to anger her. Many women know, either from threats or from past experience, that a batterer will abandon his responsibilities as a father once the relationship is over. They feel guilty about the sacrifices their children will make. They also recognize that their safety may continue to be compromised if they still have contact with the batterer through child support or visitation (Hardesty & Chung, 2006).

CONCLUSION

It has been said many times, but it bears repeating: Sometimes the physical assaults are not the worst thing a woman faces in an abusive relationship. In the VIGOR framework, understanding all risks is essential for developing the "multiple criteria" that will guide and prioritize decision making. Some risks will be more important to some women than the risks of physical danger. Depending on the nature and number of risks, some of these risks *should* be more important than their own risk of physical harm. These risks of substantial losses can powerfully influence women's protective strategies. In some cases, these risks may make leaving seem like a better choice. In others, the path to minimizing these risks may involve staying with a violent partner, who will retract his threats if she stays. Safety planning and risk management need to be personalized to reflect the risks that any individual survivor is coping with and the ways these risks have manifested in any one woman's life. The point is not to despair about the possibilities of coping with violent relationships. Women cope with violence all the time. The point is to start to appreciate that a one-size-fits-all "why doesn't she just leave" paradigm is never going to work for every woman in every relationship. In addition to constraints created by the batterer, there are other challenges that affect coping decisions and influence the protective strategies that women choose. In the next chapter we take up the two topics that have probably received the most attention in the literature: financial issues and institutional obstacles.

4

Understanding the Full Context of Violence: Financial and Institutional Issues that Constrain Coping

Many protective strategies cost money. Shelters seem to operate on the implicit assumption that within the window of time that they offer free shelter—30 days or 60 days or perhaps even just a week—it is reasonable to expect a woman to find a new living situation. Many seem to consider it a personal failure on a woman's part if she returns to her partner after a stay in a shelter. Although shelters offer many services, most shelter services are organized around the idea that the shelter will offer victimized women a bridge to a new living situation. There has been a movement to develop "transitional" housing, which provides free or low-cost housing usually for 6 months to 2 years after a shelter stay. Transitional housing is an explicit recognition that short shelter stays do not provide a workable path to new and safer housing situations for many women. Unfortunately, transitional housing is rarely available, offered only by about one in three (35%) domestic violence agencies in the United States (National Network to End Domestic Violence, 2012). It appears to be even more rare outside the United States, especially for programs specific to helping survivors of domestic violence (Novac, Brown, & Bourbonnais, 2009). Even in places where it is available, transitional housing usually offers places for only a few families, or even just one. Once a woman and her children move in, a year or more often passes before that place can be offered to another woman.

Let's unpack what is really involved in obtaining new housing. In many areas, waiting lists for low income housing ("Section 8" in the United States) are months or even years long—even for "expedited" applications for cases of domestic violence or other emergency contingencies. There is only a remote chance that someone going on the waiting list when they enter shelter will have a subsidized housing spot available within a 30- or 60-day window. Even if vacancies come open, subsidized housing "projects" or "estates" are not infrequently dangerous places. What is the advantage of trading a violent husband for a drug-selling gang on the corner? It is simply not safe to be outside after dark in many public "estates." Threats, break-ins, and pressures on one's children, especially one's male children, to get involved in local gangs are all too commonplace (Quillian, 2010). In effect, the lives of many residents in these projects are just as restricted as that of many battered women because of the high levels of community violence and the resulting pervasive fear of crime. Even if this sounds like a good trade to some, it is not a widely available solution.

So that means getting into an apartment on the retail market, which is a costly proposition. Virtually everywhere in the United States and many other countries, that will mean not only coming up with first month's rent but also a security deposit, which is most often another month's rent. In many places, leasing a home also requires passing a credit check, but assume for a moment that this is not a problem (the batterer has not ruined her credit). The average monthly rent in the United States in 2011 was $845 (U.S. Census Bureau, 2012). In the United States, the average renter spends 35% of their income on rent. There are other parts of the world where the cost burden of housing is similar or even higher, including Denmark, Greece, and the United Kingdom (Eurostat, 2013). Although I develop this example in U.S. dollars, the principles and challenges would apply in many countries. In the United States, security deposit and first month's rent is already in the ballpark of $1,700 in cash. Even in some relatively inexpensive rural and suburban areas, it costs up to $1,000 cash to secure a modest apartment in a low-income neighborhood. In many parts of the country just those two expenses alone will cost more than $2,000. In some places it is common to require not only first month's rent and security deposit in advance but also last month's rent. So now just the apartment or rental alone might cost $3,000 or more in cash. Important priorities such as good schools for children can drive these costs even higher.

Next, a woman may be interested in "luxuries" like electricity, heat, and running water. There are often deposits for each utility in the $50 to $200 range. Perhaps these can all be turned on for about $300 to $500. There is still the question of furniture—a bed to sleep on or a fork to eat with. Survivors who have gone to shelter often had to leave most of their belongings behind. In the course of a move, even survivors who are able to secure their rights to half the household property will still need to replace at least some items. Beds alone for a woman and children can easily run more than $1,000 dollars retail. Unlike rent and utilities, many household items are available used, but it can be time consuming to locate decent used items and they still can total significant costs. Anyone who has moved will also remember the costs of replacing many basic items such as cleaning supplies and kitchen staples. Survivors will either need to rent a moving truck (not an easy task without a credit card) or start frequenting yard sales and thrift shops for furniture and figuring out some way to get it to their new place. That is going to cost at least a few hundred dollars more just to get the barest essentials. So now we are probably talking about a battered woman needing a minimum of $3,000 to $7,000 in readily available cash or credit (although many of these items, like the rent, would be difficult to pay on credit). It would not be easy for many people across a fairly wide range of incomes to come up with a few thousand dollars in cash on such short notice, much less several thousand.

Perhaps a woman gets a job on her very first day in the shelter (never mind that a lot of shelters are not, to put it mildly, supportive of this). The job pays the current U.S. federal minimum wage of $7.25 for 40 hours a week. That is $290 a week, before taxes, social security, Medicare tax, and state taxes. In most places the "take home" pay from those wages would not be more than $240 at the top end, even without any payments for health insurance or anything else. Earning $3,000 would require more than 3 months and that minimal sum is only reached without any purchases for diapers or a gallon of gas or lunch or anything else the entire time. More realistically, it would take months, if not years, to even have a hope of saving that much out of the pay from a minimum-wage job.

In most parts of the United States and in many suburban, rural, and remote places across the world, the job, the apartment, the furniture, and all the rest can only happen if a car is also in the picture. There are probably not more than a couple of dozen cities in the United States—if even that many—where relying on public transportation is a viable option. In much of the world, living in areas with good access to public transportation also means living in more expensive, urban areas. Any car that actually runs and has legal registration and minimum liability insurance is probably going to add the absolute minimum of another $1,000 in expenses—more likely, two or three times that much. So now a woman is looking at something like $4,000 to $9,000 for a realistic plan for independent living, depending on the part of the country she lives in. Sometimes when people get so annoyed with women for "going back" and make up these complicated psychological explanations for why that happens, I wonder if these people have their own bills and their own bank account. Any analysis of a battered woman's situation that does not involve a realistic financial assessment is not helpful and may even be dangerous.

REAL-WORLD COPING CONSTRAINTS

As this extended example of the true costs of securing independent housing illustrates, there are many factors that influence a person's choices in any given situation This chapter focuses on areas of potential risk—financial and institutional issues--that should be included just as routinely and systematically as the risks posed by the batterer's behavior that were described in Chapter 3. Financial issues are not limited to housing; financial limitations can lead to other losses such as lack of healthcare (Logan et al., 2004). Institutional issues, ranging from limited shelter stays that do not allow time to set up a new home and job, are often phrased in terms of "barriers" or "obstacles," but the real problem behind these issues is that they increase the risk of losses—loss of safe housing, exposure to unfair treatment in the criminal justice system, loss of custody, and so forth. Many services are organized primarily around helping women leave, and if they do not wish to leave, then they may find few relevant institutional services to help them minimize risks (Davies, 2008). Beth Richie developed the idea of "gender entrapment" to capture the social and institutional processes by which victimized women are penalized for many of the responses they make to the experience of violence (Richie, 1996). Although Richie focused primarily on the unique intersecting oppressions of African-American women in the U.S. prison system, her concept of gender entrapment can inform the Catch-22s and double binds in which many victimized women find themselves, especially victimized women who are politically disadvantaged in any way. In the multiple criteria decision-making framework of the VIGOR, financial and institutional risks can affect not only priorities but also especially affect women's realistic coping choices and the derivative losses any individual might expect.

FINANCIAL ISSUES

Financial dependence may be the number one reason why many victimized women, especially those who do not experience the most extreme levels of violence, are trapped in abusive situations. Violence versus the street is an enormously difficult choice to make. Although the battered women's movement has long emphasized that domestic violence affects women in all socioeconomic classes, domestic violence is also closely linked to poverty, and failing to acknowledge this limits our ability to provide appropriate help to low-income women (Goodman, Smyth, Borges, & Singer, 2009). Economic hardship has been cited by 31% of battered women who remained with their partner as one reason that kept them from leaving (Strube & Barbour, 1983). Although lack of money is probably the most common reason, other financial entanglements exist too, such as joint ownership of a company (Cruz, 2003). However, general financial dependence can manifest in many ways. Some of these are described in more detail below and also listed in Table 4.1.

Unemployment and the Challenges of Finding a Job that Pays a Living Wage

Violence and trauma make it hard to obtain and sustain employment (Browne, Salomon, & Bassuk, 1999). This can be true even when batterers are not engaging in the workplace harassment described in Chapter 3. For most people, holding down a job requires having regular access to transportation, being able to follow a schedule, and missing limited amounts of time from work because of injury or illness. If

Table 4.1 FINANCIAL ISSUES THAT CAN INFLUENCE COPING DECISIONS

No money for security deposit and other moving costs
Unemployment & the challenges of finding a job that pays a living wage
Would lose job if missed time from work or moved
The expense of getting and maintaining transportation
Would lose health insurance for self and/or children
Would lose retirement, paid vacation, or other benefits if switch jobs
Loss of personal belongings
Cannot afford a telephone
Cannot afford to file for divorce or pay for a lawyer
Victim and her children would fall into poverty or have much lower standard of living
Joint debt with batterer, risk of bad credit rating or bankruptcy
Children would have to give up sports, lessons, or other activities
Indirect effects on employment and income
Would lose financial security—no "cushion"

a victim has children, then she will need access to daycare. Many jobs require education or training and some require travel. Most employers need to maintain professional, stable work environments. As Goodman and her colleagues (2009) have pointed out, many low-income women work in service or other nonprofessional jobs where they can be replaced fairly easily and as a result rely largely on employers' good will to tolerate the disruptions to their work that battering can cause. In addition to the direct effects of workplace harassment and other work interference, there are many cascading effects of battering that influence the ability to work and to hold a good job. The experience of battering can disrupt schedules. Batterers' efforts to isolate and control their partners may not be focused on work but can still limit access to job-related resources. As a result, many victimized women are unemployed, have limited work experience, and have an uncertain ability to support themselves economically. In samples of battered women in the United States, typically more than half are unemployed at the time they seek shelter (e.g., McCloskey, Treviso, Scionti, & dal Pozzo, 2002).

Jobs and money are often identified as the most frequent needs for abused women trying to escape violence (O'Campo, McDonnell, Gielen, Burke, & Chen, 2002). In an important study of abused women's ability to sustain work, Browne and her colleagues (Browne, Saloman, & Bassuk, 1999) showed that women victimized by partner violence had only one-third the odds of maintaining at least 30 hours a week of employment for at least 6 months, compared to nonabused women. This was true even after controlling for health, prior job training, and a variety of other factors. The erratic work histories created by a pattern of victimization create problems when women do seek work. Especially for women older than 30 years, a lack of work experience can make it very hard to get a job, especially a good job. Because so many victimized women have been forced to quit work or were fired after receiving threats, they often have not had a chance to learn any skills well and their résumé can look spotty and uneven. It is hard to obtain good references because of brief employment. Often, obtaining good references is even more difficult if the batterer stalked or attacked his victim at her workplace.

In random samples of U.S. residents, current employment status is sometimes related to recent abuse (Kalmuss & Straus, 1990), but sometimes not (Rodriguez, Lasch, Chandra, & Lee, 2001). The link between domestic violence and unemployment may be stronger for economically disadvantaged women (Lloyd, 1997). Whether unemployment increases the risk of violence is, however, a very distinct question from how unemployment affects a person's ability, once victimized, to extract herself from a violent relationship. Employed women who can support themselves financially are in a much better position to pursue separation, divorce, legal action, counseling, and many other possible actions that will increase their safety and the safety of their children. Of course this problem is not unique to women who have been battered, but the low wages for many entry-level jobs contribute to the difficulty in escaping violence. Even once the initial costs of relocating are somehow covered, many entry-level jobs simply do not pay enough to support an adult in independent living, much less an adult with children. Many victimized women have not been able to get the job skills or education they need to be competitive in today's economy. With the high rates of unemployment much of the industrialized world has experienced in the last few years, these challenges are only getting more formidable.

Would Lose Job if Missed Time from Work or Moved

More problems facing victimized women who are trying to establish financial independence are the difficulty of transferring a job to a new home and missing time from work. Many employers—for example, in retail, manufacturing, and healthcare—are very strict about time missed from work and this issue affects many low-income victimized women (Goodman et al., 2009). Requests for time off must be made weeks or even months in advance at some jobs. This makes it difficult to go to court, look for housing, search for new jobs, take classes preparing oneself for better employment, or take care of sick children. Many cities have only one or two shelters, and only about half of U.S. counties have any shelter at all (National Network to End Domestic Violence, 2012). Staying in a shelter can mean a long commute and difficulty following shelter curfews or "doing" shelter programs. This places many victimized women in a Catch-22; they cannot protect themselves if they lose their job, but they cannot maintain their employment while using domestic violence services.

The Expense of Getting and Maintaining Transportation

Transportation is another huge financial and practical obstacle for many women. Many victimized women have little or no access to a car. Although there are not, as far as I am aware, data on transportation availability to battered women, it is noteworthy that the number one purchase of battered women who participated in a special matching-dollar savings program was a car (Sanders, 2010). One focus group study also identified this as a major barrier to protection (Logan et al., 2004). Although some cities have good public transportation, much of the world is not covered by any public transportation at all, including virtually all rural areas and many small towns and suburbs. Even public transportation that is available often runs during limited times and limited schedules. Women who work the night shift or who must also make sure their children are dropped off and picked up from daycares or schools in a timely manner are often unable to find a bus, subway, or train schedule that meets their needs. Even in large cities, people may find it difficult to find adequate transportation to daycare, jobs, and victim service agencies and be able to afford to use public transportation on a regular basis (Logan et al., 2004). Even an older used car is a very significant expense and adds to the thousands already needed to start a new life in a new home. If the woman is able to take a car with her, then the car will often add hundreds of dollars per month to her expenses in car payments, insurance, upkeep, and repairs. Often a car loan is based on both people's income and many women simply cannot afford to take on the expenses themselves. Although they may eventually win child support or, much more rarely, alimony, it can take months or even years for such court cases to get settled and in the meantime the car payment is due every month.

Victimized Students May Lack Resources to Support Self or Stay in School Without Partner

Although many advocates recognize that coping is a process, there is insufficient recognition of the years it can take to establish self-sufficiency. Many women are attending college to better prepare themselves for the job market, to increase their independence from their partner, or to improve their self-esteem. Although improvements in feelings of independence and self-esteem can occur soon after the first successes in school, obtaining a degree takes time. Even as a full-time student, an Associate's degree takes 2 years and a Bachelor's degree requires 4 years to complete. Completing school, supporting oneself, and caring for one's kids can be impossible without help from someone. In the absence of help from family, help from a partner—even an abusive one—may be the only short-term solution. In the study by Roberts et al. (2008), another fairly common reason for withdrawing a protective order was needing the partner's financial resources, cited by 13%.

Would Lose Health Insurance for Self and/or Children

Obamacare (the Patient Protection and Affordable Care Act, also known as health-care reform) will hopefully improve the health insurance situation for many women in the United States. At the time of writing, however, Obamacare is only partially implemented and still facing challenges by the states and in the courts. Although health-care access is better in many other stable, wealthy democracies, there are still many countries in the world where health insurance is difficult to obtain and health-care costs are a burden. Thus, many survivors of battering have little or tenuous access to health insurance and healthcare. Some survivors receive health insurance through their spouse's employment, which they would lose if they filed for divorce. Although the poorest parents can enroll their children in Medicaid in the United States, most would still lose their own health insurance. A great many more fall between the cracks of Medicaid and private insurance systems—they work in retail or other industries where benefits are limited and insurance is prohibitively expensive, but they make too much money to qualify for Medicaid. Almost one in five Americans (17.1%) are without health insurance (Mendes, 2012). Although some victimized women may be in good enough health to feel they can take the risk of being uncovered by insurance, many have chronic health problems that cannot go without treatment. Many others are unwilling to take the risk of losing their children's insurance even if they are willing to take that risk on for themselves.

Would Lose Retirement, Paid Vacation, or Other Benefits if Switch Jobs

Divorce and separation nearly always have enormous financial costs on women's well-being, even for women who are not victims of violence (Grinstein-Weiss et al., 2008; Hanson et al., 1998; Ozawa & Lee, 2006). Women who must relocate to extricate themselves from a violent partner will often pay a considerable financial price. They will lose seniority at their work, the number of years vested in their retirement or pension plans, and the number of weeks of earned paid vacation. Many jobs have waiting periods of 1 to 2 years before such benefits are given, and it can take 10 years or even more to work up to the maximum level of benefits at a job. In addition to the possibility of losing these tangible financial benefits, there is also the stress of starting new employment, having to learn an entirely new system, and having to prove oneself all over again in a new environment.

Loss of Personal Belongings

Safety plans almost always suggest packing a bag with a few changes of clothing and personal hygiene items. It is seldom acknowledged that such plans place almost all of a victimized woman's possessions at risk, as well as those of her children. Cherished photographs and mementos, family heirlooms, modern-day electronics that have become so much a part of daily life—all of these are typically left in the possession of the batterer. You cannot bring Grandma's antique bedroom suite to a shelter or even that piece of pottery you picked up on vacation. Leaving via the shelter route turns victimized women into veritable refugees. Many batterers will take the opportunity to intentionally destroy their partner's belongings. Others will entangle them in lengthy and acrimonious legal proceedings. Victimized women and their children face the prospect of living in half-empty apartments with few of whatever personal comforts they have come to enjoy.

Cannot Access a Telephone

Although it might be hard to imagine in this day of seemingly ubiquitous cell phones, there are still substantial numbers who do not have a phone and even greater numbers who have inconsistent access to a phone because of the costs. More familiar to many readers are the gaps in cell phone networks, which can make accessing help very difficult in many rural areas. More and more people are giving up their "landlines" to rely completely on cell phones (Blumberg & Luke, 2010). Although cell phones can improve access to emergency services in some circumstances, the switch to pay-as-you-go phones and phones with batteries that must be regularly charged can also create obstacles to help-seeking during emergencies.

Cannot Afford to File for Divorce or Pay for a Lawyer

Divorce is another aspect of leaving that calls for thousands of dollars in cash. In recent years, many women I know seeking divorce have been told they need to pay between $5,000 and $10,000 up front to retain a lawyer to represent them. Buel (1999) provided a similar estimate. A contested divorce can run closer to $30,000 or even more, especially if custody of children is contested. Although mediation is somewhat cheaper, mediation is seldom a good route when violence has occurred because the batterer and the victim cannot negotiate as equals when the victim feels physically threatened. Even the cheapest divorces that cover court filing fees and little else cost several hundred dollars. These "do-it-yourself" divorces are also seldom good options for victimized women, who will have no advocate and no independent judge to help ensure a fair settlement.

Victim and Her Children Would Fall into Poverty or Have Much Lower Standard of Living

Divorce takes a financial toll on almost every woman who goes through it (Grinstein-Weiss et al., 2008; Hanson et al., 1998; Ozawa & Lee, 2006). Children are often adversely affected too. As outlined previously, many losses involve essentials such as safe housing and health insurance. Many women find themselves so impoverished that they qualify for food stamps or other types of welfare assistance. Even feeding themselves and their families becomes a challenge. There are other types of important losses too. It is difficult to face the prospect of losing the ability to provide nice clothes for children, gifts at birthdays and holidays, and participation in activities such as sports, music lessons, or scouting. Women may lose further touch with family members because they can no longer afford to travel to see them.

Joint Debt with Batterer, Risk of Bad Credit Rating or Bankruptcy

Many, many victimized women are in the position of being jointly named on mortgages, car loans, and other debt. Many batterers are as financially irresponsible as they are irresponsible in their roles as partner and father. A woman can be forced to not only pay rent on her new home, but also to continue contributing to a mortgage or other debt to preserve her credit. I have seen women make a financial agreement during separation that involves both partners contributing to a household account until the divorce is final, and then find that rather than paying the bills, their partner has spent that money on other indulgences. Because it can take months or even years to finalize a divorce, many face the prospect of paying their husband's bills for a long time to come. Even when loans are not delinquent, a survivor's joint debt with the batterer can make it hard to qualify for new loans. Couples often hold second mortgages, fairly new car loans, or high amounts of unsecured debt. When a woman applies for financing to move into a new home or get her own car using only her own income, she may find that she is unable to obtain more credit even if her payments on other debt are current. Unless she has access to large amounts of cash, this can really limit her options. Debt and bills were identified as a major risk by approximately one in five women in the VIGOR 1 study (Hamby, 2013b).

Children Would Have to Give Up Sports, Lessons, or Other Activities

Unlike many advocates, police, and human service professionals, victimized women typically engage in a sophisticated assessment of pros and cons to ending a relationship. Few cons can be perceived as greater sacrifices than the losses that would be experienced by children. Some of these losses are caused by economic constraints. As already discussed, establishing a new household and legally separating and divorcing from a spouse are extremely expensive, cash-intensive undertakings. These financial demands can mean there is little room for other costs, including the price of participating in sports, lessons, scouting, youth groups, or other activities. The prices of uniforms, instruments, and lesson books may have seemed manageable before, but simply cannot be afforded on one income. It is thought that there are optimal periods for children to get introduced to athletic, musical, citizenship, and other skills, and having to cancel or delay such experiences for a year or longer can have a lifelong impact on the level of achievement children will attain in those areas.

Indirect Effects on Employment and Income

Chapter 3 discusses the ways that batterers can have enormous influence in job settings (Browne, Salomon et al., 1999). In addition to a batterer's direct workplace
interference, there are other ways that the experience of violence can adversely affect
employment. Women who become sole caregivers of children will have less flexible
schedules. They may not be able to work multiple shifts or may not be able to attend
overnight business trips, conferences, or other after-hours events. Women who have
lost a job because of violence will not be able to get a good reference when they apply
for new positions. Time needed for court appearances, moving, and so forth, will
either eat into paid hours or potentially even put a job at risk. These are vastly understudied examples of derivative losses.

Would Lose Financial Security—No "Cushion"

Many people already live paycheck-to-paycheck, or something close to that, and leaving a batterer often costs a person's entire savings. Women with children and older
women do not have the luxury of decades to establish financial security. Although
young, single women may experience less financial anxiety because they still have time
to plan for the future, even women in their 30s and 40s will have trouble recouping
lost opportunities for savings. It is enormously stressful to lack any kind of financial
cushion to cover unexpected emergencies, such as healthcare and car repair. Fears
about loss of financial security were one of the most commonly mentioned risks in the
VIGOR 1 study, reported by more than half of the women (53%) (Hamby, 2013b).

INSTITUTIONAL ISSUES THAT INCREASE THE RISKS
OF LOSSES FOR VICTIMIZED WOMEN

Institutions cannot realistically meet the needs of every victim in every situation, no
matter how much providers and other personnel might like to do so. Institutions of all
kinds face their own constraints. Like the constraints facing victimized women, many
of these are financial but others include access to needed resources, such as sufficiently
trained personnel. Institutions can also, inadvertently or otherwise, engage in practices that reinforce sexism, racism, and classism. They are not equally helpful to all victimized individuals (Richie, 1996). Regardless of the reason, many victimized women
encounter substantial obstacles when they engage in formal help-seeking from human
service agencies of all types. Table 4.2 lists a variety of common institutional obstacles
and these are described in more detail in the following.

Most Shelters Provide Services for 5 Days, 30 Days, 90 Days,
or Other Brief Periods

As we have seen, it takes thousands of dollars to move out on one's own and initiate
divorce proceedings. Ninety days is not enough for many women to get that kind of

Table 4.2 INSTITUTIONAL ISSUES THAT CAN INFLUENCE COPING DECISIONS

Most shelters provide services for 5 days, 30 days, 90 days, or other brief periods
Local shelters are often full
Local shelters often do not accept women with substance abuse or psychological problems
Shelters may not admit victimized women who have previously returned to batterer
Many programs encourage leaving or divorce as the only effective options
Unwanted treatment required by many domestic violence agencies
Police and the courts respond in unhelpful ways
Police may arrest victim if she has used violence, even in self-defense
Arrest and jail time for batterers is unlikely, especially if first or second conviction
Victim at risk for child protective services report for "exposing" children to violence
Risks losing custody of children in divorce proceedings
Courts and batterer's programs support idea that treatment will change batterers
Immigration laws hamper help-seeking for documented and undocumented immigrants
Divorce orders may force child visitation with batterer without offering protection
Many religious institutions oppose divorce for any reason, including violence
Health-care providers may give victimized women stigmatizing psychiatric diagnoses
Insufficient child support payments and lack of enforcement for nonpayment
Welfare reform imposes time limits on eligibility for public assistance
Takes weeks to forward TANF or other public support to new address
Community services are set up so that the victim is the one expected to leave her home
Unequal treatment of members of politically disadvantaged groups
Control of batterer is only substituted by control of law enforcement and social agencies

money together, much less 30 days or even 5 days. Short-term shelter stays are supposed to be emergency housing for life-threatening situations, but what do you do when your month is up and you have only a few dollars to your name? Is it less of an emergency a few weeks later? The batterer's immediate rage may have subsided, but some will be even angrier at a woman for trying to leave and "abandoning" him and leaving him to care for himself for a while. It is increasingly recognized that victimized women need longer term transitional housing, but this is not widely available (National Network to End Domestic Violence, 2012) and can itself fail without other supports, such as job-finding assistance.

Local Shelters Are Often Full

Many nights I have called shelter after shelter looking for room for a woman and her children. Despite time limits to their services, many shelters stay at or near full capacity (Kulkarni, Bell, & Wylie, 2010). The results of the 2011 domestic violence shelter census found that across the United States, there were more than 6,000 unmet requests for housing *on a single day* (National Network to End Domestic Violence, 2012). It can be especially challenging to find room for women with several children, for women who need cribs and other supplies to care for infants, or for women who need accessible equipment because of a physical disability. In rural areas, the situation can be even more difficult because there are even fewer beds and it can be very hard to maintain confidentiality (Kulkarni et al., 2010).

Local Shelters Often Do Not Accept Women With Substance Abuse or Psychological Problems

Some women who need help escaping violence suffer from depression, trauma symptoms, and substance abuse. Many times these problems are the direct result of their victimization. It is equally true, however, that psychological problems found throughout the general population are also found among women who have experienced domestic violence. Some battered women live with bipolar disorder, schizophrenia, cognitive disabilities, and other serious psychological problems. Few shelters are equipped to support women with special needs for therapy or medication. Almost all require women to stay sober, which, as understandable as this is, sets up another barrier to service access (Kulkarni et al., 2010). Regrettably, too many shelters have a "one strike and you're out" policy with women whose symptoms make it impossible for them to adhere to shelter policies. These women often have nowhere to go except the street or back to their batterer. In addition to these issues, shelters often are not well equipped to serve women with complex medical needs or physical disabilities (Kulkarni et al., 2010). According to one woman in the Kulkarni et al. study, one shelter would not admit women more than a certain weight if only top bunk beds were available. These problems persist despite the Americans with Disabilities Act (ADA) and are widespread worldwide.

Shelters May Not Admit Victimized Women Who Have Previously Returned To Batterer

Shelter programs can be surprisingly harsh to women who seek a second stay, if they returned to their batterer in the interim. This is true even though it is widely known that leaving a batterer is often a process. In the advocate community, one frequently hears that it takes an average of seven attempts to leave a batterer. Although the original source of that estimate is unclear, it does reflect a widespread understanding that once may not be enough. Women sometimes hope that the first attempt will serve as a wake-up call to the batterer and that he will change or seek treatment. In other cases, the financial and other risks will only fully become apparent as women try to leave. Many victimized women have no understanding of the shelter system before their first stay—why should they?—and are surprised to learn how limited and short-term services are. Despite these well-known issues, too many shelters are very unforgiving of victimized women who do not follow their advice, even when that advice would be almost impossible to implement. Physicians treat diabetics who continue to eat cake. Therapists help those who repeatedly injure themselves. Alcoholics Anonymous embraces those who fall off the wagon as they make another attempt to stay sober. Why do shelters turn victimized women away when it is widely recognized that creating safety and protection is a process that may take multiple attempts?

Many Programs Encourage Leaving or Divorce as the Only Effective Options

Another problem with the advice offered by shelters is that few, if any, options are offered with the exception of immediate termination of the relationship. Few shelters offer any long-term planning options beyond the month or two of housing they make available. This stubborn adherence to a one-size-fits-all approach is one reason why so many women refuse shelter services or quickly terminate their associations with shelters. Immediate relationship termination is not feasible or desirable for many women. The growing literature on interventions for batterers and even couples-based interventions suggests that relationship termination may not be necessary for all victimized women—some may be able to work things out with their partner (Stith & McCollum, 2011). It is still widely considered heresy to even mention such possibilities in the advocate community, but a refusal to at least address them is one reason why so few women fully follow the advice of shelter workers.

Unwanted Treatment Required by Many Domestic Violence Agencies

In the early days of shelters, most shelters ran entirely on volunteer help and with the contributions of a few passionate activists. Many early advocates campaigned tirelessly for more public support of programs for victimized women. In this regard, the movement against partner violence has been very successful, with the Violence Against Women Act and numerous other programs now allocating billions to reduce violence against women and provide assistance to victimized women. One of the unintended consequences of the institutionalization and bureaucratization of shelters, however, is a huge increase in the burden placed on residents to participate in required programs to receive any assistance. Many of these programs are implicitly victim-blaming. For example, many battered women are forced to participate in parenting skills programs, regardless of whether any specific difficulties in their own parenting have been identified. Many more shelters require participation in support groups or other venues where women are expected to disclose details of their abuse and be "good" group members, whether they are comfortable or ready for such interventions or not. To refuse is to be kicked out of the shelter.

Shelters can be quite controlling in other respects. One study heard reports that a shelter required women to quit their jobs to attain shelter services (Kulkarni et al., 2010). Another shelter program I know focuses on job training in restaurant work and food preparation. Women who do not need job training or who do not want to learn food preparation have much less access to services in their community. Programs can also set up substantial barriers to services by requiring things like identification and complicated forms and admissions interviews (Kulkarni et al., 2010).

Police and the Courts Respond in Unhelpful Ways

Calling the police is often a desperate act of a woman who has used every other option she could think of. Years ago, the main problem with the police was that they seldom treated "domestic disturbances" as real crimes and many women died because their calls were repeatedly ignored. Often, calls to the police resulted in little more than officers telling the batterer to take a drive and cool off for a few hours. Today, although this does sometimes occur (Kulkarni et al., 2010), it is less frequent, but other problems have emerged. Although police training is improving, police are still taught that the prototypical situation for them to respond to is a crime perpetrated by a stranger, usually with the goal of financial gain. The perpetrators and the motives of partner violence do not fit this pattern and police often struggle with appropriate responses to acts committed by known assailants. Often, they are more expert at handling acts committed by strangers, despite the fact that the former is more common than the latter.

Mandatory arrest is one of the biggest legal changes that have occurred for victimized women in recent years in many jurisdictions. Mandatory arrest for domestic violence requires police officers to make an arrest if there is probable cause that a physical assault has occurred, as indicated by evidence such as injuries or knocked over furniture. One study of New York City women seeking helpline assistance for cases involving the police found that despite the existence of mandatory arrest policy, more than one in four (27%) reports to police did not lead to any arrest (Frye, Haviland, & Rajah, 2007). Even more problematically, almost the same number (24%) reported retaliatory arrest—incidents where the victim was arrested as a result of a false or exaggerated complaint by the perpetrator, and 9% reported dual arrest (Frye et al., 2007). Mandatory arrest can create problems both for victimized women and for police to the extent that this policy inhibits flexible, situation-specific responses (Goodmark, 2012). The courts are not always victim-centered in their services, either. In one study, nearly one in five married women (19%) seeking a restraining order were themselves ordered into counseling (Shannon et al., 2007). Thanks in part to the federal Violence Against Women Act, many U.S. jurisdictions now prohibit so-called "mutual" orders of protection, where the victim seeking help also has her movements restricted, rather than just the perpetrator's movements, but protection orders are still not always written in victim-centered ways. Despite ongoing efforts by advocates to keep human service institutions from re-victimizing women, some police officers and courts seem to repeatedly find avenues to blame the victim. Certainly victims of other crimes are not ordered into counseling or required to restrict their own movements to receive criminal justice intervention.

Police May Arrest Victim if She Has Used Violence, Even in Self-Defense

Dual arrest is one of the biggest problems with which survivors must contend. Police now often arrest both parties and "let the courts decide" who acted in self-defense and who was the primary aggressor. Although it can be difficult to sort out what is going on in a seriously troubled family, the result of this is that many women are now reluctant to call the police because they are afraid they themselves will be arrested. The number of dual arrests for partner violence and arrests of women for simple assault has risen dramatically since the introduction of mandatory arrest policies. Mandatory arrest has led to sharp increases in arrests of women in many jurisdictions, usually as part of a dual arrest of both partners, which have comprised more than 30% of partner violence arrests in some jurisdictions since mandatory arrest was introduced (Hirschel & Buzawa, 2002; Martin, 1997). Many advocates believe that the increase in arrests of women reflects, at least in part, overenforcement of mandatory arrest policies by some police departments (Martin, 1997). According to this view, women are being mistakenly arrested—for example, after engaging in self-defense or because their male partners make false countercharges.

Trends in arrest data show some surprising patterns in an analysis of gender patterns in arrest (Hamby, 2005). Ten-year arrests trends from 1993 to 2002 indicate a slight drop of approximately 2% in the total number of persons arrested in the United States (FBI, 2003). There were important gender differences, however—arrests of males fell 6%, whereas arrests of females increased 14%. Certain offenses show even larger differences. For aggravated assault, arrests of males dropped 12%, whereas arrests of females increased by 25%. The category of "other assaults," which includes simple assault, was virtually flat for males (1% drop) but increased a startling 41% for females. Despite this huge change in trends, males were still arrested for assault more than three times as often as women. There is no known social change that could account for increasing arrests of women, especially given that the pattern is not found in victimization data, but it can be explained by a backlash response to mandatory arrest policies. Although there may be other explanations, at the very least these large and relatively sudden changes raise important questions about arrest patterns.

Despite the presence of "primary aggressor" laws in many jurisdictions, dual arrest continues to be common and one source of this marked change in gender patterns for arrest. Primary aggressor laws are supposed to focus the attention of law enforcement on the party who perpetrated the greatest injury and has the most potential for causing future injury (Finn & Bettis, 2006). Police are also supposed to consider whether one party acted in self-defense in many jurisdictions. But research has suggested that there is often not systematic attention to these issues. Surprisingly, one qualitative study of police officers' beliefs found that many officers seem to believe that there are many benefits to criminal justice system involvement and especially that it is a path to receiving counseling (Finn & Bettis, 2006).

Arrest and Jail Time for Batterers is Unlikely, Especially if First or Second Conviction

Despite many changes in the laws regarding domestic violence in virtually every U.S. state and many other jurisdictions, few batterers serve any time in jail, especially for a first or second conviction. Although programs for batterers have increased society's efforts to stop offenders from continuing their violence, they have also served as a favorite alternative to jail in many courts. As a result, even those who are convicted of assault do little more than pay a fine and attend a group for a fixed number of sessions that typically ranges from 10 to 30. Technically, although failure to attend the group is often considered a violation of probation and can lead to jail time, unfortunately in reality there is often very little follow-up of attendance at these groups and many batterers get away with one excuse after another for missing sessions. As time passes, the public will to incarcerate them fades and many are soon back in the home, unsupervised and unrepentant. There they are relatively free to retaliate against their partner for involving the police in the first place.

Victim at Risk for Child Protective Services Report for "Exposing" Children to Violence

As the problem of partner violence has become more prominent in the public's eye, more attention has been given to the adverse effects on children of living in violent homes (Kitzmann, Gaylord, Holt, & Kenny, 2003). Although there is little doubt that living in a violent home has an adverse effect on children, some of the ways that has been dealt with make the problem worse, not better, for victimized women (Goodmark, 2012; Hamby & Grych, 2013; Radford & Hester, 2006). One frequent problem that has emerged is the use of child maltreatment accusations to force victimized women to comply with orders to leave their home and their partner. Rather than substantiating abuse by the perpetrator who is actually committing the violence, women are being accused of child endangerment or neglect because they have been assaulted in their home. This creates the surreal situation of the victim being legally defined as a perpetrator, even if she has committed no violence herself. Some women have become fearful of all victim services because of fears of being accused of being an unfit mother because they had the misfortune of getting hit. In the VIGOR 1 study, nearly one in five women (18%) reported concerns about child protective services (Hamby, 2013b).

Risks Losing Custody of Children in Divorce Proceedings

Shockingly, survivors of battering are often at no advantage when custody is determined in divorce proceedings (Araji, 2012). It may seem obvious that a perpetrator of family violence would not make a good candidate for physical or joint custody of children, especially when evidence suggests that a substantial number of partner abusers also abuse children (Edleson, 1999; Hamby et al., 2010). Nonetheless, being a victim is not only no advantage in custody hearings, it can even be a disadvantage (Goodmark, 2012; Radford & Hester, 2006). The stigmatized portrayal of victimized women can make the victim seem weak in comparison to the perpetrator. Perpetrators can drain the financial resources of their partners and make it hard for them to fight for legal custody. There have even been instances when help-seeking by battered women has been used against them in court as evidence of emotional instability—because they have documented records of visits with counselors or symptoms of post-traumatic stress disorder or depression. In the VIGOR study, more than one in four women reported concerns about losing child custody (Hamby, 2013b).

Courts and Batterer's Programs Support Idea that Treatment Will Change Batterers

Batterer's programs are a welcome attempt to address the issue where the problem lies: with the perpetrator. Nonetheless, like any intervention, they have unintended consequences and unforeseen side effects. There are two main problems with batterer's programs. One, they do not work a great deal of the time (Feder & Wilson, 2005). Two, despite their low success rates, they can create expectations with survivors that they will work. Some women postpone protective strategies when their partner is mandated to an intervention program, because they think that the batterer will change (Roberts et al., 2008). Although some do change, many do not. Estimates of the percentage vary quite widely, but when all of the program dropouts and failures are considered, many studies indicate that fewer than half the men who attend remain violence-free for even a single year.

Immigration Laws Hamper Help-Seeking for Documented and Undocumented Immigrants

Many batterers take advantage of the fear of deportation to control their partners, even those who are legal residents. Many women are not experts in immigration law and may not be aware that they will not lose their naturalized citizenship upon divorce. Others may genuinely be subject to deportation and consider the abuse a lesser evil than a return to a homeland where they may be confronted with joblessness and violence. Few shelter advocates are sufficiently familiar with immigration laws, and access to legal aid is limited. In many parts of the country, a high percentage of victimized women seeking help are foreign-born. For example, in one large survey of battered women in California, 20% of shelter residents were born in Mexico, and another 13% were born elsewhere outside of the United States. (Sorenson & Wiebe, 2004). Many women may be concerned about their residency status and the implications of divorce for their residency status, even if they are legal residents where they currently live.

Divorce Orders May Force Child Visitation With Batterer Without Offering Protection

Shelters advocate termination of the relationship as if that offers complete freedom from the batterer. In reality, batterers are frequently able to obtain the legal right to have regular contact with their victim through child visitation orders. These orders can be as often as twice a week. In most cases, visits are unsupervised and offer a batterer frequent opportunities to continue to terrorize, threaten, and abuse their former partners. A batterer may remain angry and resentful about a divorce for many years, with little respite. In contrast, there may have been extended periods of relative calm when the family was intact, and it is not always clear whether a victim's or her children's safety is actually enhanced through divorce or relationship termination.

Many Religious Institutions Oppose Divorce for Any Reason, Including Violence

Some major religious groups staunchly oppose divorce. Clergy from many different religious institutions maintain that divorce for any reason is wrong. In some cases, religious dogma indicates that problems in a marriage can be addressed by better submissiveness and piety on the part of the wife. Even religions that allow divorce often restrict women's roles. For example, in traditional Jewish law, a divorce is accomplished by a husband giving a *get* and a wife accepting it, which can restrict women's ability to obtain religious (versus civil) divorces without their husbands' cooperation (Jewish Orthodox Feminist Alliance, 2005). Hindu traditions discouraged divorce, often considered re-marriage a lesser form of marriage (full religious rituals only for first marriage), and granted men more access to marriage dissolution than women. Divorce in Hindu culture is still highly stigmatized (Holden, 2008). Islam permits divorce but, as with other religious traditions, discourages it (Mashhour, 2005). Islamic societies vary, but typically women are supposed to be obedient. In Islamic law, men have more divorce rights than women and traditionally women may have to return all or part of their dowry to divorce. Although legally women can obtain civil divorces in some Islamic countries, often harm must be proven (i.e., they cannot obtain a "no fault" divorce) and reconciliation efforts are often required. In some Islamic traditions, men can file "obedience" claims against wives for lack of submission (Mashhour, 2005).

Religious literature is complex and multifaceted. The New Testament of the Bible has many passages that advocate nonviolence and respect for others (*see* Chapter 9 for more discussion of this). Other religious works, such as the Quran, espouse similar principles. Examples from the Quran include emphasizing that marital relationships should be based on "love and mercy," that "women shall have rights similar to those against them, according to what is equitable," and that the relationship between men and women should be reciprocal; "They are your garments and ye are their garments," but these principles are not always the ones emphasized in modern Islamic societies today (as cited in Mashhour, 2005, p. 576).

Religious texts, however, can also include passages that do not easily align with secular egalitarian principles. I live in the so-called "Bible belt" of the United States and most of my own experiences dealing with these issues have been with regard to the Christian Bible. For example, in some conservative Christian churches, Ephesians 5:22-24 is commonly read at weddings and other services. In the King James translation of the Bible, they read:

> *Ephesians 5-22 Wives, submit yourselves unto your own husbands, as unto the Lord.*
> *5-23 For the husband is the head of the wife, even as Christ is the head of the church: and he is the saviour of the body.*
> *5-24 Therefore as the church is subject unto Christ, so let the wives be to their own husbands in every thing.*

Although the chapter goes on to include admonitions to the husband, his duties are outlined differently. The full section reads:

> *5-21 Submitting yourselves one to another in the fear of God.*
> *5-22 Wives, submit yourselves unto your own husbands, as unto the Lord.*

5-23 *For the husband is the head of the wife, even as Christ is the head of the church: and he is the saviour of the body.*

5-24 *Therefore as the church is subject unto Christ, so let the wives be to their own husbands in every thing.*

5-25 *Husbands, love your wives, even as Christ also loved the church, and gave himself for it;*

5-26 *That he might sanctify and cleanse it with the washing of water by the word,*

5-27 *That he might present it to himself a glorious church, not having spot, or wrinkle, or any such thing; but that it should be holy and without blemish.*

5-28 *So ought men to love their wives as their own bodies. He that loveth his wife loveth himself.*

5-29 *For no man ever yet hated his own flesh; but nourisheth and cherisheth it, even as the Lord the church:*

5-30 *For we are members of his body, of his flesh, and of his bones.*

5-31 *For this cause shall a man leave his father and mother, and shall be joined unto his wife, and they two shall be one flesh.*

5-32 *This is a great mystery: but I speak concerning Christ and the church.*

5-33 *Nevertheless let every one of you in particular so love his wife even as himself; and the wife see that she reverence her husband.*

Some pastors do not believe these passages justify domestic violence, as they are sometimes interpreted. The Reverend Al Miles wrote, "These verses clearly instruct husbands to love their wives as they do their own bodies, just as Christ loved the church. Christ never cursed, raped or threatened harm upon the church in any other emotional, psychological, physical, or spiritual manner. Husbands must follow Christ's example of self-sacrificing love." (Miles, n.d.-a). Nonetheless, other Biblical passages and parables also send messages that vary quite substantially from the "active coping" encouraged by most people in the psychology and advocacy communities. Examples mentioned in interviews with victimized women conducted by Nash and Hesterberg (2009) included the Biblical story of Job, which teaches patience, long patience. The story of Daniel's deliverance from the den of lions is another archetypal story that also focuses on handing over to God the timing and nature of change, and emphasizes that the role of the individual is sincere prayer and righteous living (Nash & Hesterberg, 2009).

Many women have been given no option except to "stay, pray, obey and [hope] everything will be okay" (Miles, n.d.-b). Sometimes these interpretations are disputed by Christian scholars, who insist that nothing in the New Testament can be used to condone abuse and maltreatment (Farley, 2008). See Chapter 9 for an extensive discussion of the positive aspects of faith and the involvement of faith-based organizations for many victimized women. Nonetheless, studies have shown some women's partners use scripture as seen through some church interpretations to enhance power and control over them, or that the rules of some organized religions hamper their efforts to protect themselves (Hage, 2006; Hassouneh-Phillips, 2001, 2003; Potter, 2007). It is still common for some members of the clergy to be unsupportive to battered women seeking help and suggest they keep quiet and stay (Potter, 2007).

Health Care Providers May Give Victimized Women Stigmatizing Psychiatric Diagnoses

Aspects of the health-care system can harm victimized women. One of the worst harms perpetrated by health-care providers is applying psychiatric diagnoses such as "borderline personality disorder" to victims of violence. Although it is true that some victimized women may be depressed, anxious, or emotionally overwrought, it is the victimization itself that has produced these symptoms for many, if not most, victimized women. The same can be said of substance abuse. Unfortunately, the use of even more benign diagnoses such as Post-traumatic Stress Disorder and Major Depression can hurt victimized women when they go to court and try to seek custody of their children. It is preferable to use V codes, an option in the Diagnostic and Statistical Manual for psychological disorders (American Psychiatric Association, 2013) that simply state a person is a victim of violence without making a stigmatizing psychiatric diagnosis. Institutional needs to apply Axis I diagnostic categories for insurance reimbursement should not take precedence over survivors' needs.

Insufficient Child Support Payments and Lack of Enforcement for Nonpayment

Although child support determinations are improving, many fathers put up surprisingly aggressive battles to give as little financial support to their own children as possible. They do all they can to demonstrate a financial inability to make much of a contribution. Some of the more common tactics include working at jobs where their income is "under the table" and not reported to tax authorities, hiding financial assets, or exaggerating financial liabilities (Bryan, 1999). Although many states now have fairly explicit guidelines as to what child support should be, in many cases these guidelines still represent a precipitous drop in children's standards of living. It is still also possible to find judges who do not adhere to these guidelines in all cases and will sometimes set lower amounts. As a society, we tend to value the preservation of the parent's standard of living over the children's. Many women find this unacceptable.

Getting a decent sum for child support in a divorce settlement is only the first hurdle. Every single month, a victim must wait hopefully for the money to arrive, often not knowing whether or not it will. Although child support enforcement is improving, largely because states have realized that is a way to reduce their own assistance to needy children, it still takes time to establish a pattern of missed or chronically late payments. Often several thousand dollars are owed by the time state enforcement has made any progress. Although states will garnish wages, suspend driver's licenses, and take other actions to increase the chances of payment, these methods only work if there are wages to garnish or assets to seize. Some batterers will purposefully avoid employment just to avoid giving their former partners any assistance, even when that assistance is for their own children.

Welfare Reform Imposes Time Limits on Eligibility for Public Assistance

In the United States, the 1996 welfare reform legislation imposed lifetime limits for receipt of welfare benefits. Although there are extensions possible by filing for a Family

Violence Option extension, these extensions are underused by victimized women and not offered enough by social service workers. Victimized women who have received benefits in the past are at particular risk for running out of eligibility before they are able to establish themselves financially (Goodman et al., 2009). Temporary Assistance to Needy Families (TANF) requires single parents to cooperate with child support enforcement, which can be dangerous for survivors of domestic violence (Goodman et al., 2009; Renzetti, 2009).

Takes Weeks to Forward Temporary Assistance to Needy Families or Other Public Support to New Address

The mills of bureaucracy grind slowly. Many victimized women will be forced to rely on food stamps, TANF, housing, and childcare subsidies. Some also receive social security or disability benefits. Unfortunately, it can take several weeks to forward these benefits to a new address. In the meantime, it is not uncommon for perpetrators to access checks or other benefits or to withhold them from their partners unless they return home.

Community Services Are Set Up So That the Victim Is the One Expected To Leave Her Home

Shelters have become such institutions in the United States that they seem a "natural" response to the problem of partner violence. Although the modern shelter movement largely emerged from the efforts of feminist activists, shelters are in some respects fundamentally anti-woman, because they have set up the expectation and the formula that the solution to partner violence involves sacrifice and loss on the part of the victim, not the perpetrator. Rather than being treated like other crime victims, who are helped to reclaim their statutory right to life and property after a crime, women who experience domestic violence become refugees from their own homes. Why should the victim leave? Let her violent partner find someplace else to go—if not jail, then at least some sort of transitional housing for men who cannot conform to the standards of basic civil behavior.

Unequal Treatment of Members of Politically Disadvantaged Groups

The shelter and feminist movements were started in Europe and North America primarily by middle class women of European descent (hooks, 1984/2000). In many places, people from other racial and ethnic backgrounds, including African-American, Asian, Mexican, other Latin@, and American Indian, have not been readily welcomed or accommodated in shelters and other programs that are dominated by majority culture staff (Donnelly, Cook, & Wilson, 1999; Hamby, 2000). Even if they are "welcomed," it is often on majority culture terms only. bell hooks recounts, "Many white women have said to me, 'We wanted black women and other non-white women to join the movement,' totally unaware of their perception that they somehow 'own' the movement, that they are the 'hosts' inviting us as 'guests.'" (hooks, 1984/2000, p. 55). One study found that some White shelter staff assumed other ethnic groups would "take care of their own," even when there was only one shelter in a community (Donnelly et al., 1999, p. 724).

The same can be true for women of varying religious beliefs. In the U.S. South (a.k.a. "Bible belt"), it is common, in my experience, for shelters and domestic violence agencies to use Christian decorations and Christian program materials. I have also found this to be common in Indian country, partly as a result of centuries of active efforts by Christian missionaries. I have heard that some residents at some shelters are pressured to participate in Bible study groups or to use Biblical metaphors for survival and healing. As described in detail in Chapter 9, I think the anti-violence movement has underutilized religious institutions and undervalued religious approaches to coping with violence. Nonetheless, it is equally important to make people of all faiths, including people with no faith or no active participation in religion, feel welcome when seeking help.

Only offering materials in the language of the dominant culture is another problem. Even in states with large Latin@ populations, many services are not offered in Spanish, or Spanish services are limited to a few translated brochures and bilingual advocates are unavailable or only sporadically available. An inability to offer translators and bilingual staff was cited as a major reason for unmet service requests in a national survey of shelters (National Network to End Domestic Violence, 2012). Simply translating materials is often insufficient—for example, some materials use examples of verbal abuse that include printed curse words, but even in the context of providing an example, the use of such language is considered inappropriate in many cultures, particularly in professional settings. As a result of widespread insensitivities to cultural and ethnic backgrounds, many women feel excluded from services available to members of majority culture groups. In many communities, most shelter residents are members of minority groups. In a California-wide survey of shelter residents, Latinas comprised the largest single ethnic group (37%), with 16% describing themselves as Black, and 13% of other ethnicities. Only 35% were White (Sorenson & Wiebe, 2004). Research on this issue often refers to barriers or obstacles, but the literature on racism and prejudice uses the term "microaggression" for many forms of unequal treatment (Sue et al., 2007). Microaggression is an important concept for understanding coping with violence, because it shows women might be trading one form of victimization for another if they choose to engage with many social institutions as help-seekers. It is important that services meet the needs of the entire population, not just members of the dominant culture.

Control of Batterer Is Only Substituted by Control of Law Enforcement and Social Agencies

Advocates frequently describe power and control as the worst feature of battering, but a woman who must access law enforcement, shelters, or social service agencies to escape violence often finds herself under a different system of power and control. Child protection agencies threaten loss of custody of one's children unless their plans are followed, law enforcement mandates the type of programs a victim must engage in to obtain legal protection, and shelters have curfews, chore assignments, and myriad other rules that few adults are forced to live under. More than one victim has questioned whether these new enforcers are really much improvement over the one she faced in her home.

CONCLUSION

Many protective strategies are easier said than done. "Why doesn't she just leave?" makes it sound like it is a simple matter to acquire and set up a new household, but this is an expensive and complicated proposition in most parts of the world. Institutions, both those that were originally designed to help victimized women and those created for other reasons that now find themselves serving substantial numbers of battered women, are not always set up in ways that actually promote their mission. Much of what women do to protect themselves is oriented around dealing with these issues as much as with the batterer. An MCDM analysis allows these other issues, which often represent derivative losses and cascading effects, to be more explicitly incorporated into protective coping plans. Even this rather daunting array of challenges does not yet outline all of the relevant factors. In the next chapter we take up the social, practical, and personal issues that can also present challenges when women are trying to protect themselves and their loved ones.

5

Social Issues, Practical Concerns, and Personal Values that Influence Coping Strategies

The previous chapters examined how the batterer can present many obstacles beyond the threat to the victim's personal safety (Chapter 3) and how the largely impersonal risks of financial and institutional issues complicate self-protection (Chapter 4). Now we turn to the eminently personal factors. Losing the support and esteem of loved ones and a victim's community are major risks for many women that can constrain protective strategies or at least limit honored and valued choices. De-valued options include pursuing divorce or relationship termination and other potentially stigmatizing choices such as seeking counseling. These are common forms of derivative losses and cascading effects. We also will examine how a woman's personal values influence her protective strategies. Multiple goods are often in conflict. All of us face situations where different values point us in different directions. Women strive to minimize the social and personal risks when they cope with violence as well. These issues are listed in Table 5.1 and described in the sections that follow.

SOCIAL ISSUES AND PRACTICAL CONCERNS

Victim's Family Wants Couple to Stay Together

Many women experience significant pressure from families to stay married to their partner or continue in a nonmarital relationship (Buel, 1999). There are many reasons for this family pressure. Sometimes family members are completely opposed to divorce for any reason, sometimes on religious or cultural grounds. Other family members feel that any father in the home is better than no father. Some parents worry about experiencing stigma themselves if their adult children are perceived to have "failed" marriages. Perhaps for these or other reasons, some family members refuse to believe that the relationship is abusive or blame the victim for provoking the violence (Trotter & Allen, 2009). Some may feel they are recommending the safest course of action, knowing that separation can increase the risk of homicide. For whatever reason or combinations of reasons, many women receive surprisingly little support when they turn to family. Sometimes this can even turn to outright betrayal. Trotter and

Table 5.1 SOCIAL ISSUES, PRACTICAL CONCERNS, AND PERSONAL VALUES THAT INFLUENCE COPING STRATEGIES

Social and Practical Issues
Victim's family wants couple to stay together
Victim's family and friends are afraid to get involved
Victim's family unwilling or unable to give social support or money
Batterer's family or others in community want couple to stay together
Batterer's family uses violence against victim
Victim and children would lose support of friends and family if they move
Family would have to change churches if they move or separate from partner
Would lose partner's help with child care and chores
Children would have less time with both parents because victim has to go to work
Victim is pregnant and needs help with delivery and caring for newborn baby
Victimized woman has a serious illness or disability
Victimized woman is elderly and unable to live alone
Victim is criticized for having a failed marriage
Being called a "battered woman" is stigmatizing
Being a single woman, single mother and help-seeker are stigmatized
American indian victimized women face unique obstacles
Options for new relationships are limited
Personal Values
Holds religious beliefs that divorce for any reason is wrong
Believes a violent father in the home is better than no father
Believes the success of marriage is the wife's responsibility
Believes the man should make the major decisions in a relationship
The roles of wife and girlfriend are important to many women's self-esteem
Believes batterer's claims that problems are her fault
Belief that her own use of violence, even in self-defense, ends her right to be safe
Believes that should not cause legal or job problems for her partner
Remembers happier times, believes those are possible again
Doubts ability to take care of herself and children on her own
Feels loss of control when she "gives up" on relationship
Believes children should be raised at home, not in daycare
Worries about risk of re-victimization in any close relationship
Loyalty and sense of duty
Commitment
Love

Allen (2009) documented cases where the victim's family actually told the batterer where the victim was hiding. Children often miss their father and pressure the mother to return (Cavanagh, 2003). In one study, 15% of women withdrawing a protection order said the reason was because their children missed their father (Roberts et al., 2008). In the VIGOR 1 study, more than one in four women (27%) said rejection by their families was a major risk they were facing (Hamby, 2013b).

Victim's Family and Friends Are Afraid to Get Involved

Sometimes family and friends have been threatened directly, as described in Chapter 3. Other times they may just worry about what the perpetrator might do. A victim's parents or siblings must also take into consideration not only their personal safety but also the safety of themselves and other family members. It can be genuinely frightening to consider opening one's home to someone who is being stalked, threatened, or assaulted. Although sticking by friends and extended family is instinctive to many, it is also instinctive to do what one can to protect one's own and one's family's safety. Some families and friends choose not to get involved.

These risks can be quite real. I know of a case, for example, when a woman married to someone with considerable financial resources wanted to leave. He pursued her and her child—though he was not the biological father—when she got her own place. One morning, to give one example, she woke to find her car doused in acid. He intimidated many people around her. My husband expressed concern about my staying in contact with her. Her parents took her in at considerable personal risk to themselves, which did help, but it was a scary time. As so often seems to be the case, he finally stopped harassing her when he got into a new relationship. Crime data (on any type of crime) show that sometimes third parties are injured (Planty, 2002). Unfortunately, domestic violence research provides scarcely any data at all on threats to others, much less on how that affects social support and constrains coping.

Victim's Family Unwilling or Unable to Give Social Support or Money

Going home is not an option for many victimized women. Some victimized women have no family to turn to. Going home would not increase the safety of other women—victims of partner violence have higher-than-average rates of childhood victimization in their family-of-origin as well (Hamby & Grych, 2013; Widom, Czaja, & Dutton, 2008). Ongoing lack of social support from abusive families-of-origin is an understudied mechanism for the intergenerational cycle of violence. Other family-of-origin problems, such as alcoholism, are also common. Although some families are able to help victimized relatives with the costs of divorce and establishing a new home, other families are barely making ends meet and can offer little financial support. In some cases, past family conflicts make family members unwilling to help. Still other family members may simply be trying to avoid contributing to the support of their daughter or grandchildren and may especially be trying to avoid housing them temporarily. Some do not want to provide the needed help with childcare or other concrete resources that victimized women need (Trotter & Allen, 2009). In the VIGOR1 study, almost half of the women (45%) said that lack of social support was a major concern (Hamby, 2013b).

Batterer's Family or Others in Community Want Couple to Stay Together

In-laws often play a substantial role in the dynamics of violent relationships. Many of them fear a divorce would mean greatly reduced contact with their grandchildren. This is a legitimate concern. If the victim succeeds in obtaining custody, then she will almost certainly spend less time with her ex-husband's family, so this is a very concrete loss for many in-laws. Of course, on average, the parents of perpetrators are more likely to have histories of violent perpetration too (Hamby & Grych, 2013; Murphy, Meyer, & O'Leary, 1993). They may excuse their son's behavior or expect his wife to make the same concessions that were made in their relationships. Even if they are not themselves violent, some in-laws will nonetheless sympathize with their child. As with other family members, many would also prefer to avoid the stigma of divorce and the public airing of family problems.

In-laws are not the only ones who sometimes wish to avoid the public airing of "family" problems. Women whose partners are police officers or members of the military, for example, can also be pressured to keep quiet about abuse (Buel, 1999). Despite efforts to improve institutional responses, individual colleagues or supervisors can still exert pressure on men's partners. This conception of "family" can even extend to broader groups such as others of the same race or ethnic background. Hill Collins and Garfield, for example, have written about a reluctance to "air dirty laundry" in the African-American community, especially in ways that might reveal it to White people (Garfield, 2005; Hill Collins, 1998a).

Batterer's Family Uses Violence Against Victim

In some cases, usually involving the most severe violence, parents or brothers of the perpetrator have also assaulted the victim. In my experience, this is most common in communities where divorce is so stigmatized it would disgrace both extended families. Violence between other family members—not limited to just between partners or between parents and children—is far more common than recognized. The National Survey of Children's Exposure to Violence found that at least 1 in 12 has been exposed to violence between other family members (Hamby, Finkelhor et al., 2011). Mothers were the victim in 28% of these incidents and male relatives and adolescent male children were common perpetrators. These can be very dangerous situations. The added threat makes it even harder to extricate oneself from the situation.

Victim and Children Would Lose Support of Friends and Family if They Move

Moving to a new town is sometimes the only way to escape from stalking, threats, and stigma, but moving extracts a high price. Some of this price is monetary, as discussed in Chapter 4, but much of it is social. It can take months to establish new friendships and years to put roots down in a new community. Residential instability is associated with numerous adverse outcomes, including emotional problems, teenage pregnancy, illicit drug use, and reduced quality of healthcare (Jelleyman & Spencer, 2008). If the victim lived in a town where she had a lot of family, it is likely that those bonds will never be replaced unless her family relocates to be near her. Although the loss of social support might seem similar for adults and children, it can be harder for a victim to impose losses on her children than on herself. Whereas an adult might move 10 or 15 miles and still have fairly easy access to her family, friends, and job, a move of just a few miles will put most children in a different school district. For many children they might as well move across country, for they will have to establish all new friendships and learn the rules and norms of a new school system. Although many people in our society are fairly mobile and move frequently for career advancement or other reasons, there are still many people who have deep roots in their hometowns and who do not take relocating lightly. Both family structure changes and more residential mobility have long-lasting negative effects on children's behavior problems and other important youth outcomes (Fomby & Sennott, 2009).

Family Would Have to Change Churches if They Move or Separate From Partner

Another issue that is underappreciated by many in social and human services professions is the deep attachment that many people have to their home churches and to the members of the congregation. As mentioned earlier, social work, psychology, medicine, and the grassroots feminist movement are all heavily influenced by a secular and humanist approach to intervention. There are many benefits to a secular approach. Principally, it helps keep services available to people of all faiths and denominations. However, it has in many cases also created blind spots about the importance of religion in many people's lives. It can be hard to find a new place to worship where one is comfortable. It can be even more difficult to continue attending the same church as one's former partner or, of course in the case of a long-distance move, geographically impossible. This is another loss that is little recognized by most advocates and providers.

Would Lose Partner's Help With Childcare and Chores

If you have not spent a significant amount of time caring for small children, then it is hard to appreciate the importance of a partner. Even a partner who contributes little to childrearing cannot help but offer some assistance, however inadvertent. His mere presence in the home will make it easier to do the simplest activities, such as taking a shower, carrying groceries in from the car, or taking out the trash. Otherwise even mundane chores require arrangements to accomplish while also keeping an eye on an infant or toddler. Most partners, even abusive ones, offer some additional assistance, such as carrying children or hauling strollers and other baby furniture. Even in the least egalitarian homes, men usually still contribute to some household tasks, even if they are limited to stereotypically male tasks such as home repair, car maintenance, and yard work. A woman without a partner must find a way to accomplish all of these alone.

Children Would Have Less Time With Both Parents Because
Victim has to go to Work

Children who live with only one parent are likely to see less of both of them. Although it may be preferable that they have less contact with the abusive parent, they are likely to see less of the nonabusive parent too, even when she has physical custody. Many women who would otherwise stay home or work part-time must return to full-time work following separation or divorce. Some women who are already working full-time will have to take a second job. Children will see less of the custodial parent too on the nights and weekends that they spend with the noncustodial parent. Batterers often have unsupervised visitation rights and even joint custody (Bryan, 1999). When the parents and children are home together, a single parent will have more household responsibilities and less free time to spend with her children. Although children cope with full-time childcare (which for children often means 50+ hours a week including a parent's commuting time), many parents value a home environment, especially for young children. Although high-quality childcare has a modest positive association with later academic achievement, evidence shows that long hours in even high-quality childcare during the infant and toddler years are associated with more behavioral problems. Recent longitudinal data indicate that this is a long-lasting effect that persists at least into adolescence (Vandell et al., 2010). Yes, exposure to violence is stressful, but so is exposure to daycare, which produces elevated cortisol levels (a biological marker of stress) in children compared to staying at home (Geoffroy, Côté, Parent, & Séguin, 2006). This is not to suggest that daycare is never an appropriate option but, rather, to point out that concerns about the effects of daycare are not unfounded and this option does have potential costs. A comprehensive analysis of multiple risks would incorporate these other risks into the decision-making process.

Victim Is Pregnant and Needs Help With Delivery and Caring
for Newborn Baby

Although the responsibilities of childcare are always significant, caring for a newborn is one of the busiest times of parenthood. Pregnant women need someone to help get them to the hospital, stay with them when the baby is born, and help trade-off the round-the-clock duties of parenting an infant. Babies also require a significant financial investment in equipment such as car seats, clothes, and diapers. Although some victimized women may be able to turn to their own parents or other family members, some will have no one to rely on except the baby's father. In one study, being pregnant with the perpetrator's child was cited as the reason for withdrawing a protective order by 1 in 13 battered women (7%) (Roberts et al., 2008).

Victimized Woman has a Serious Illness or Disability

People often speak of "victim" as a unitary concept and imply that all victimized women have similar abilities and needs. Some women need assistance with activities of daily living or seeking required medical help. Unfortunately, not much is known about victimized women with disabilities or other medical needs, but existing data suggest that people with physical disabilities and chronic illnesses are very vulnerable to abuse and neglect and have fewer options than most to cope with victimization. One of the largest studies on victimized women with physical limitations was based on a nationally representative sample of Canadian women (Forte, Cohen, Du Mont, Hyman, & Romans, 2005). Women with activity limitations reported more severe physical violence (60% vs. 47%), more emotional/financial abuse (88% vs. 80%), and more sexual violence (29% vs. 18%). Even in this community-based sample, physical injury rates were much higher for women with activity limitations (57% vs. 37%). Women with activity limitations reported more fear (43% vs. 33%) and increased caution (20% vs. 11%). They also had higher rates of depressive and anxiety symptoms (32% vs. 20%). Women with physical disabilities may also find it harder to access resources and information (Buel, 1999). As hard as it is to find an apartment or other living arrangement, accessible apartments equipped with ramps, low counters, and specialized bathroom equipment are even rarer (even with the advent of the Americans with Disabilities Act in the United States). Shelters also struggle with meeting the needs of victimized women that require accessible equipment (National Network to End Domestic Violence, 2012).

Victimized Woman is Elderly and Unable to Live Alone

Older women who have experienced domestic violence are another particularly vulnerable group (Buel, 1999). Older adults are also likely to have more health needs that require assistance. Older adults often live on fixed incomes and have fewer opportunities to acquire the funds needed to move. Older adults are more vulnerable to crime, sudden changes in health status, and social isolation than many other segments of the population, and these may also contribute to justifiable concerns about living alone. Although some older adults will be able to move in with family, many victim's children may fear the perpetrator themselves or hesitate to take sides between their parents. Other children may not have the resources to support a parent or may already be providing caregiving to children or other adult relatives. Some children, particularly those who were exposed to family violence as a child, may be simply unwilling to let a parent move in with them.

Victim Is Criticized for Having a Failed Marriage

Although not as strong as they used to be, many social forces still converge to support the continuity of marriage. Although supporting family stability has many social benefits, the social support for marriage creates difficulties at the individual level for those in problematic relationships. Stigmatizing divorce, and by implication the people who divorce, is one way that the value placed on marriage is communicated. In today's world, divorce no longer leads to social ostracizing but it is still a far less desirable social status than being happily married. Two or more divorces are significantly more stigmatizing than one, and some victimized women may hesitate to be a "two-time loser." It is hard to overstate the power of stigma—for many women the desire to keep up the appearances of a happy marriage is one of the last powerful motivators to remain with an abusive partner (Hamby & Gray-Little, 2007; Merritt-Gray & Wuest, 1995). Their status in their community is more important than the happiness, and even sometimes the safety, of their personal life.

Being Called a "Battered Woman" Is Stigmatizing

Before women engage in public protective strategies, partner violence is often a concealable stigma—many victimized women successfully hide the abuse (Hamby & Gray-Little, 2007). Although the stereotype of the battered woman is someone whose face is bruised and swollen, in fact many perpetrators do not seriously injure their partners, and some intentionally injure their partners in places where injuries are not easily seen by others, such as the back or scalp. Sexual assaults also often do not result in publicly visible injuries. Thus, the decision to "go public" confronts many victimized women, who are seen as "normal" as long as they hide the abuse, but in an instant can become objects of pity and fear (Goffman, 1963). A woman who previously seemed smart, talented, and capable is now seen as pitiable and helpless. Many victimized women who disclose to one or two trusted confidantes will still hesitate to separate or divorce, which will effectively disclose their stigmatized condition to the whole community (Merritt-Gray & Wuest, 1995). Women who already have devalued attributes, such as being a member of a politically disadvantaged racial or ethnic group or identifying as a sexual minority, may hesitate to add another devalued characteristic to their public identity or just see this latest episode of oppression as part of a continuum of oppression, not a distinct aspect (Potter, 2006).

Being a Single Woman, Single Mother, and Help-Seeker Are Stigmatized

Yet another way that victimization leads to stigmatization is through acquiring the devalued roles of "single woman" and "single mother" (Hamby & Gray-Little, 2007). Although both conditions are extremely common and even becoming normative, these identities still fall short of the social status ascribed to women in intact marriages with children (Perilla, 1999). Single mothers who qualify for food stamps or other government assistance will have to adopt the stigmatized status of "welfare recipient" to obtain those benefits. There are harsh terms such as "welfare queen" that communicate this stigma. These terms change little despite regular changes in the names of the laws or funding mechanisms used to minimize hunger in the United States and provide support to needy families. Although there are advantages to society of encouraging two-parent homes, victimized women must choose between several stigmatized conditions—single woman, single mother, divorcée, battered—or between trying to continue to hide the violence through information management.

I have even heard some human service providers express resentment about the "free ride" they perceive welfare benefits to offer. I remember one training where a provider complained vehemently that "food stamps" (as they are still commonly called in the United States) could be used on what she perceived to be frivolous food choices. I was expecting her to at least say something about "junk" food, but her example was peanut butter. I was even more shocked when she suggested that welfare recipients and their children should buy dried beans and live off of those. I am not certain why she thought a bean diet would help them break out of poverty but it does illustrate how negative and powerful the stigma associated with needing help can be.

American Indian Victimized Women Face Unique Obstacles

In addition to the prejudices that all ethnic minorities face, American Indian women living on U.S. reservations must deal with the lack of criminal justice and victim resources on most reservations. If they have a non-Indian partner, tribal law enforcement will not be able to arrest or detain him, no matter what kind of violence he commits because of Federal laws limiting tribal sovereignty (Hamby, 2009b). Some attempts to address this legal loophole passed in the 2013 U.S. Violence Against Women Act, but many loopholes remain. The law will not take effect until 2015 and does not include sexual assaults or crimes committed by non-Indians who do not live or work on the reservation. The result is much less justice for American Indian women who have experienced domestic violence, because Federal law enforcement personnel are almost nonexistent on many reservations. Further, most American Indian communities are a fraction of their size before European colonization of the Americas, and many American Indian women have few opportunities for intratribal remarriage. With most tribes well less than 50,000 members and many under 5,000, victimized women may feel that they are personally contributing to the extinction of their tribe if they leave a relationship with a fellow tribal member (Hamby, 2000). In the United States and most of the rest of the world, there are few ethnic groups in this sad and unique position. Although it has long been noted how these and other long-lasting effects of the oppression suffered by American Indian people when Westerners came to North America contribute to high rates of violence in American Indian and First Nations communities (Hamby, 2000), it has less often been acknowledged how some of these issues, such as lack of law enforcement and limited within-group relationship choices, also affect American Indian women's protective strategies and coping choices.

Options for New Relationships Are Limited

Many victimized women are young and do not yet have children. These women may have numerous other opportunities for future relationships. Other women are in more complicated situations. Older women may well be committing to a life of solitude if they separate from their current partner, because there are few available older men. Victimized women with children may find it difficult to find a partner who is willing to become a stepfather. Lots of people have ex-boyfriends and even ex-husbands, and these can complicate new relationships, but exes who may stalk or threaten or assault their former partner and her new romantic partner may make it difficult for survivors to get beyond the first date with someone new. New romantic interests can scarcely be blamed if they hesitate to get involved in a situation that might lead to their own bodily harm. Worry that that they would not be able to find a future partner was reported by a few women in the VIGOR studies. Perpetrators often tell women that no one else will ever want them; more than half of survivors (61%) in one study reported this (Anderson et al., 2003).

PERSONAL VALUES THAT CONSTRAIN COPING

Holds Religious Beliefs that Divorce for Any Reason Is Wrong

> *"One of the things that kept me bound to my marriage for 13 years, too, though, was being committed to marriage and saying you know this is my vow in front of God and everything else." (Werner-Wilson, Zimmerman, & Whalen, 2000, p.170)*
> *"In this country, religious values are pretty strong. Growing up, everyone told me that it is a wife's duty to take of her husband and children and make the marriage work – no matter what." (Hornosty & Doherty, 2002, p. 24)*

The anti-violence community has strong roots in the feminist, psychological, and health-care communities. Many members of these groups hold secular perspectives on social justice and individual well-being. Conservative religious ideals are not common among these groups. When conservative religious values are mentioned in the materials of many organizations, it is largely in reference to why women should still leave even if they hold conservative religious values. Although not all victimized women belong to fundamentalist churches or hold such views, many do and this effects how they approach the challenges of protection (Werner-Wilson et al., 2000). Sometimes it is easy to talk about religious institutions and lose sight of the fact that these are personal values as well. Some women are willing to sacrifice their own safety to preserve their religious beliefs. This is true for women from a variety of religious backgrounds, including Christianity, Judaism, Islam, Hinduism, and others. They are inspired by powerful, archetypal stories that have survived millennia and guide the decisions of millions. As noted in Chapter 4, many of these stories teach patience, endurance, and handing over one's life to God. I include it again here under Personal Values to emphasize that these are both institutional and personal issues. Their importance to many women who have experienced violence should not be dismissed. The field needs to do more to find ways to help women take protective steps without disavowing or, even worse, asking them to disavow their religious and spiritual beliefs. Steps toward separation and divorce are particularly likely to be rejected. Women who believe their religious views are belittled or ignored are more likely to stop seeking help than to give up their spirituality, which may also be a source of great strength for them. *See* Chapter 9 for a more extensive discussion of the ways women with strong religious ties approach protection and how the field can better support them.

Believes a Violent Father in the Home Is Better Than No Father

Most people value having two parents in a home with children. Research supports these traditional family values: There are many advantages to having both a father and mother in the home, including increased financial stability, less parental stress, male and female role models for children, and, in many cases, increased emotional support (Grinstein-Weiss et al., 2008; Ozawa & Lee, 2006; Turner et al., 2012). As mentioned earlier, single parenthood is difficult and stigmatized. Although society as a whole benefits from promoting family stability, problems arise where the assumed benefits of staying together do not exist in individual relationships. Society has not really worked this problem out. In fact, if anything, society seems to have it backwards. People who divorce over "irreconcilable differences" with no hint of scandal are stigmatized less, although perhaps many of those marriages could continue with no irreparable harm to husband or wife and perhaps even some benefits to the spouses and their children. The taint of scandal is a powerful stain, however, and when marriages really should end, it is those people who are whispered about, stared at, and often endure a new aloofness among their friends and acquaintances. These are not only social or community values, but the values of individual women too. These combined social and personal values create a climate where many women choose to stay "for the sake of the children." They are choosing between losses: loss of a parent in the home and the inevitable distancing with at least one parent after divorce and loss of a peaceful family environment to which all children are entitled but so many children lack. Research indicates that many women stay for the sake of the children. Almost one in five cited this as a reason in one study of battered women (Strube & Barbour, 1983). In the National Violence Against Women Survey, the sake of the children was the third most common reason given for returning to a violent partner, reported by one in six women victimized by their current partner (16%) (according to calculations on archived dataset done for this book).

Believes The Success of Marriage Is the Wife's Responsibility

Although our attitudes and standards about relationships are slowly changing, the responsibility for relationship maintenance still falls largely on women in most heterosexual relationships, violent and nonviolent alike. Women still, even in the twenty-first century, do considerably more childcare and housework than men (Kimmel, 2008). However, this issue is not only about housework. There are dozens of other relationship maintenance duties, many seemingly small, that are typically done by women, such as remembering and acknowledging family birthdays, staying in touch with extended family, and planning events such as graduation and marriages. How many women purchase and package cards and gifts even for their in-laws? This extends also to more intimate and intangible efforts, such as initiating discussions regarding relationship issues and expressing affection. Because of these and related social patterns, there can be a sense that any failed marriage is more a failure of the wife than the husband. Certainly at the very least there is often the perception that it is a shared failure. Many victimized women do not want to feel that they have failed so they continue to try and make the marriage work. The values related to the role of wife and mother vary across cultural groups. For example, the concept of "marianismo" is still influential in many Latin@ communities. The concept of marianismo emphasizes that good women keep families together, stand by their husbands, and, if necessary, put others' needs before their own (Perilla, 1999).

Believes the Man Should Make the Major Decisions in a Relationship

Although our society and our relationships are becoming increasingly egalitarian, we are a long way from being fully so (Kimmel, 2008). Throughout society, major moves and career decisions are more likely to be based on the man's career than the woman's. Households with stay-at-home moms are more than 50 times as common than ones with stay-at-home dads (Fields, 2003). Although people are, on average, more likely to endorse joint decision making than in the past, there is considerable individual variability and many women and men still endorse a traditional model with the man as chief decision maker. They avoid an adversarial position with respect to their husbands.

The Roles of Wife and Girlfriend Are Important to Many Women's Self-Esteem

Part and parcel of all of the gender-defined roles are gender-specific possibilities for obtaining self-esteem. Being in a relationship is esteemed for women. It is a good thing for men, too, but the difference is that being single is okay for a man too—that just makes him an "eligible bachelor." On the other hand, being single is not a valued status for a woman, although we no longer say "spinster" very often. Many women have other avenues of esteem open to them and women have more opportunities than ever before. Still, on the societal level, these are not equally distributed across class or race. Further, on the individual level, many of these other avenues have been cut off for women in violent relationships because their partners stop them from working, going to school, or maintaining friendships.

Believes Batterer's Claims that Problems Are Her Fault

When your primary source of information and feedback is biased and blaming, it is hard to maintain your own sense of perspective. Many batterers purposefully shut off access to other perspectives and other sources of information by isolating victimized women from family, friends, and health providers. As a consequence, some victimized women experience feelings of guilt and self-blame for the violence. They have been told over and over that it is their inadequate behavior or flawed personality that triggers the violence (Anderson et al., 2003). That is the story that the batterer tells anyway, although the true underlying dynamics have more to do with the batterer continually watching for an excuse to explode and emphasize his control over her and their life together. Women are taught to say "I'm sorry" easily and often.

Belief that Her Own Use of Violence, Even in Self-Defense, Ends Her Right to be Safe

Women's use of violence is probably the biggest controversy in the provider and advocate communities. Women are injured and sexually assaulted much more often than men. Nonetheless, it is increasingly clear that some women do use violence against their intimate partner. Although this is sometimes called "mutual violence," that term is really a misnomer. Men are, on average, 5 inches taller, 30 pounds heavier (McDowell et al., 2008), and possess 50% more upper body and 30% more lower body strength than the average woman (Powers & Howley, 1997). Further, in the United States as in many other countries, social norms encourage romantic pairings in which the man is taller than the women, with the result that height differences, and by extension weight and strength differences, are maintained in most couples (Pierce, 1996). Few male partners have reason to fear women's violence, and in many romantic comedies and other movies, a slap by a woman is played for laughs. Although not really very funny, violence by women, even in self-defense, can make women doubt whether they "deserve" a nonviolent existence. The court system and trends toward dual arrest are spreading blame and criminal culpability equally in many extremely lopsided cases, such as instances where a woman scratches a man while trying to push him off of her. He may have been hitting her repeatedly, but because he is the one bleeding, both or even just the woman are arrested. These scenarios are becoming all too common and are creating false impressions in many people's minds. It is possible to identify the primary aggressor, and there is a difference between violence used in self-defense and other violence. Everyone deserves to be safe and free from violence. If a woman is acting violently, then her partner should call the police, rather than engage in vigilante justice that so often results in her receiving a beating far worse than she could be physically capable of perpetrating herself.

Believes She Should Not Cause Legal or Job Problems for Her Partner

The question of getting the law involved looms large for many people, and especially so for members of many oppressed groups. In the United States, African-Americans, American Indians, Latin@s, and other ethnic minorities often have especially good cause to wonder whether calling the police will create more problems than it solves (e.g., Buel, 1999; Garfield, 2005; Hamby, 2008; Hill Collins, 1998b). Elsewhere, ethnic and political minorities are also often treated unfairly by law enforcement. In the United States, males from most politically disadvantaged communities are already jailed at incredibly high rates and often receive punishments more severe than members of the dominant culture. Other politically disadvantaged groups, such as gays, lesbians, and documented and undocumented immigrants, also have good reasons to fear the legal and societal response to their help-seeking (Perilla, 1999; Renzetti, 1992; Villalon, 2010). They may not want to contribute to removing another person from their community—that price may seem too high no matter what the person has done.

   Even members of the majority community, however, face a difficult dilemma. Criminal charges that result in either a criminal record or jail time can create employment problems for batterers, which create financial problems for families. A victim may face eviction if her partner serves a month or more in prison and loses substantial income. It is easy to encourage them to seek "justice" without considering whether they themselves will in effect also be punished for using the legal system. A law-and-order response may not meet the needs of many women who have experienced violence (Garfield, 2005). Most women are carefully weighing these unintended outcomes when they make decisions about how to respond to violence.

Remembers Happier Times, Believes Those Are Possible Again

Not every moment, in even the most abusive relationship, is spent in violence. Advocates, providers, and the general public tend to treat battering as the overwhelming feature of any relationship. In nationally representative studies, however, most violent relationships experience only one or two episodes a year and few more than one a month (e.g., Hamby et al., 2011). Even in shelter populations, violence is far from an everyday occurrence. Ellen Pence, one of the founders of the Duluth model, was one of the first advocates to appreciate that battered women often do not see their lives the ways human service professionals do. Just as health-care providers tend to speak of "diabetics" and "schizophrenics," there is a tendency to treat "battered women" as if that is the main, if not only, relevant feature of their existence. However, just as diabetics, alcoholics, and schizophrenics are more than their disorders, so battered women are more than their victimization, and their relationships include elements other than violence and abuse. Many of their relationships started the way most relationships do—with a period of dating and romance that produced many happy memories. Even after the violence starts, there can be extended periods—weeks or months—when things are "going well." Holidays come and go, children are born and celebrate birthdays, and vacations are enjoyed. Some of the happiest days of a woman's life are likely to have been spent with her partner. Not only do many women remember these times, they still periodically experience happy moments that can give them hope that more good times are ahead and the violence can be put behind them.

Doubts Ability to Take Care of Herself and Children on Her Own

As we discussed earlier, anyone who has ever taken care of an infant or small child knows how exhausting that can be. Being a single parent can be a 24-hour endurance test during which it can be hard to find a moment to take a shower, much less get 8 hours of uninterrupted sleep or some time for oneself. The practicalities of taking time off from work to care for sick children and managing all the other day-to-day responsibilities can be overwhelming in the best of circumstances. Although some people have good family support or can easily afford extra babysitting, not everyone is in that position. Personal doubts about whether one can handle these challenges are common.

Even women who do not have children may doubt their ability to take care of themselves. Many women are still raised to think they need to find a partner to rely on for financial and other support. They may never have been financially independent. Some victimized women come from families, often single-parent homes, where there was never any financial stability and sometimes not even a stable home environment. They may not have learned the basic tools to care for themselves or they may have learned, from their parents' struggle, that financial ruin is always just around the corner and doubt their own ability to succeed where their parents failed. Of course, there are all the other situations we have already mentioned—illness, disability, infant care, depression, poor family support, college, and so forth—that limit a person's ability to live completely independently.

Feels Loss of Control When She "Gives Up" on Relationship

An advocate in training once asked me if victimized women needed to reassert control over their lives. I responded that many victimized women I know are in considerably more control than the rest of us. At that very training I was already running over my scheduled time—I had told my husband I would be done at 11:30 a.m. and it was already after noon. I had also already offered to return after lunch to continue the training, without checking with him first (I probably should have). Among other things, that meant he would be home alone with our two young children for another couple hours on a Saturday. I was not worried about staying on schedule or waiting 45 minutes to tell him I was going to be late. I had no reason to fear his response.

In contrast, many battered women go to extraordinary lengths to control all the vagaries of life and present a perfectly ordered environment to their partner. In many, if not most, situations, responding to adversity or stress by stepping up your own efforts to make things better is a good idea. Health outcomes, for example, are better when heart attack patients or diabetics take better control over their diet, exercise, and stress reduction. Victims of other crimes often respond with actions that some criminologists refer to as "hardening the target" (Podolefsky & Dubow, 1981). These include protective steps such as installing security, locking doors, getting a dog, and not walking alone at night. It is not surprising many women try to "fix" their partner's violence by trying to control the apparent triggers. Although these apparent triggers are often simply avenues for expressing a batterer's need to control and dominate, they often appear to be problems that can be addressed. Don't be late, don't speak to other men. Some of them are versions, albeit extreme ones, of normative and appropriate expectations for relationships. For women who have been trying to address these issues by trying to live up to their partner's expectations, giving up on the relationship can feel like loss of control. Advocates often do not seem to understand that the prospect of leaving does not necessarily create a sense of relief. In addition to the huge issues we have already discussed (the financial challenges, separation violence, the possibility of losing custody of the kids), there is also the sense of helplessness and failure that is difficult and unpleasant to face.

Believes Children Should be Raised at Home, Not in Daycare

There is considerable public controversy regarding whether children in full-time daycare are disadvantaged over those who are at home with their mothers. Several studies have documented increases in behavioral problems among those in daycare at the earliest ages or in less-than-high-quality daycare (Vandell et al., 2010). On the other hand, children in daycare often have better school achievement than children who stay at home. Researchers and commentators frequently look at the same data and come to very different conclusions, so it is not surprising that opinions vary among the general public as well. Many women believe very strongly that children, especially infants and toddlers, should be raised at home. They are exposed to fewer illnesses at a young age, children have more time to participate in other activities, and in general it can be less stressful for families when both parents do not work full-time. After three decades of increasing work force participation by mothers of the youngest children, the current trend is for mothers of infants and toddler to prefer to work fewer hours outside the home (Pew Research Center, 2007). There are pros and cons to all choices regarding work–life balance for families with young children. Although victimization certainly changes the cost–benefit ratios of these choices, it does not eradicate the costs of other choices. Many providers and researchers assume that the costs of violence exposure are worse than the costs of losing time with a parent, changes in family structure, residential mobility, and increased time in daycare (to name just a few common ones with known adverse outcomes), but we do not have research evidence that specifically tests this assumption. It should not be surprising or disparaged when women value staying home with their children and weigh that value heavily in their decision making.

Worries About Risk of Re-Victimization in Any Close Relationship

Many victims of partner violence have a lifelong history of victimization. Although this is not true of all victimized women (nothing is true of *every* victim), re-victimization is an important pattern (Hamby & Grych, 2013). Although the reasons why past victimization increases the risk of future victimization are not fully understood, it is likely that several factors contribute. A history of violence, by creating chronic stress among other possible mechanisms, can affect women's ability to appraise and respond to threats (Macy, Nurius, & Norris, 2006; Noll & Grych, 2011; Norris, Nurius, & Dimeff, 1996). Risky routine activities can increase risk (Wittebrood & Nieuwbeerta, 2000). "Risky activities" are not euphemisms for victim blaming. Women may find themselves in risky situations because they live or work in high crime areas and cannot afford to move. Substance abuse and other issues may also lead to riskier routine activities. Although this topic has more often been addressed in the conventional crime and sexual aggression literatures, people's environments may also affect the relationship choices that they have. Regardless of the mechanism, it is clear that involvement in violence can create a cascading effect for some people that place them at higher risk for later re-victimization.

Loyalty and Sense of Duty

Here is where I may as well mention that I am a cousin of Tammy Wynette, most famous for the song "Stand By Your Man" (my grandmother was her aunt). Wynette was married four times so she did not necessarily live by the lyrics herself, but that does not mean they have not become an iconic expression of loyalty and perhaps forgiveness to one's partner. Loyalty is an old-fashioned virtue and one that is not entirely in favor in this age of divorce, but there are still people who hold loyalty dear. Loyalty can be a more personal commitment to the man than to the marriage—they do not want to hurt their partner, they worry about what will happen to him, and they do not want to see themselves as a fair-weather friend. This is especially true of violent partners who struggle with problems such as alcohol, depression, and suicidal thoughts. It can be hard to know when loyalty is a virtue and when it is a disadvantage.

In the twenty-first century, loyalty is endorsed more than one might think. A 2007 poll found that 56% of American voters said Hillary Clinton's decision to stand by Bill after the Monica Lewinsky affair was a sign of *strength* (Lonnstrom, 2007). Not a sign of denial, not a sign of passivity, not even just an okay thing to do, but an actual *strength*. There was a gender difference too—women were more likely to say so than men: 62% to 50%. Although these findings are not about violence per se, they are important because they show that sticking with a relationship even in the face of serious troubles is respected by the majority of the population—even when those troubles are splashed all over the national media for months. It is not weak or deviant to have these values—it is normative.

Commitment

"I wasn't the type of person to walk out and leave....I'd rather do a lot to sort out the problem and work it out...." (Lempert, 1996, p. 274)

It might seem surprising in this time when most new marriages end in divorce, but there are many people who commit completely to marriage. Many times commitment has a religious foundation. The new idea and, in some U.S. states, legal category of "covenant marriages" embodies this idea of an especially strong marital commitment (Baker, Sanchez, Nock, & Wright, 2009). Some have a more secular orientation but take vows such as "for better or worse" to heart. Some are determined to live up to their parents' example of a long marriage. Others are equally determined to live down their parents' example and break the cycle of divorce.

Commitment is an idea that has caught the fancy of researchers and so there are many studies showing that more committed women are more likely to stay in violent relationships (e.g., Rusbult & Martz, 1995). Sometimes the implication of such research is that commitment, or perhaps excess commitment, is bad. But what is excess commitment? All marriages face difficult times and periods of greater strife. Providers and advocates speak as if there is a bright line demarcating the kinds of strife that need to be worked through by committed partners and the kind that should sever a committed relationship. However, rarely is there such a bright line, when one day things are fine and the next life-threatening violence is perpetrated. The early stages of abusive relationships can look much like the problems that most couples face—first there is an increase in problems, then more arguing. Many people say and even do things during heated arguments that are, most charitably, regrettable. The line between unwise comments and full-fledged psychological abuse is fuzzy and often emerges over time through the frequency and intensity of words and behavior.

Love

Yes, love. Many women retain feelings of fondness, affection, and attraction for their partners even after episodes of victimization (Buel, 1999). To many victimized women, this is not unlike the persistence of love through other hard times and despite the flaws that all of us have. To love despite someone's flaws is what it means to truly love someone. Within the last year, I have heard battered women described as "confused about love," but many conceptions of love place the highest value on unconditional love. Unconditional love means loving someone even after they have done something terribly wrong. It does not mean that people still "seem" to love them or still have feelings of attachment. We stigmatize batterers in the same way that we stigmatize victims—a husband and father becomes a "batterer"—that is his master status attribute, and the only important piece of information that most advocates, providers, and researchers ever learn about perpetrators. Anything else they do learn is subsumed under the "batterer" status—Are they drunks too? Mentally disturbed? We seldom ask whether a batterer might have any positive traits (for an exception, *see* Lehmann & Simmons, 2009). These outsider perceptions are not like the perceptions of many women. In fact, many, if not most, batterers are not Hitler-esque characters who are pure evil. They can be charming, fun-loving, irreverent—or serious and traditional. They are not all the same, but very few of them are monsters who never show their good sides to their partners or their children. It can be confusing and complicated for a woman to sort out what it means that the most special person in her life and her most constant companion can be hurtful and injurious. It is easy to see how the hurtful behavior could be seen as an aberration and the rest of it—which after all occupies a much greater percentage of time in almost everyone's life— shows the "real" man. The love can be real, too. Humans have an almost infinite capacity to experience multiple, contradictory emotions at the same time, and love can indeed be present even when fear and anger are there too. To fail to acknowledge this is to fail victimized women, because advocates just won't "get it" when they are trying to explain these compli-cated mixes of emotions and sort out how to deal with them all at once. People do not identify the worst days of their and their partner's life and let those represent their partner and their relationship. If advocates and health-care workers do not understand this basic fact of relationships, then they will never be able to help the vast majority of victimized women. In a study of 98 victimized women, 22% said love was a factor of initially staying—and it was mentioned by more women, 38%, who were still with their partners at follow-up (Strube & Barbour, 1983). *See* Chapter 13 for additional discussion of how stigmatizing perpetrators hampers the movement against domestic violence.

CONCLUSION

The range of potential social risks is considerable. They include objections by victims' or perpetrators' families to divorce or relationship termination. Members of some cul-tural groups or communities may also experience pressure not to disclose the violence or cope with it in ways that will keep it private. This is one example of how social and institutional risks are often exacerbated for certain groups such as immigrant women, elders, youth, pregnant women, lesbian and bisexual women, gay men, transgender people, people of color, women with disabilities, and other groups who may have spe-cial needs, complicated legal issues, or other considerations that are not always met by existing services.

Finally, there are also personal values that can complicate some women's choices as they try to remain true to those ideals, such as beliefs that divorce is wrong, while also trying to protect themselves and their children. The costs of giving up these values can be substantial and are not only psychological but also can be social. For example, if their church or other organization rejects them for appearing to breach its values, then a victim might lose considerable social support and possibly even a likely source of financial and in-kind assistance. Together with an understanding of all of the ways that a batterer can act to constrain choices, financial issues, and institutional concerns, a picture emerges of a complicated set of circumstances that no single solution is likely to solve. The examples presented in these chapters are not meant to be exhaustive or to apply to every victim but, rather, to suggest the dozens of constraints facing most women as they strategize about what to do. Violence in relationships is an extremely complex problem and successfully addressing it will require attending to all of these cascading effects and derivative losses. The solutions (almost certainly plural) will require bearing in mind the need to minimize all of these risks. With this fuller context in mind, it will also be possible to develop a more holistic understanding of the many ways in which women act to protect themselves, protect their loved ones, and persevere against sometimes formidable odds. The wide ranges of women's protective strategies are the focus of the next several chapters.

6

Immediate Situational Strategies

The first opportunity to protect oneself and one's loved ones comes right in the moment of the attack. One theme of this book is that many responses that battered women make are similar to any person's response to a crime or to a relationship problem. Immediate situational strategies, or actions taken during or immediately after an attack, are no exception. Immediate situational strategies especially favor the sort of emergency and defensive acts that are typical of any assault victim. More research has focused on long-term protective strategies than heat-of-the-moment responses, but there are data showing that there are many important strategies women employ in the immediate context of a physical or sexual assault to try and protect themselves. For the most part, these protective strategies are focused on the risk of physical danger. Derivative losses and cascading effects, including the financial, institutional, social, and personal issues addressed in Chapters 4 and 5, tend to occur after the immediate attack and so do protective strategies aimed at minimizing their effects. Chapters 7 through 11 focus on protective strategies that are usually better suited to these risks.

As we will also see with longer term protective strategies, rather than a coherent effort to understand women's responses in the moment of an attack, our current thinking on this topic has developed in a rather piecemeal fashion. There are no standardized questionnaires on immediate situational strategies. Existing methods for studying these have not been well validated. As you read about individual strategies, it is important to keep in mind that these are not static processes. Rather, they ebb and flow over time. Most of the research has also focused on a single moment in time or asked women to think back retrospectively about all of the choices they have used. The fluidity of coping strategies gets lost with this research approach. For example, a woman who called for help after one incident may not do so after another. Calling for help may not have gone well, she may not be able to call for help on another occasion, or she may choose another protective strategy for other reasons.

Immediate situational strategies also raise the issue of self-defense and legal issues related to distinguishing between justifiable self-defense and retaliatory violence. Many scholars have also drawn attention to the role of gender in understanding these legal issues and how male-on-female violence presents issues that are not captured in laws that were initially designed primarily for male-on-male crime. These topics will also be covered in this chapter.

BACKGROUND

Safety plans are one place in the field of domestic violence where one can find numerous references to immediate situational strategies. Many safety plans

emphasize planning ahead for future assaults and suggest different immediate protective strategies. Indeed, many safety plans are largely comprised of immediate
and fairly short-term suggestions for coping with violence (e.g., Hart & Stuehling,
1992 and their many imitators). Longer term strategies are surprisingly absent from
many safety plans (Hamby & Gray-Little, 2007). As mentioned in Chapter 2, almost
all existing safety plans are based on Barbara Hart's groundbreaking work (Hart &
Stuehling, 1992). Hart, a lawyer and one of the first important advocates for victims
of domestic violence, adapted a law firm's list of suggestions about what to do in case
of an attack by a partner. She was personally instrumental in the widespread dissemi-
nation of safety plans. Safety plans have since become a cornerstone of interventions
with victimized women. Googling "domestic violence" and "safety plan" generates
more than 160,000 hits. Common recommendations include luring the perpetrator
away from rooms with guns and knives, practicing escape routes, keeping cash on
your person at all times, and developing codes or signals to alert neighbors or children when to call for help. Measures to take in anticipation of future attacks are also
often recommended, such as trying to remove weapons from the house and hiding a
bag of clothing and emergency items should such an attack occur (such recommendations can be found on websites like www.domesticviolence.org or the National
Domestic Violence Hotline).

   The elements of a safety plan seem an obvious choice for research, especially
because there is so much similarity in the suggestions given from one organization
to another, as discussed in Chapter 2. Surprisingly, however, safety plan-centered
research seems lacking. As we will see in more detail below, some protective acts,
such as calling for help, have been assessed in multiple research investigations,
whereas others, such as luring perpetrators away from danger spots, have received
almost no research attention. Another seriously understudied area is immediate protective strategies that are designed to protect others. These have been documented
in a number of qualitative descriptions. There are many instances of women putting
themselves between the batterer and their children or other family members and taking other steps to protect children. Protecting others will be addressed in more detail
in Chapter 7. This chapter focuses on steps women use primarily to protect themselves from the harm of an attack.

THE IMPORTANCE OF PERSPECTIVE

Another theme that weaves throughout this book is the importance of perspective
and the lens one adopts when thinking about battered women. Whether something is seen as protective or passive can depend on small changes in viewpoint and
use of language. This is very true of immediate situational strategies. "Avoidance"
is often labeled a passive strategy, but sometimes avoiding a problem is the best
course of action. In fact, outside of the context of battering, walking away from a
fight or otherwise taking steps to calm a potentially escalating situation is often
considered *wise*, not passive (Graham et al., 2012). "Defusing" and "de-escalating"
are just two examples of words with very different connotations from "avoiding"
that could easily be used to describe the same acts that are sometimes dismissed
as poor coping.

THE WIDE RANGE OF IMMEDIATE SITUATIONAL STRATEGIES

There are a wide range of protective acts that can be part of one's immediate response to an assault (*see* Table 6.1). They vary somewhat in the degree to which they focus on the elements of the attack and the degree to which they focus on the perpetrator–victim

Table 6.1 IMMEDIATE SITUATIONAL STRATEGIES

Escaping the scene
Leave the house
Run to another room
Lock oneself in a room
Get into (or out of) a car
Walk away calmly
Luring away from dangerous parts of the house
Keep perpetrator away from gun cabinets, kitchens, etc.
Find a way to get guns out of the house (store elsewhere, etc.)
Calling for help
Signal a neighbor or child
Teach children how to get help
Get an emergency phone
Get a pay-as-you-go phone
Keep a landline telephone
Scream
Pass a note or leave a message for an employee in a public place
Defusing strategies
Distract with other activities such as making tea or coffee
Hold hands or cuddle with perpetrator, even if not feeling affectionate
Keep things quiet around house
Talk batterer out of abuse
Protecting children or others from the attacker
Self-defensive actions
Use force to stop perpetrator's assault
Protect one's body
Stop perpetrator from destroying objects around house

Note: This is a list of strategies derived from the research literature on women's protective strategies and from women I have known who have developed creative strategies. Inclusion on this list is not meant to be an endorsement or recommendation for any particular woman in any particular situation.

relationship. Most of them are actions that could be taken just as easily in cases of a mugging or home invasion. Other actions reflect the fact that the perpetrator is not a stranger. These latter strategies could also, in many cases, be used to avoid fights or confrontations in other distressed or high-conflict relationships. Seeing the connections to other criminal assaults or other stressful situations helps take battering out of the realm of the unique or bizarre and focuses on how this is just one of many similar life problems. Immediate situational strategies can be constrained by the severity of the violence perpetrated against a woman. Certain injuries, such as knocking a woman unconscious, can prohibit immediate protective strategies. The physical environment can also constrain victimized women's ability to flee or other responses. Nonetheless, despite these constraints, it is clear that many women respond protectively in the moment that violence occurs.

ESCAPING THE SCENE

People who believe they are in imminent danger of becoming a crime victim will usually try to get away if they can. A person under threat of violence can run to the safety of a locked car or apartment or get back to a more populated area where attacks are less likely. Women who are in danger of being attacked by their partners often do these things too. Many of us take steps to become "harder targets" (Podolefsky & Dubow, 1981) by locking ourselves in our homes at night or avoiding dangerous parts of town. The steps that battered women take, both in the moment of the attack and by planning ahead to make it easier to get away if they are attacked, fall into this same general category of responding.

A substantial number of women being attacked by their partners try to get away from them. Leaving the house or escaping the immediate scene of the assault has been reported by 15% to 32% of women in studies of battered women (Follingstad, Hause, Rutledge, & Polek, 1992; Magen, Conroy, Hess, Panciera, & Simon, 2001). A study of Mexican-origin women also found high rates of walking away (81%) and locking oneself in a room (51%) (Brabeck & Guzmán, 2008). The latter has been asked about so few times it is almost an invisible strategy (*see* Chapter 11), but it is clearly a useful way of escaping the scene. In a randomly drawn community sample involving mostly minor and moderate violent incidents, Hamby & Gray-Little (1997) found that one in five (20%) endorsed at least one immediate self-protective strategy, such as leaving the situation, getting someone's help, or calling the police. Downs and his colleagues found slightly higher rates (26%) of similar nonphysical strategies among women seeking help for substance use who had also been victimized and still higher rates (57%) among domestic violence shelter residents (Downs, Rindels, & Atkinson, 2007). Unfortunately, in both of these latter studies, several different types of protective strategies were combined into a single summary score.

More specific data are available for a nationally representative U.S. sample, in which it was found that 16% ran to another room and 8% left the house (Kaufman Kantor & Straus, 1990). Leaving the house was reported by one in five victimized women in a nationally representative Swiss study (Gillioz, De Puy, & Ducret, 1997). Community-based samples such as these primarily involve cases of less injurious and less frequent violence. The lower rates of actions such as trying to escape probably reflect that the threat, on average, is less serious in most of these situations compared to the ones facing women who have sought help from domestic violence shelters. Although all forms of violence are certainly concerning, lumping all instances together into a single category of "abuse" or "violence" does not reflect the very wide range in severity of violence (Hamby, 2000). Women do make these distinctions when thinking about their own experiences. It makes sense that coping responses will vary according to the severity of the act (Hamby & Gray-Little, 1997). The data show that escaping the scene is chosen by women in a range of situations.

LURING AWAY FROM DANGEROUS PARTS OF THE HOUSE

Sometimes completely leaving the house is not possible and sometimes may not be safer, especially depending on where one lives. Examples of places that hardly offer an escape from danger by running outside include areas with a heavy gang presence or extreme climates, such as remote villages in far northern regions. Many safety plans mention trying to stay away from rooms such as the kitchen, with all its knives, during an argument. Gun cabinets, tool cabinets, and other places with weapons or items that can be easily converted to weapons are also well-known danger spots. Despite the very common advice in the advocacy community to avoid weapons and other danger spots, little to no research has been conducted on this specific topic. For example, it seems likely that some of the instances that Kaufman Kantor and Straus identified as running to another room might have been with the purpose of getting away from the most dangerous areas in the home, but the research is not precise enough to say so. "Leaving the situation" is even more vague. Thus, it is difficult to estimate how common this strategy actually is, although the intent of it is clearly protective.

Safety plans also often suggest that it is good to pursue the longer term goal of getting guns out of the house, and one study found that 77% of women who had been threatened with a gun had done this (Glass et al., 2010). That was a small subgroup in that study, but more broadly, in the same sample, 40% of those who had been threatened with any kind of weapon (including knives, etc.) had removed the weapon from the home. There are many ways weapon removal can be accomplished. In one instance, after a batterer made a suicidal gesture, a woman was able to get his father to intervene and remove the guns from the batterer's house and bring them to his own home. The father had apparently not seen a need to remove the guns earlier to protect his daughter-in-law or even to protect his grandchildren, but at least it turned out that there was some level of risk that spurred him to action, and I know the woman was glad to have the extra measure of safety regardless of the reason for it.

Help with removing weapons from perpetrators is now more readily available in many places. In recent years, thanks to Violence Against Women Act provisions, this is becoming part of many orders of protection (also called restraining orders) in most U.S. jurisdictions. Obtaining an order of protection against someone will typically lead to that person losing his gun permits and/or permission to keep guns in the home. As with most institutionalized practices, however, these legal changes can have unintended consequences. According to advocates at one shelter, a judge had been routinely converting temporary orders of protection in domestic violence cases, which can be obtained without judicial review, into permanent protection orders when they reached his bench. The advocates had been generally satisfied with the ease of attaining permanent orders of protection. Federal and state law changed, however, so that anyone with a full protection order (i.e., not a temporary one but one where the perpetrator has been served notice about the hearing and had the opportunity to defend himself) is not allowed to keep a gun in his possession or buy one (WomensLaw.org, 2011). This reportedly seemed unreasonable to this judge, who then became reluctant to grant protection orders because he did not think it was right for a man to lose his guns as a result of domestic violence. The advocacy community in this district viewed this as a net negative outcome, although they had supported the VAWA legislation. In defense of the judge's position, however, this change in the laws regarding protection orders was made without evidence of effectiveness and the difference, if any, it makes in terms of lower injury and fatality rates among victimized women. Research on important topics such as real-world implementation of policy changes is sorely needed. Because so many policy changes have unintended consequences, policy changes should be as evidence-based as other prevention or intervention (Haynes, Service, Goldacre, & Torgerson, 2012).

CALLING FOR HELP

Calling for help can be accomplished in a lot of ways that are not well-represented in the research literature. "Calling" probably conjures images of a telephone to many people, but it is not limited to that. Calling can also mean literally calling out loud enough to get the attention of a neighbor or passerby. In some cases it can mean creating a signal, such as a code word, with children to go and get help from a neighbor. There are other ways of "calling" for help too. I have known women who have created signals with a neighbor. For example, women can draw a shade (or pull a shade), or open or close curtains at a particular window that can be easily seen by a neighbor if they think the situation may be turning dangerous. If you are in a public place, such as a restaurant or gas station, then calling for help can mean passing a note or even scrawling a message on a bathroom mirror. Sometimes calling for help is not a shout—it is a whisper.

Further, making a phone call is not always as easy as it sounds. Not everyone has a telephone. Many people have pay-as-you-go cell phones that require having money available to buy minutes to use them, especially to call family or friends for help (emergency calls are usually free). Not all assaults happen in homes with landlines or in areas with good cell phone coverage. There are still many parts of the world, including many rural parts of the United States, where cell phone reception is spotty. Sometimes batterers intentionally take their partners to remote locations. Further, making a telephone call can be a fairly obvious move that may be risky in some situations, as the batterer may respond to attempts to get help with escalated violence. Depending on the circumstances, physically accessing the telephone during an assault may be difficult or impossible. Calling the police will be addressed in more detail in Chapter 10, which addresses classic domestic violence services. There has been less research on calling for other kinds of help, but one nationally representative study found that 6% had called someone other than the police (Kaufman Kantor & Straus, 1990). Another study found more than one in three women (36%) had developed a danger signal (Goodman, Dutton, Weinfurt, & Cook, 2003).

DEFUSING STRATEGIES

As mentioned at the beginning of the chapter, some research findings that have been labeled as evidence of passivity or avoidance could represent conscious attempts to defuse a situation (Cavanagh, 2003). Although defusing strategies can be used with strangers and are also used by law enforcement (such as in hostage negotiations) and by other professionals (Graham et al., 2012), violence in a relationship context creates possibilities for using defusing strategies that are based on knowing the perpetrator. Cavanaugh, for example, conducted interviews with women who reported steps such as distracting their partner by making tea and coffee. This could start a different script of behaviors rather than one that leads to violence. One woman in Cavanaugh's study spoke of holding hands or cuddling—even when she did not feel affectionate—as a strategy to keep her partner calm.

Although these types of strategies have been noted in several qualitative studies, they have seldom been included in quantitative research. Goodman and colleagues (2003) found that 70% had tried to keep things quiet in the home for their partner and 64% had tried to do what their partner wanted to avoid a fight. Another study found that 88% had used placating, and the women in their comments clearly communicated that they viewed placating strategies as an active choice about how to survive (Brabeck & Guzmán, 2008). Almost as many women had tried to talk the batterer out of the abuse (81%). Women also try to avoid potentially violent situations (63% in Yoshihama, 2002), which could refer to a range of indirect strategies. Although "avoid" may sound passive, women often described avoidance as an effective protective strategy in Yoshihama's study. Goodman and colleagues obtained similar results. Although defusing strategies were far from being rated as universally helpful, more than half of women found defusing helpful in reducing the risk of violence (54% said keeping things quiet was helpful, and 63% said doing what he wanted was helpful).

SELF-DEFENSIVE ACTIONS

Self-defensive actions have received relatively little attention in the literature on battered women's coping with victimization, but self-defense has been a topic of interest in several studies of motives for intimate partner violence perpetration. These data are somewhat different from most data in this book, but they do offer evidence that self-defensive acts are common in incidents of intimate partner violence. Unlike most of the research we have been discussing, this research is less likely to focus on samples of battered women who have experienced extreme violence. Rather, these studies are often based on samples of college students and others who report committing what are mostly less injurious acts of violence such as pushing, whether in self-defense or as the primary aggressor. Typically, the main purpose of these studies is to understand why people commit aggressive acts, not how they respond to victimization. Still, they suggest that substantial portions of individuals who have been aggressive, approximately one in five, report engaging in violence to defend themselves (Cascardi & Vivian, 1995; Follingstad, Wright, Lloyd, & Sebastian, 1991). Some studies have found even higher rates (Saunders, 1986). In a more recent study of women who had been arrested for domestic violence perpetration, more than one-third (37%) said they had used violence in self-defense (Stuart, Moore, Hellmuth, Ramsey, & Kahler,

2006). Despite being arrested as perpetrators of assault, the high rates of self-defense suggest that some of these women would not have been arrested if a careful appli-cation of laws regarding self-defense had been followed. Although it is questionable whether the term "perpetration" should still be used for people acting in self-defense, these data also show that self-defensive violence is a common behavior in serious incidents of intimate partner violence. We discuss some of the conceptual issues this raises later in the chapter.

There are other means of self-defense too. In Brabeck and Guzman's study, two of three women (68%) had tried to protect their bodies (2008). Some other research has indicated that preventing a partner from destroying one's personal belongings is a common motive for self-defensive acts (Shorey, Meltzer, & Cornelius, 2010). These other forms of self-defense have received much less study.

SELF-DEFENSE, FIGHTING BACK, AND THE LINES BETWEEN THEM

Some strategies are controversial. Hitting back is perhaps the most controversial strategy because although it might stop an assault and therefore be protective, it can also contribute to victim-blaming and the perception that both relationship partners are equally victimized. Although virtually any response can lead to an escalation of the batterer's violence, hitting back may be more risky than most. It may also create legal problems for women, including leading to assault charges against women that could be damaging to their positions in custody contests. A few women do choose this strategy, however—12% in one nationally representative U.S. sample and 7% in a representative Swiss study (Gillioz et al., 1997; Kaufman Kantor & Straus, 1990). In help-seeking samples, reports of "fighting back" or pushing one's partner away have ranged from 21% to 82% (Brabeck & Guzmán, 2008; Campbell et al., 1998; Downs et al., 2007; Goodman et al., 2003). Unfortunately, these measures are very impre-cise, and it is impossible to tell how much of this "fighting back" is self-defense and how much is retaliatory. The following scenario from Downs and colleagues' study is a vivid illustration of how "physical force" can be protective:

> He beat me up the day before, and he was on charges the next day. He had to go to court for domestic violence. He came to my house and broke the window....My son was standing next to me and my little girl was sitting in a chair away from the window. My son could have got....he could have just....it was crazy. [Interviewer: Were you able to protect yourself?] Yeah. [Interviewer: What did you do?] I picked up my son's baseball bat and started swinging at the window to make him stay out or he would have climbed in and who knows what he would have done? (Downs et al., 2007, p. 37)

Looked at from a broader perspective, hitting back is a common response to get-ting hit, engaged in by everyone from toddlers in a daycare to elderly crime victims. Although in some respects it is perhaps one of the simplest responses to describe, rec-ognize, and measure, in other ways it proves to be one of the most complex. As noted above, if you simply ask people whether their physically forceful acts were motivated by self-defense, substantial numbers describe their behavior as self-defense, but on confidential surveys, many also endorse other less noble motives. In studies asking people to endorse one motive from a list of possible motives for aggressive behavior, self-defense is seldom the most commonly named. Anger, jealousy, and "getting back" at a partner for some perceived offense are all freely endorsed more often than self-defense (Cascardi & Vivian, 1995; Follingstad et al., 1991; Harned, 2001). In the sample of women arrested for domestic violence, many other motives were also commonly reported (Stuart et al., 2006), although more than one in three did say they were acting in self-defense to protect themselves. More than one-third of this group of women also said they did not know what to do with their feelings or that they were provoked by their partner. Retaliating or punishing their partner was also reported by more than 30% of respondents (it was possible to endorse more than one motivation). It almost seems surprising that more people do not claim self-defense, given the incentives to be absolved of guilt for any violent actions in which they engaged. Even if people were willing to admit guilt on confidential questionnaires, one might think that more people might have self-serving views of past aggressive incidents and that they might perceive their actions as self-defense, even if a third party might not agree. This would also lead to high reports of self-defense on questionnaires. The lack of any attempts to validate past measures of motive limits our understanding of this important form of self-protection.

Self-Defense and Gender

Self-defense is a more gendered phenomenon than often recognized. Many feminist scholars have pointed to problems in the so-called "reasonable man" standard in the law (e.g., Randall, 2004). In Western law, it has for centuries been legal to respond with "reasonable" force to prevent an impending injury (Kopel, Gallant, & Eisen, 2008). The definition of "reasonable" has been worked out over decades of case law and scholarship. The force should only be strong enough to repel the attack. Deadly force can only be used as defense against what is also potentially deadly force. In some cases, there is an obligation to try and retreat, but there are exceptions, particularly the "castle" defense, which stipulates no duty to retreat from one's own home. The threat is supposed to be immediately present, not a potential future threat. There are many situations where it is also acceptable to defend others, especially family members. Assaults that meet these criteria are justified and are not criminal. The "reasonable man" standard suggests that although the true perceptions and intentions of any actor might be unknown, the law must base views of unreasonableness, and hence potential criminal responsibility, on what an "average" person would do in a situation. For many years, feminist legal scholars have argued that the "reasonable man" standards of the law are problematic when talking about gendered interactions (e.g., Browne, 1989; Mahoney, 1991). A detailed review of these issues is beyond the scope of this text, but a basic understanding of them is important to understand victimized women's use of aggression as a protective strategy.

Briefly, many of these critiques focus on the "man" part of the "reasonable man" standard (Browne, 1989; Mahoney, 1991). There are many assumptions built into what may seem to be a straightforward definition. For example, if self-defense occurred, then by definition the assailant did not (successfully) use deadly force. So this requires a judgment about whether the actions of the perpetrator did indeed amount to (unsuccessful) deadly force. This is especially important in cases where the self-defense led to the fatality of the would-be perpetrator. It is a critical judgment, for example, in investigations of deadly force by police officers. Built into the "reasonable man" standard is that all reasonable men would perceive the situation similarly. However, acts that may not be deadly force against an adult male may be deadly to an adult female.

Interpreting these situations gets even more complicated when examining the issue of force sufficient to repel the attack. Intentionally or not, the reasonable man standard implies two fairly evenly matched individuals. Again, this does not accurately represent most situations of male-on-female violence. In the use of physical force, men and women are not similarly "situated," to use the legal term (MacKinnon, 2005). As mentioned in Chapter 3, in the United States, men are, on average, 5 inches taller and 30 pounds heavier than women (McDowell et al., 2008). Further, romantic scripts in many societies promote the partnering of a taller male with a shorter female (Pierce, 1996). A typical adult woman, and even more specifically a typical female intimate partner, cannot match the physical force of a typical adult man or male intimate partner. Many women will be faced with the choice between ineffective force and using a weapon such as a gun. The only way for many women to repel an attack may indeed be to use more force than was used in the original attack.

The other component of standard self-defense arguments is the immediacy of the threat and the opportunity to flee. This again may not accurately represent the situated reality of many women. They may recognize that a severe threat is imminent and take steps to pre-empt it by acting when their batterer is asleep or too drunk to present a severe threat. Although pre-emptive force presents difficult legal questions that have not been resolved, this does show the complexity of understanding the battering situation. These formulations also offer an important alternative to Battered Woman Syndrome (Walker, 1984), which sees pathology instead of nuanced judgment in these cases. For the purposes of this book, regardless of their legal standing, many of these cases can be seen as self-protective and sometimes protective of others as well.

Self-Defense and Retaliation

Another conceptual problem comes from the pairing, in some research, of the concepts "self-defense" and "retaliation." Although there may be situations when these are both part of the same response to violence, from a legal or criminal justice perspective they are entirely distinct entities. I have been to some feminist conferences where "self-defense and retaliation" are nearly always uttered together, as if they both comprise appropriate responses to someone else's violence. Self-defense is justified, and retaliation, or vigilante justice, is not (Hamby, 2009a).Although retaliation can and does look very similar to self-defense in that it also involves hitting back or some other forceful act, it is not necessarily self-protective. On the contrary, retaliation can lead to an escalation of force rather than the repulsion or termination of an attack. Unpacking retaliation is complicated. Some aspects of retaliation are not protective at all. Retaliation is not protective to the extent that it is motivated by a desire to punish the assailant, regardless of whether this leads to escalation, makes the situation worse, or even if it does result in ending the immediate attack. On the other hand, some women may perceive that hitting back and showing that they are a worthy adversary in a physical fight may be one way of deterring future violence. Deterrence is very hard to prove and is one of many invisible strategies that have received essentially no empirical study, but anecdotally there are stories of it working.

Challenges in Distinguishing Self-Defense, Retaliation, and Other Motives for Aggression

Unfortunately, none of these complexities are well captured in the research literature. Part of this results from the limitations of measurement and statistics. It is very difficult to assess and analyze moment-by-moment dyadic interactions and there have been few attempts to do so. The motive literature has so far relied almost exclusively on face validity. "Face" validity assumes that if you ask a question about self-defense, then you will get an accurate report about self-defense. Face validity is generally considered one of the weakest ways of establishing whether something is a good measure. In the case of self-defense, even the most cursory analysis reveals many problems with this approach. The general public may not be very familiar with the legal concept of self-defense and all of the elements that can be part of its definition. Some victimized women may not always appreciate that their actions could be excused that way. The questions on emotional experiences during an aggressive episode may be more salient for respondents and easier to understand. One can be angry and acting in self-defense at the same time. The will to survive can be very emotionally arousing. If a survey only allows a respondent to choose one motive, then they may choose "angry," although both are true.

Another problem often seen in research on self-defense in the domestic violence literature is using simple proxies such as who hit first, or initiation. Many incidents involve multiple hits, and someone who started off escalating and/or retaliating could switch to self-defense at any time they feel the need to protect themselves. Some incidents with multiple "hitters" could involve self-defense by both parties; others, neither. There are other problems with self-report about self-defense. Some people may think that self-defense applies only to stereotypically "criminal" incidents, and they do not think of partner violence as a crime. Or some may feel that self-defense implies that they were feeling threatened and they do not want to admit that. Much more research is needed on the validity of self-reports of the motives of aggressive acts.

The literature on assessing so-called "mutual violence" is, if anything, even more problematic. This is another way of looking at the issue of hitting back. The way it is usually studied in domestic violence research can provide a distorted picture of the violence in a relationship. Most troublingly, a woman who has been beaten regularly for 20 years and then hits back one time would be classified as a member of a "mutually violent" relationship by the most common methodology in place (Hamby & Grych, 2013). Even in cases where there are a fairly equal number of reports of violence by both partners, there is rarely any situational or dyadic analysis so there is no way of knowing whether "mutual" means hitting back during every incident or whether there are some instances of one person being the sole perpetrator. Most behavioral checklists of partner violence do not formally even assess the number of incidents involved, so if someone reported that she had hit her partner five times and he had hit her five times, then there is no way to know if she hit him five times on one occasion in an attempt to stop or get away from him, while he hit her on five separate occasions, causing injury each time (the reverse could also be true).

The domestic violence literature is not the only place where perpetrator-victims are studied. Perpetrator-victims refer to any individuals who have been involved in violence as both a perpetrator and a victim (Hamby & Grych, 2013). They have also been studied extensively in the bullying literature and the delinquency literature, where it is well-known that counter to many stereotypes, children who bully are more likely than other children to be bullied themselves and that bully-victims are the largest group of children in many studies—larger than those who only bully or those who are only victims of bullying. Delinquent youth also commonly both perpetrate and sustain considerable violence (Cuevas, Finkelhor, Turner, & Ormrod, 2007). These literatures tend to be somewhat more sophisticated than the domestic violence literature in measuring and defining this phenomenon, however. It is common in the youth victimization literature to screen out cases like the first example above—one episode as either a victim or a perpetrator is not enough to get a youth classified as a "bully," "delinquent," or "victim." Although higher thresholds are obviously inappropriate for some offenses, such as rape, they can be useful for studying many forms of aggression. They can show, for example, that the habitual, instrumental aggression of many bully-victims is different from the infrequent and mostly reactive aggression of primary victims of bullying (Salmivalli & Nieminen, 2002).

This kind of approach could vastly improve our understanding of "hitting back" and "mutual violence" in domestic violence by helping us to identify different subtypes of women who have used violence and/or subtypes of relationships. There are probably many important differences between a battered woman who routinely uses violence against her partner and a woman who has only resorted to violence once or twice. In contrast, there are also cases where the woman does not typically or frequently fight back, but who in extreme situations resorts to violence or violence ends up being part of the effort to terminate the relationship. This pattern may often also be one that can be classified as protective, perhaps in some cases even as protective as acts that meet traditional legal definitions of self-defense.

CONCLUSION

Like dealing with most major crises and adverse events, coping with violence is not something that just occurs at a single point in time. There are many opportunities to figure out how to respond to violence. The first opportunities come during the attack itself. Despite the challenges of responding in a moment of crisis (the shock of the attack could make it difficult to respond or the violence of the attack could make it virtually impossible to respond), many women do find ways to act protectively in the immediate moment. Help-seeking and protective behaviors occur even in the first moments following an attack. Understanding self-protection and self-defense requires a nuanced contextual analysis, not just an inventory of acts. Immediate situational responses are just one aspect of a coping response that will typically involve multiple actions to deal with the complex problem of battering. In the next chapters, we look at the wide range of protective strategies that can be pursued in the days and weeks following an assault.

7

Protecting Children, Family, Friends, Co-Workers, and Pets

It is a classic, even clichéd, scene from hundreds of action movies. The bad guy tries to get to our hero by inflicting personal pain on said hero. Our hero—usually a man—is tough, however, and refuses to bend to his enemy's will. The offender is undeterred, because, every movie evil-doer knows how to really get to a hero—by threatening a loved one. Somehow, the hero finds a way to thwart his enemies, but only after his family is safely secured. No one ever seems to question the hero's judgment in these scenarios. Perhaps it might just be possible that even if it meant the sacrifice of one's child, it would be worth it to save *every single other person* in North America? Of course, in these movie fantasies the hero gets to have his cake and eat it too. The world was never seriously imperiled because the hero still had 30 seconds to save everyone after making sure his children were safe and secure.

The scenarios facing many battered women have, by comparison, much lower stakes and are perhaps not as dramatic. However, unlike most of the rest of us, they face these sorts of threats in real life. Many batterers have had the same insight that Hollywood screenwriters have had. Sometimes it is easier to get to someone by threatening a loved one than by threatening a person directly. Now that I am a mother, my perspective on the issue of protecting children and other loved ones has changed dramatically. Not infrequently, the situation between a victim and her batterer amounts to this: The mother knows she will be insulted and micromanaged in every aspect of her life and beaten up occasionally when she does not live up to her partner's demands, possibly among other reasons. In return, however, the partner stops threatening the children and leaves them alone. He does not kidnap the kids and take them to where she will never find them. Sometimes, maybe it is her parents that will be safer. Or it is understood that he will not disembowel her dog and hang the carcass on the front porch. The choices that some women face are sometimes much more difficult than implied in the question, "Why doesn't she just leave?"

As shown in Chapter 3, many batterers' most serious threats are aimed at children and other loved ones, rather than at their partners. Many women prioritize protecting their children or other loved ones and take numerous steps to make sure they are not harmed. This is yet another area that has received shockingly little research attention, but the information we have offers important insights into the strengths of victimized women. As will become apparent in the sections below, some strategies that focus on protecting loved ones can be part of a larger effort to leave the relationship or disentangle oneself from a batterer, and some of them can be executed regardless of whether or not the intention is to leave. Most of these protective strategies are not mutually exclusive and can be used in combination with other efforts. Table 7.1 lists some protective strategies focused on protecting others. These are described in more detail below. This chapter also includes perspectives on the goals of preserving and protecting the family unit through the lens of couples therapy and the literature on divorce. These literatures provide another opportunity to show that views, such as anti-divorce attitudes, that are often pathologized when expressed by victimized women are seen as more reasonable when viewed from other perspectives.

IMMEDIATE PROTECTIVE STRATEGIES FOCUSED ON CHILDREN AND LOVED ONES

Following the theme from Chapter 6, there are many steps women take in the immediate context of the fight to protect children, pets, and others who may be present. They may physically insert themselves between the batterer and other people or pets. They may try to get the batterer to focus on them instead of others. They create safety plans with children so they know where to run or hide during an assault or create a code word so children know when to call for help. They may attack the perpetrator physically, not in defense of themselves but in defense of children or other loved ones.

One study involving in-depth interviews with a small group of mothers involved in child protective services yielded evidence of numerous protective strategies, many of which were responses in the immediacy of the threatening moment (Haight, Shim, Linn, & Swinford, 2007). Haight and colleagues found that 65% had physically separated the children from the violence by either moving away from them (and so creating distance between the children and the target, the mothers) or putting children in their bedrooms. More than half (53%) called for help when they thought the children were threatened. As mentioned in Chapter 6, many safety plans suggest developing code words with children so they would know when to get away from their mother's partner. This turned out to be a fairly common strategy in the Haight et al. study. Seven women (42%) had developed specific signals with their children to warn them about impending violence, including verbal signals such as "don't referee" or "go to your room." One-third (33%) of the women in another study had taught their children to call the police (Brabeck & Guzmán, 2008). Another recent qualitative study also found that mothers prioritize their children's safety and frequently attempt to protect their children during dangerous moments (Lapierre, 2010). As in the study by Haight et al., trying to get children to another room or keep them away from their partner was frequently mentioned. So was turning up the stereo to keep them from hearing the argument. The women in Lapierre's study also told several stories of intervening directly to keep their partner from striking their children.

LONGER TERM STRATEGIES FOR PROTECTING CHILDREN

> "Volunteered more at school—in fact made "Volunteer of the Year"—able to get a little closer to the staff while making sure my children knew they had the support from at least one parent."
> "I am seeking full custody."
> "Let my children be in my custody and maintain a drama-free home for my kids."

Table 7.1 STRATEGIES FOR PROTECTING CHILDREN, FAMILY, FRIENDS, AND PETS

Immediate protective strategies focused on children and loved ones
Women may physically insert themselves between batterer and others
Try to get batterer to focus on them
Create code words and safety plans with children or others
Use aggression to defend children or others
Send children to their rooms or other safer location
Teach children to call police
Turn up stereo or television so children cannot hear violence
Longer term strategies for protecting children
Send children to stay with relatives or friends
Seek full legal custody
If joint custody, seek primary physical custody
Seek financial child support
Help children process experience
Tell children it is not their fault
Tell children it okay to still love their father despite his violent behavior
Volunteer at children's school to protect them and spend more time with them
Delay leaving to protect children from batterer's threats
Protecting pets
Delay leaving to protect pets from batterer's threats
Return to batterer for sake of pets
Enroll pets in "doggy daycare"
Place pets in kennel
Keep animals outside house
Use domestic violence shelter resources to find safe places for pets to stay
Protecting other family members, friends, and coworkers
Quit job to protect coworkers
Stay away from family and friends to protect them
Arrange to see family and friends only when partner is at work
Create separate e-mail account that batterer does not know about to contact others
Create alternate Facebook or other social media profile to maintain private contact
Arrange to see family and friends at church or other safe venues

Note: This is a list of strategies derived from the research literature on women's protective strategies and from women I have known who have developed creative strategies. Inclusion on this list is not meant to be an endorsement or recommendation for any particular woman in any particular situation.

The quotes above and throughout the next several chapters are from the VIGOR studies, which allowed women to describe their analysis of their situation in their own words (Hamby, 2013b). Children were often mentioned in women's plans. Concerns about children were one of the most commonly mentioned in the VIGOR, with 47% of women describing concerns about children's well-being. Among women with children (91% of the sample), one in five (20%) reported seeking custody of their children. In situations where it is possible to pursue legal custody, this can be a powerful tool for protecting oneself from the risks posed by the batterer. Approximately 1 in 12 (8%) said they either had, or intended to, file for child support (Hamby & Clark, 2011).

Many protective strategies are accomplished over a longer period of time, including many that are focused on protecting children. Some of these include the historically favored alternative of separation. In a study by Lapierre (2010), the children were a main motivation for asking their partner to leave the house. Other ways to keep children out of harm's way include sending them to stay with relatives. Several mothers (29%) in one study had made such arrangements for their children (Haight et al., 2007). More than two of five women (42%) had done this in a larger study of battered women (Goodman et al., 2003). Although this was mentioned by only two women in the VIGOR study, this is clearly a possibility considered by some, despite the difficulties in separating from children. The women in the Haight et al. study also spoke of a number of other strategies, including reassuring children, emphasizing it was not their fault, doing their best to minimize children's exposure to the violence, and instilling hope that things would get better. Some of them spoke about the difficulties in trying to present their children's father as someone who still loved them despite his violent behavior. As one woman put it, "He was 'Daddy.' I explained to them that it was the best decision I could have made to leave their father and I told them it was okay if [they loved their] dad... Even though it was painful—to tell my children it was okay to love the same man that I could not." (Haight et al., 2007, p. 54). In the first VIGOR study, one of the more innovative protective strategies mentioned by one woman was volunteering at her children's school. The VIGOR studies were specifically designed to help identify such innovative steps that are not commonly included in research questionnaires or safety planning instruments.

More fundamentally, a nationally representative sample of Australian women did find that help-seeking of all types was more common among women with children who had witnessed violence (88%) than among women without children (68%) (Meyer, 2010). Further, of those who did seek help, women with child witnesses were more likely to seek formal help (such as calling police) rather than only informal help (such as reaching out to a friend). Child witnesses also proved to the best predictor of shelter-seeking in the Australian study. Victimized women were more than seven times more likely to seek shelter if they had children who had witnessed the violence compared to other women (Meyer, 2010). As important as these findings are, it is important to distinguish between concerns about exposure to the violence and coping with batterers' threats to escalate violence against children if victims leave or make other changes.

PROTECTING PETS

The importance of protecting pets can be hard for some people to understand. Yes, in true life-or-death circumstances, one would hope that most people would choose their own lives over that of a companion animal. For many people, however, and not just battered women, companion animals (especially dogs and cats) are important parts of their lives and an important source of emotional comfort. Companion animals and other domesticated animals play a variety of important roles and functions in people's lives. Dogs and cats do not judge. They do not ask judgmental questions like "Why don't you just leave?" or imply that the victim has failed as a spouse. Under some circumstances the bonds between humans and animals can become very strong indeed. In both rural and urban areas, dogs have important roles as watchdogs. It is well documented that animals can have therapeutic benefits and that pet ownership can be a great buffer against depression, loneliness, and the stress of dealing with a variety of health issues (Braun, Stangler, Narveson, & Pettingell, 2009; DeCourcey, Russell, & Keister, 2010; Friedmann et al., 2011). Often the choice faced by pet-owning women is not "my life or Fido's" but "stay here and protect Fido until I can figure something else out."

Even if pets were less emotionally important, it would still be another matter entirely to feel somehow partly responsible for their violent death. Threats against animals are real and perhaps even more likely to be acted on, perhaps because perpetrators may think they are unlikely to be punished for crimes against animals in comparison to the risk of arrest for crimes against people. As reviewed in Chapter 3, there have been several studies on this and the numbers are troubling. Almost half of pet-owning women report that their pets have been harmed or threatened. Far from being an especially deviant form of violence experienced in only the worst cases, violence or threats against pets is a common batterer behavior.

These threats against pets are important considerations in women's decisions about how to proceed, especially for women in shelter. Staying in the house with the batterer is one way to protect pets, and it is a common protective strategy. Across a series of studies conducted in shelters, a significant number of women who own pets reported that they delayed leaving because of concerns about the safety of their pets. This ranged from 18% in one study (Ascione, 1998) to 48% in another (Carlisle-Frank et al., 2004), with an average across studies of about one in four women trying to protect their pets by staying with their partner longer (Ascione et al., 1997b; Carlisle-Frank et al., 2004; Faver & Strand, 2003; Flynn, 2000; McIntosh, 2004). Returning to the batterer for the sake of pets is another protective strategy. One study of women who were residing in shelter at the time of the survey found that 25% said they had gone back to their batterer on previous occasions because of concerns for their pets, a figure that jumped to 35% when limited to women who had seen their pets previously abused (Carlisle-Frank et al., 2004).

There are also other possible protective strategies that have been taken on behalf of pets that have received almost no scholarly attention. As Haight and colleagues found, it is possible that some women might find safer places for their pets to stay, as some women had done for their children, until they could offer more permanent protection from the batterer. Some women—because not all victimized women are poor—might be able to arrange protection through "doggy daycare" or stays in kennels. They might be able to rearrange the pet set-up at home to offer more protection to pets. For example, keeping pets outside at night might be helpful in some circumstances. There are probably others yet to be identified.

There has been considerable academic attention given to the plight of pets in comparison to some other ancillary victims of domestic violence, especially in comparison to threats against friends, coworkers, and neighbors. This results in no small part from the efforts of Frank Ascione to bring attention to this issue. Ascione's work is a great example of the ability of a single person to raise awareness about an issue. Nonetheless, there are also other areas that could be fruitfully explored. Almost all of the research has focused on common household pets such as cats and dogs, but in some parts of the country (such as where I live) other domesticated animals can be a big part of a family's life and sometimes an important part of a family's livelihood. These include horses, goats, pigs, cows, even chickens. These animals are not immune from the threat of violence. In the case of animals like horses, strong bonds are common between an animal and its owner. These animals also have more financial value than most dogs and cats, and threats to them can also be substantial economic threats. The desire to protect these kinds of animals can influence a victim's behavior too.

PETS AS A PROTECTIVE STRATEGY

"Get a dog to watch my apartment."

Pets not only need protecting, pets can also offer protection. This is another area that needs more research. One recommendation I have commonly offered to battered women is to get a dog. There is evidence in criminology that a dog can deter some offenders and that the noise of a barking dog especially might deter prospective perpetrators (Cromwell, Olson, & D'Aunn, 1991) or help alert neighbors or witnesses that there is a problem and the police should be called. Getting a dog was one of the options identified in the VIGOR study (Hamby & Clark, 2011). Although only described by two women, this is another example of the sort of innovative strategy that might be better identified if victimized women were more frequently asked to brainstorm about their options for coping with violence.

The field could be much more supportive of women's concerns about their pets and other animals. There need to be safe havens for pets as much as for people. There are shelters that can accommodate companion animals, either in the grounds of the shelter itself or through foster animal programs not unlike some of those run by "no-kill" animal shelters. Unfortunately, these programs are fairly few and far between and do not even come close to meeting the need for them. The National Network to End Domestic Violence makes a yearly census of 30 different services provided by domestic violence agencies and shelter for pets is not even on the list (National Network to End Domestic Violence, 2012). The challenges of responding to the needs of pets also point to problems with the shelter system itself. Group housing is not really an ideal setting for anyone, and putting a bunch of strange dogs and cats together is a touchy proposition, touchier even perhaps than expecting people who are strangers to live in close quarters. However, expecting women to abandon their pets is another form of cruelty inflicted on battered women.

PROTECTING OTHER FAMILY MEMBERS, FRIENDS, AND COWORKERS

The issue of protecting friends, colleagues, neighbors, and others outside women's immediate families has had no champion and as a result we have very little information on what women do to accomplish this. It seems likely that some of the data show-ing examples of workplace interference, such as high rates of quitting jobs (Browne, Salomon et al., 1999), might have unrecognized protective elements embedded in them. Some women might quit their job to protect people at their workplace. I have known women to quit for this reason. Some of the social isolation that is so common among battered women might also be efforts to protect friends or family members. The possibility that there are protective motivations undergirding these behaviors has not been explored.

There are numerous other steps victimized women can take to protect family and friends. They might take care to only see family and friends while their partner is at work. They could use an e-mail address that their partner does not know about or create an alternate Facebook profile so they can have some privacy in their relation-ships. They might arrange with friends and family to meet in public places. They might organize many of their social activities around church activities or community orga-nizations that are less likely to arouse the batterer's suspicion or anger (Davies, 2009). Some research has found that many women (41% in one study) avoid contact with family members to protect them (Brabeck & Guzmán, 2008).

RESEARCH ON BATTERING VERSUS OTHER RESEARCH ON FAMILIES

Protecting family members also raises the issue of preserving the family, either for the "sake of the children" or other reasons. Here is another area where there is disconti-nuity between different areas of scholarship within psychology and the other social sciences. On the one hand, research and policies regarding battered women are rou-tinely extended to anyone who has experienced any relationship violence, at all levels of severity. In the violence against women field, divorce appears to be considered a universal good. Leaving the relationship is the primary recommendation for essen-tially all women who have experienced violence. In many U.S. states, policies have been put in place to discourage or forbid any kind of couples-based intervention when the presenting problem is domestic violence (Stith & McCollum, 2011).

On the other hand, there are other domains in which divorce is not seen in such a glowing light. Two of the most important are the field of couples' therapy and the scholarship on divorce. From the perspectives of people immersed in these fields, "Can this marriage be saved?" is a legitimate question for almost any marriage. Although the answer is not always yes, the question is one that is routinely carefully considered. Recognizing that there are almost always pros and cons to any relation-ship choice is standard, not heretical. Protecting the relationship itself is another pro-tective strategy.

The populations of distressed couples seeking therapy, unhappy couples seeking divorce, and couples who have experienced relationship violence are often treated as distinct, but there is much more overlap among them than is generally acknowledged. (This reflects a general problem in the field to treat issues as distinct that are really highly interconnected; see also Hamby & Grych, 2013). As described in more detail below, several studies have suggested that it is typical that couples who seek therapy will have experienced some level of violence by one or both partners. The high-conflict relationships that are typical of divorcing couples also have very high rates of violence compared to the general population (*see* below). Some of the literature in favor of two-parent families does seem to stem, at least in part, from a conservative world-view that is different than that of many advocates and feminists working in the field of domestic violence. Recognizing this helps to illuminate the political aspects of schol-arship on domestic violence and scholarship on divorce. Women who abhor divorce are disparaged in some of the domestic violence literature. Most would probably agree that there is not a single right or wrong view on divorce. Recognizing that anti-divorce sentiments are not only fairly common, but also have some research to support them, is another step toward depathologizing battered women and the personal values that some of them hold.

THE FIELD OF COUPLES THERAPY

It is well documented in the marital therapy literature that violence is a very common problem faced by distressed couples presenting for therapy. When given an intake questionnaire that includes something like the Conflict Tactics Scales (Straus et al., 1996), as many as one-half to three-fourths of couples seeking counseling will disclose that at least one partner has been violent (Holtzworth-Munroe, Waltz, Jacobson, & Monaco, 1992; Simpson, Doss, Wheeler, & Christensen, 2007). About half of these couples have engaged in severe violence (O'Leary et al., 1999). Violence is so preva-lent in therapy-seeking couples that Holtzworth-Munroe and colleagues suggested it was challenging to find distressed nonviolent couples for research comparing treat-ment for violent and nonviolent couples. Violence, however, is seldom identified by couples as the "presenting problem," to use psychotherapists' term for the main reason someone seeks counseling (Doss, Simpson, & Christensen, 2004; Ehrensaft & Vivian, 1996). Violence is not the problem that brings most couples in for treatment or what they identify as the most pressing issues. Communication problems or emotional estrangement are more likely to be the presenting problem.

Historically, couples therapists have not routinely assessed for violence or other safety issues at intake. Even today, difficult topics, including violence, are avoided by many therapists, leaving the onus on the clients themselves to raise them (Stith & McCollum, 2011). Some traditionally trained couples therapists also refuse to see each member of the couple individually, which can be a positive in terms of keeping the focus of the therapeutic alliance on the couple as a unit but also leaves no room for a fearful spouse to disclose issues that they are afraid to raise in front of their part-ner. An emphasis on brief treatments and insurance that pays for only a few sessions puts pressure on therapists and clients alike to stick to the presenting problem and not conduct comprehensive assessments of all relationship areas. The result is that many couples therapists are treating violent couples, whether they realize it or not. Although many couples therapists will help couples progress to the most amicable divorce possible, the very nature of couples therapy leads to a focus on improving and sustaining the relationship. Some couples therapists consider a decision to divorce the natural termination point of their work, rather than a time when even more help may be needed.

An important study came out recently that shows how common couples therapy for violent couples actually is. DeBoer and her colleagues (2012) followed up couples who had sought help at a program where they did actually assess and screen out those reporting significant levels of violence. If the male partner was reported to have perpetrated six or more acts of mild violence in the past year (such as grabbing or pushing), two or more acts of moderate violence in the past year (including punching, slapping, or kicking), or one or more act of severe violence ever in the relationship, the investigators met with the woman alone and referred her to single-gender, violence-focused services such as domestic violence shelters and batterer intervention programs.

It turns out, however, that a substantial portion of those couples later sought couples therapy elsewhere—and received it. Nearly one-third had been in couples therapy somewhere else by the time the researchers re-contacted them 2 years later. Violence levels were unfortunately stable over that time period for all couples (75% of the sample was still experiencing male-perpetrated violence 2 years later), including those who did and did not receive couples therapy. Surprisingly, however, relationship satisfaction had increased anyway for the couples who had received conjoint therapy in comparison to those couples who had not received couples therapy. Perhaps satisfaction improved because of other changes in the relationship. Perhaps they were invested in believing the couples therapy had helped, especially because they had acted counter to the professional advice they had received from the people who were re-interviewing them.

Although this study is not exactly an advertisement for couples therapy for violence, it does illustrate several important points. First and foremost, that there is a real demand for couple-focused help among people who have experienced frequent and moderate (not just minor) levels of violence, and if they cannot get it from one therapist, many will find it somewhere else. We do not know how many felt punished for disclosure when they were excluded from therapy at the first clinic. Perhaps the violence did not get better because the other therapists never found out about it. Those therapists may have been sending them out on date nights and teaching "fair fighting." (This is perhaps not the best choice of terms for healthy conflict resolution in a population so troubled by physical violence—but as good an indicator as any of how oblivious therapists can be to the dynamics of violence and abuse in intimate relationships. It is still a term that can be found on tens of thousands of sites from a Google search, including mainstream advice sources such as Dr. Phil.) Another important conclusion from this study is that sometimes the violence may stop. One in four women reported no recent violence 2 years later, adding to the existing literature indicating desistance for some.

Although treating violent couples without realizing that violence is occurring is clearly problematic, couples therapy may be a reasonable approach to working with many couples even after violence has occurred. Couples therapy is becoming a politically problematic approach despite some evidence of its efficacy, with some state standards forbidding it because of safety concerns (Stith & McCollum, 2011). There are data in support of the safe use of couples therapy for at least some couples in which one or both partners has been violent, however. Early research on interventions for domestic violence showed that couples therapy works as well as gender-specific group therapy for some violent couples (O'Leary et al., 1999). Of course, it should be said that this partly results from the limited efficacy of batterers' interventions, which do not work very well. Certainly, at least there is room for improvement in the effectiveness of single-gender batterers' intervention (Gondolf, 2011). Couples therapy for violent couples has continued to receive some study with evidence of promising outcomes, at least for couples who are experiencing mild to moderate levels of violence (Stith et al., 2004). It is premature for policies and laws to restrict choices for helping couples when one or more partners have been violent, especially given that there is some evidence base to support them (McCollum, 2012). These couples are trying to make things better in their relationship and the field should support these protective efforts.

THE LITERATURE ON DIVORCE

The violence against women movement coincided with huge changes in divorce laws in the U.S. and many other democracies. "Irreconcilable differences" and no-fault divorces made their way on to the scene around the same time the first shelters for battered women opened in the United States and in many other parts of the world. This was no coincidence, as both changes are closely tied to the broader women's liberation movement and to the still broader movement toward expanding civil rights for all. These are widely known social changes of the 1960s and 1970s. These changes were accompanied by a shift in social norms for divorce (Ishida, 2003). These shifting norms are apparent in many ways. For example, being divorced was no longer something treated as scandalous and no longer only a characteristic of bad or disturbed people in popular media, much in the same way that the media has now shifted its portrayal of gay characters by making diverse sexual orientations a salient feature of many sympathetically portrayed television characters. Pro-divorce propaganda served its purpose at the time, by making divorce seem like something that was a win-win situation for everyone. Many people in very unhappy and unsafe marriages are now able to end those relationships more easily.

But we also now know that divorce can have significant adverse effects, and women and children disproportionately experience many adverse effects. Most women take a permanent hit to their lifetime net wealth (Grinstein-Weiss et al., 2008; Hanson et al., 1998; Ozawa & Lee, 2006). Men, on the other hand, often see their standard of living go up substantially, especially with the decline in alimony. Stress, conflict, and loneliness have marked effects on people's health and life expectancies, which are, rather remarkably, statistically significantly shorter for divorced people (Marmot, 2005).

Although divorce and joint custody have long been treated as if they are neutral or even positive outcomes for children, the reality is more complex and more negative. This is a complicated message and I want to be clear that I am *not* against divorce. Divorce should be a viable option in any open, democratic society. At the same time, divorce has enough common adverse consequences that it should not seem wrong, passive, or deluded not to want one. These adverse consequences apply to victimized as well as non-victimized women and it is not pathological for women to consider them. The adverse consequences can be especially far-reaching when women have children, especially children in common with the batterer. Having a child in common with your ex-husband changes everything. It changes how much a woman still has to deal with her ex-husband, how often she has to interact with him, how often he comes up in conversation, and how often she sees his family. If the main reason for divorcing is to terminate an unpleasant or harmful relationship, then it basically does not work for many people with minor children.

Women know this. But if divorce is less than a panacea for many women, it is even more problematic for children. Children's standards of living also typically fall

(Grinstein-Weiss et al., 2008). They often move to more dangerous neighborhoods. They often have to change schools (Brooks, Hair, & Zaslow, 2001). Their routine can be disrupted, because many children, post-divorce, will typically spend 1 or 2 week-days and every other weekend in a different house. This also disrupts children's rela-tionships with their peers, because they have to schedule all of their other activities and relationships around their parents' custody arrangement. Children may spend more time in daycare, which, like exposure to parental conflict, can raise levels of the stress hormone cortisol (Geoffroy et al., 2006). Deciding which outcome is best is complex, and any decision is likely to incur costs for parents and children.

"Amicable" divorces are better than high-conflict ones, where the fighting carries on even after the marriage ends, but unfortunately high-conflict ones are common. We all know people who cannot say a good word about their exes, sometimes even 10 or 20 years after the end of the relationship. The acrimony lasts longer than the marriage in some cases. Some people make the calculated decision that they can better protect their children and manage these situations from inside the marriage.

It would be hard to overstate how unsympathetic many family court judges are to battered women. Joint custody is routinely granted to violent fathers (Araji, 2012; Bryan, 1999). In cases involving spouses with multiple citizenships, the Hague Child Abduction Convention has created many unintended effects regarding custody issues and the ability to seek safety that have harmed battered women and their children. This act was intended for cases when a perpetrator takes children but can compel vic-timized women to return to their batterers when they try to return to their home coun-tries with their children (Lindhorst & Edleson, 2012). So not only does a battered woman have to continue to deal with her violent partner, she is now in the situation of being *legally mandated* to leave her children unsupervised with a man she knows to be violent. If she is there, then she may have a better chance of protecting them—bodily, if need be. Some of these men are so violent that in many jurisdictions it is now com-monplace to have supervised exchanges of custody. However, this kind of supervision begs the question of whether someone who is so violent that he cannot be trusted to pick up his children without beating up their mother should be allowed to have unsupervised access to the children. Sometimes, staying with a man so you can keep an eye on him around your kids is one way of protecting your kids. Another is violat-ing the custody agreement and trying to hide your kids from their violent partner, and that happens too. In the National Survey of Children's Exposure to Violence, mothers were more likely than fathers to engage in what is legally known as "custodial interfer-ence," which involves trying to deny one parent access to children. Most of these cases involved domestic violence (Hamby et al., 2010).

CONCLUSION

Protecting loved ones is a top priority for many women. Political and sociocultural views color the perception of some protective strategies that focus on the family, because the desire to protect the intactness of the family is not the primary focus in the field of domestic violence or of many human service providers who focus on domestic violence. (I have heard more than one advocate refer to their agency as "Divorces 'R Us.") However, looking at the desire for family preservation and protection from the standpoint of couples therapy or the research on divorce shows that this may be too rigid an approach. Divorce is a tough decision with common adverse outcomes. All efforts to protect a family should be recognized as efforts to minimize as many negative outcomes as possible while maximizing positive ones. Protection of families and other loved ones are is often top priorities of women who have experienced violence, and their coping efforts often reflect these priorities. The MCDM approach, using the VIGOR framework or other method, offers a flexible way to approach risk management and problem solving that respects these personal priorities rather than questioning or disparaging them.

8

Reaching Out for Social Support and Navigating the Challenges of Information Management

Protection is often equated with formal help-seeking. To many professionals, "help-seeking" primarily refers to victimized women contacting professionals in relevant human services. This is not how most people seek help, however, especially for interpersonal problems. This is also true for other types of crime; about half of all violent victimizations (by any perpetrator) go unreported to authorities (Truman, 2011). Assaults by known perpetrators and sexual victimizations are less likely to come to the attention of authorities than other crime (Tjaden & Thoennes, 2000a, 2006). Similarly, fewer than half of people with clinically significant mental health problems seek treatment for their condition (Bland, Newman, & Orn, 1997; The ESEMeD MHEDEA investigators et al., 2004; Wang et al., 2005). This is another way in which violence by spouses and other intimate partners is similar to other life problems. "Informal help-seeking," or seeking help from family, friends, or other noninstitutional sources, is the main way people get assistance and support for the problems that they face. This is true of both females and males, a point that illustrates how important it is to be careful to avoid viewing social support through the lens of gender stereotypes by suggesting it is an approach to coping that is especially typical of females (Banyard & Graham-Bermann, 1993).

SOCIAL SUPPORT AND THE CHALLENGES OF INFORMATION MANAGEMENT

Social support is an important coping and protective strategy, but to fully understand decisions victimized women make about social support requires understanding issues related to information management (Hamby & Gray-Little, 2007). Social support refers to turning to one's family or friends for help with problems or stresses. Probably most people reading this can recall a time when they reached out to someone who did not respond in the way they had hoped. Telling someone something negative is always a risk (Foynes & Freyd, 2011). We all have people in our lives who do not respond well when problems are disclosed. In the literature on domestic violence, however, disclosure is almost always portrayed as a universal good. Tell everyone. The potential downsides of this are never explored, but research indicates that whether disclosure has beneficial effects depends in large part on whether a supportive response is received (Foynes & Freyd, 2011). The varying rates of disclosure to different people suggest battered women may be taking a more nuanced approach to this situation than many researchers and advocates are. Sometimes the smartest move is to keep quiet.

Another major limitation in writings about domestic violence is the near-constant equation of lack of disclosure with denial. People know they are getting beaten up. I used to work with psychotic patients in two different state mental hospitals and, in my experience, even the most delusional and hallucinatory schizophrenics know when they are getting beaten up. Just because a person does not admit victimization to a parent, physician, or researcher with a questionnaire does not mean that they do not understand what is happening.

HOW STIGMA AFFECTS DECISIONS ABOUT SEEKING SOCIAL SUPPORT

Seeking social support is much more closely tied to the issue of social image than much of the psychological literature on social support would suggest. To seek social support for victimization involves disclosure of having been victimized, by definition. As Erving Goffman first identified 50 years ago in his classic work on stigma, disclosure of many types of imperfections and difficulties "spoil" a person's public status (1963). As discussed in Chapter 5, the possibility of being assigned a stigmatized identity is one of the many negatives that battered women try to minimize. Unfortunately, stigmatized characteristics are often treated as a person's "master status." Master status characteristics are attributes that affect so many social contexts that they become the primary identifying characteristic of the person who possesses them (Goffman, 1963). Stigma is another stressor in the lives of people with devalued characteristics. Thus, like victimization itself, stigma can be understood in the framework of coping (Miller & Kaiser, 2001). Unlike the direct physical threats to oneself or the direct physical threats to loved ones, stigma can be considered a derivative loss in the VIGOR framework. Losses resulting from stigma are more like the risks to stable housing or stable employment that may not have been part of the original damage caused by the batterer or even part of the intent of the batterer but are still an almost unavoidable result of victimization.

There are many different types of stigma, and they are often divided into two categories: visible and concealable stigma. Visible stigmas include observable signs of disease, scarring from past injuries, and disability. Visible stigmatized conditions also include being obese or a member of a disadvantaged minority group. These stigmas are considered to be "visible" because they are apparent in most social encounters. Concealable stigmas can include identifying as a sexual minority, many psychological disorders, and many chronic physical conditions such as sexually transmitted diseases, asthma, or diabetes. A few poorly timed words can mean that one moment a person is seen to be "normal," and the next she becomes an object of pity and even fear. The concept of "information management" arises from the recognition that people with concealable stigma must carefully decide who to talk to, what to tell them, and when to broach the stigmatized topic (Goffman, 1963; Herek & Capitanio, 1996).

The stereotypes of battered women typically include visible injuries such as swollen faces and bruises (Hamby & Gray-Little, 2007). Certainly these kinds of serious and visible injuries occur. It is worth noting that assault injuries are more stigmatizing than many others. The cliché "I ran into a door" helps illustrate that accidents are considered less blameworthy than injuries resulting from fights. Many people with broken arms or sprained ankles are assumed to be victims of accidents or sports injuries. Although some sports injuries can be repetitive and result in part from people repeatedly putting themselves in harm's way, these are not devalued. Contrary to stereotypes, however, most women who have been assaulted by their partners will be capable of concealing this stigma, because most women who are assaulted by their partners do not suffer visible severe physical injuries (Straus & Gelles, 1990; Tjaden & Thoennes, 2000a). Even those who have been injured may not have visible injuries following every attack or may be able to disguise their injuries with turtlenecks, long sleeves, or calling in sick to work.

The perceived controllability of a stigmatizing attribute also affects how people respond to devalued individuals. For example, race is considered uncontrollable whereas being overweight is perceived as being controllable by most in American culture (Crocker, 1999). Although these are both examples of visible stigma, this factor applies to concealable stigma as well. Some concealable chronic illnesses, such as seizure disorder, are perceived as uncontrollable, whereas being a victim of abuse is seen as controllable. People are more likely to offer social support if they perceive that the stigmatizing condition is uncontrollable versus controllable (Menec & Perry, 1995).

It is essential to recognize the importance of stigma and the legitimate questions about information management that most people face when coping with victimization. The costs of adopting a "victim" role are substantial. Failure to disclose is often called minimization or denial, but it could also be "disidentification" with a devalued condition, a well-recognized process in the stigma literature (Hamby & Gray-Little, 2007). It is difficult to distinguish between minimization and denial versus disidentification with a stigmatized domain (C. Miller & Kaiser, 2001). Minimization and denial of battering may be one way to disengage from the stigmatized condition of victimhood. Professionals seldom consider, however, that disengagement and disidentification are the reasons for lack of disclosure. Further, "disengagement" is sometimes used as a term to characterize poor coping by victimized women (e.g., Taft, Resick, Panuzio, Vogt, & Mechanic, 2007). This is unfortunate because it is well recognized in the stigma literature that disengagement has benefits and in some situations can increase well-being. Information management is a major task of individuals with concealable stigma and to manage information means to selectively control the disclosure of it (Goffman, 1963; Herek & Capitanio, 1996).

A woman, especially one who has left the relationship (which includes many respondents in research on minimization and denial), may fully recognize what she has been through, but wish to disidentify with the stigmatized label "battered woman" as she tries to move forward with her life. Women who remain with their partners may also reject "battered" as their "master status" characteristic and still recognize that they are survivors of violence. Ironically enough, research on so-called "denial" actually typically relies on women disclosing at some point in the questionnaire or to the agency where they were recruited—somehow they are getting identified as victims and most of the time that is because they told researchers or providers that they had experienced violence. Professionals conclude victimized women are in "denial" because they have not disclosed to enough people or adopted a victim-based identity, not because they don't report having been assaulted. Few women who have sustained partner assault choose to describe themselves as battered (Hamby, 2000). Women who primarily identify with their career, as a mother, or with other roles in a community are not necessarily less competent than women who more publicly adopt an identity as "battered." Indeed, it seems possible the opposite may be true. In some articles (e.g., Dunham & Senn, 2000), authors recognize that omitting information may be active information management yet still use the pejorative term "minimization." We should give women who have experienced violence the benefit of the doubt and examine whether there are ways advocates, researchers, and other professionals can be safer recipients for disclosure.

The most important conclusion of all this is that there are many good reasons why the percentage of women who seek social support is not 100%, nor should it be. Some women have families that will not be supportive and who should not be told, because the survivors will only get blamed for their victimization. Not all friends, employers, and coworkers are appropriate candidates for disclosure either. The differences in rates of disclosure across these groups also make sense from the viewpoint of information management. For example, as described in more detail below, victimized women disclose to family members and friends far more than they do to coworkers. This is not a sign of denial but a sign of active information management choices that are similar to ones that we all make.

ACCESSING SOCIAL SUPPORT

> "My family has helped me out financially as I was a stay-at-home mom when I left my husband. They have given my son and I shelter, food and even clothing. My brother has given me a car... Through the help of my family, I was able to retain an attorney to resolve custody issues."

Understanding information management is one key to developing a more nuanced understanding of disclosure and seeking social support (Hamby & Gray-Little, 2007). Another important aspect of social support is that it is multifaceted. This is not well captured by the simple questions on most surveys that simply ask whether a woman disclosed to a particular person or sometimes, even more generally, whether they disclosed to anyone at all. The short questions on most surveys do not even begin to capture the richness of what can be involved in reaching out for social support. Most of the research in this area—including the qualitative research—just asks whether anyone was spoken to or sometimes breaks down those contacts into separate categories such as family, friends, and coworkers. A few studies get somewhat more specific, such as distinguishing turning to parents from other relatives or distinguishing turning to relatives in one's own family-of-origin from seeking help from in-laws. Yet even these distinctions just scratch the surface.

The range of things that can happen once that contact is established is vast. Table 8.1 provides just a few examples. We know that disclosing to friends and family sometimes develops into very concrete protective actions. The National Violence Against Women Survey (NVAWS) shows that most women who left their partner for any

Table 8.1 TYPES OF PROTECTIVE STRATEGIES DONE WITH ASSISTANCE
OF SOCIAL SUPPORT

Obtain emotional support
Obtain counsel and advice
Stay with family or friends
Get financial help with costs of moving
Get financial help for legal expenses
Get financial help for other protective strategies
Get practical help with moving, such as loaning truck or furniture
Ask family or friend to accompany women to court
Ask someone to accompany women to other agencies and providers
Ask for help filling out legal forms, applications for housing, and other paperwork
Obtain advice about lawyers or leads on jobs
Offer financial help with educational expenses
Get help with childcare
Get help with transportation
Ask family or friends to store belongings or extra keys
Ask family or friends to hold bank accounts or other assets in their name
Ask family to help negotiate a plan for reconciliation
Ask family to remove guns from household
Ask boss or coworkers to rearrange schedules
Explain to boss or coworkers issues related to performance or absenteeism
Explain to boss or coworkers batterer's behavior
Ask for security plan at the workplace

Note: This is a list of strategies derived from the research literature on women's protective strategies and from women I have known who have developed creative strategies. Inclusion on this list is not meant to be an endorsement or recommendation for any particular woman in any particular situation.

period of time did *not* go to a shelter. Only 5 women in the survey had ever done that. The most common strategy, used by about half of the women who had ever left (52%), was to go stay with family and friends (analyses conducted using archived NVAWS dataset). More than half (59%) of the women in a help-seeking sample had also stayed with family and friends (Goodman et al., 2003).

The field's focus on whether a woman has "disclosed" misses an appreciation for these kinds of concrete sources of support and protection obtained by reaching out to one's social network. It is even possible that responses such as obtaining a new home might have been accomplished with the help of family and friends. Support from one's social network could range from the financial, such as helping someone come up with a security deposit, to the physical, such as providing labor for the move. Household furnishings could be donated or loaned. As far as I am aware, there are no quantitative data indicating how often these things happen but I know from talking with countless women that is the path to protection for many.

There are all sorts of ways that victimized women obtain help from their social network. The assumption of most research is that the main benefit of social support is emotional and provides some insulation from feelings of depression and other adverse psychological consequences of victimization. Obtaining informal counsel and advice is also often assumed and no doubt occurs frequently. However, there are numerous other possible benefits. Sometimes family and friends provide services that are very much like the ones that domestic violence advocates provide. They accompany women to court. They help women fill out legal forms. They accompany them as they try to navigate the myriad social systems by helping them apply for low-income housing, petition for child support, or seek job training. They may have advice about lawyers or connections that can lead to jobs. They might offer money for tuition so women can go back to school. They can provide transportation. They can babysit. They can help with home maintenance and repair tasks that either take two people to easily accomplish or that go beyond the skills a particular woman might possess (although, as with all of these examples, I by no means intend to suggest that most victimized women are particularly helpless in any of these regards.) I have known some women who, following common safety plan advice, have asked parents or trusted friends to keep belongings or an extra set of keys for them. Some women go even further than that and will put savings or other assets in the name of a parent, sibling, or close friend to protect the assets from the batterer. Sometimes the only way to save money is by ensuring that no bank statements or other information come to their house or workplace.

RESEARCH ON OVERALL RATES OF SOCIAL DISCLOSURE

Contrary to the stereotype that most people keep domestic violence a secret, research suggests that disclosure is common and that the vast majority of women tell at least one person in their social circle about their victimization. One community-based study in New England found that 82% of victimized women had disclosed their victimization to at least one person, and the average number of people to whom they had disclosed was 3.6 (Sullivan, Schroeder, Dudley, & Dixon, 2010). A nationally representative Canadian survey found that 80% of victimized women sought some form of informal help, usually by contacting a family or friend (Barrett & St. Pierre, 2011). A survey of Mexican-origin women found that 83% went to people in their social network for help (Brabeck & Guzmán, 2008). An analysis of British Crime Survey data found that nearly two of three women (63%) who had experienced domestic violence in the past year had disclosed to relatives or friends (Walby & Allen, 2004). In 10 countries that participated in the International Violence Against Women Survey, approximately three of four women had reached out for social support (H. Johnson, Ollus, & Nevala, 2008).

These overall rates help to communicate that reaching out to one's social support networks is a common strategy. A *normative* strategy. Much of the research on informal help-seeking has examined this at another level of detail by asking about classes of people to whom women have disclosed or sought help. It is important to remember, as one reviews this research, that at least four of five women are engaging in some kind of social support seeking. Women disclose to some people more than others and it is essential to bear in mind that individual categories, such as "family" or "friends" are not mutually exclusive and there could even be multiple disclosures within these categories. It is possible to disclose to one's family, multiple friends, and several people at one's workplace. The study by Sullivan and colleagues (2010) shows that it is the norm to disclose to multiple people. The more specific data on who women disclose to provide a sense of the range of people women turn to for help. These data also provide a sense of who women rely on and who they judge to be the most likely sources of support.

FAMILY MEMBERS

"I stay strong by talking to mom, grandma, aunt…. I can rely on my mom, grandma, grandpa, aunt."

Women most consistently reach out to family members according to a large number of studies. In the first VIGOR study, when we invited women who had experienced domestic violence to list their strengths in open-ended descriptions, family support was the single most common resource identified, reported by more than half (54%) of the participants. Beyond just disclosure, more than one-third (35%) said talking to their family was one of their best options for coping with the violence (Hamby & Clark, 2011). In one nationally representative Canadian study, two of three (67%) of victimized women had talked to a family member about their situation (Barrett & St. Pierre, 2011). A similar percentage (69%) was found in another study (Goodman et al., 2003). More specifically, 55% of women in another study reported turning to immediate family for help (Brabeck & Guzmán, 2008). About one-fifth of this sample (19%) had also sought help from extended family, providing a useful comparison that is not included in most other research. In a sample of women whose victimization had reached the courts, almost all (94%) reported that at least one relative knew about it (Belknap, Melton, Denney, Fleury-Steiner, & Sullivan, 2009). The higher rates in this study may have resulted from the fairly public nature of having one's case reach the criminal justice system. In this same sample, more than four of five women (81%) also reported that their relative had been somewhat or very supportive.

Studies outside North America remain relatively few. An Australian study found that turning to family members was one of the most common forms of help-seeking, reported by 58% of help-seeking women (which was 44% of all victimized women) (Meyer, 2010). A nationally representative Swiss study also found that victimized women were most likely to disclose to family members. The rate of disclosure to family was 38% in Switzerland, which is lower than most other samples, although it is not clear if this reflects cultural differences or differences in the nature of the violence (Killias, Simonin, & De Puy, 2005).

Turning to family was one of the primary protective strategies reported in a qualitative study of Egyptian women (Yount, 2011). Given that approaching police or other officials was considered shameful by the women interviewed in these studies, appealing to male relatives was considered one of the strongest protective steps women could take. Appealing to a father or uncle was especially seen as a protective strategy, albeit one only to be used in cases of the most extreme violence (Yount, 2011).

Families-of-origin were the most common source of safe shelter, usually used as a safe base from which to negotiate reconciliation. The Yount study suggests that some people may disclose to different family members for different reasons. Mothers, fathers, or other family members may be better able to assist with different protective strategies. The domestic violence literature has paid almost no attention to the different types of support that may be sought from different family members, beyond a very few qualitative studies such as Yount's. Other literature on social support, however, suggests that in some cases, people are more likely to disclose to mothers or other female relatives than to fathers or male kin and that they find female relatives more supportive than male ones (Kalichman, DiMarco, Austin, Luke, & DiFonzo, 2003). Especially regarding problems having to do with relationships, it seems plausible that victimized women might be more likely to approach mothers or sisters than other family members when seeking help for violence. Studies on younger women are also relatively rare, but reaching out to parents is, if anything, even more important when the victims are minors involved in dating relationships. In the National Survey of Children's Exposure to Violence (NatSCEV), we found that about 40% of youth had disclosed to parents (Finkelhor, Ormrod, Turner, & Hamby, 2011).

Reaching out to family members will probably never reach 100% because 100% of people do not have family members to reach out to. Some have lost their parents to death or illness. Others may have lost their parents to addiction or other problems. Not everyone has siblings and this trend is accelerating as family sizes continue to shrink. Just because someone does not approach their family members does not mean that they have made a mistake. In fact, with research suggesting that 70% to 80% of battered women are approaching their families for help, they may already be close to the maximum feasible level given the wide range of family-of-origin situations that women will have.

FRIENDS

"I had a very supportive friend that helped me get through the hardest time of my life."

Friends are also a form of social support used by most battered women. In our project to identify women's perceptions of their own resources, having friends was one of the most commonly mentioned strengths, identified by more than two in five women (42%) (Hamby & Clark, 2011). In many respects, friends can, in principle, offer the same kinds of social support that family members can offer. In practice, there tend to be differences. Research on social support for other kinds of problems has suggested that many people find friends more supportive than family, at least for certain stigmatizing conditions such as being HIV-positive (Kalichman et al., 2003). Friends may be more likely than family to be at developmentally similar life stages and perhaps more likely to share values. Thus, perhaps it is not surprising that they are sometimes seen as more supportive than parents or other family. In many cases, however, friends may also be less easy to approach about concrete forms of assistance such as financial help or a place to stay, especially while avoiding a dangerous man. In the Canadian study, two of three women (68%) had also talked to friends (Barrett & St. Pierre, 2011). In the nationally representative Australian survey, talking to friends was the most common form of help-seeking, chosen by more than two in three help-seekers (70%) and adopted by 52% of all victimized women (Meyer, 2010). Other studies have also found that disclosure to friends is common, ranging from 53% to 92% (Belknap et al., 2009; Brabeck & Guzmán, 2008). The Swiss study is somewhat lower here, too, with only 21% disclosing to friends (Killias et al., 2005). Notably, this was lower than disclosure to police, health-care professionals and victim assistance programs, suggesting Swiss women may be more comfortable using formal services than informal social support.

IN-LAWS AND FAMILIES OF PARTNERS

Regardless of whether a woman is married to her partner, the relatives of her partner fall into a gray area for many victimized women. For simplicity's sake, I will use the term "in-laws" for all of them although in some cases they may be the family of a cohabiting partner or boyfriend. Although in some families the extended families of both partners are very much considered part of a single family unit, in others the distinctions between one's family-of-origin and those of one's in-laws is never completely forgotten. Not quite family, not quite friends, they can still have a large role in the lives of many women. Although, as mentioned in Chapter 5, in-laws can sometimes be a source of considerable risk to victimized women, they can also be a source of support and help. Sometimes a violent partner will listen to his parents when he will not listen to anyone else. A partner's parents can be powerful allies.

Most research on reaching out to families has not been specific enough to separate reaching out to families-of-origin from reaching out to other relatives. British Crime Survey data indicate that approximately one in nine domestically victimized British women have disclosed to their partner's relatives, friends, or neighbors, at least distinguishing the partner's social network from the woman's (Walby & Allen, 2004). As noted above, Brabeck & Guzmán distinguished between immediate and extended family in their study of help-seeking among women of Mexican origin. They also asked specifically about in-laws and found that nearly one-third of women (31%) had turned to their partner's family for help (Brabeck & Guzmán, 2008). It is possible that their focus on understanding the help-seeking patterns of one specific cultural group may have helped them decide to focus on possible differences within family relationships. Distinctions between immediate, extended, and partner's families are hardly unique to Mexican culture, however. Rather, it is the dominant U.S. culture that is unusual in the extent to which it tends to focus on the nuclear family and downplay other family relationships, and that may be why so little attention has been paid to them in past research.

COWORKERS

Disclosing to coworkers provides additional opportunities for protective efforts. Of course coworkers can be friends or even family members as well as workplace colleagues. In this regard, disclosing to coworkers can often involve seeking the same types of emotional support or advice that women might seek in any relationship. Coworkers, and perhaps especially bosses and supervisors, can also provide other types of assistance that are unique to the workplace environment, such as helping to rearrange schedules if needed.

There are also risks involved with approaching colleagues in addition to the risks of rejection and stigma that apply whenever a disclosure is made. Most of us try to maintain more polished personas in the workplace than we do with family members and close friends. The potential to "spoil" one's image might be greater in an environment when many people may know little about one's private life. Opportunities for promotion or the ability to maintain one's personal authority can be compromised when people know that there are problems at home. This is somewhat true of almost any stigmatizing problem, such as going through a divorce, but can be especially true for violence. Here it is important to remember that the stereotype of battered women, which suggests that most, if not all, are economically disadvantaged and, if employed at all, are working in menial jobs, is not true. Many victimized women have active careers and protecting those careers is important to them. Thus, disclosing to coworkers may only be chosen when that seems the only path to protecting a job or career.

Probably as a result of these and other factors, research consistently indicates that women approach coworkers less often than other people in their lives. Still, it is far from a rare occurrence and a substantial number of victimized women do seek help at their workplaces. More than one in four women (28%) had disclosed to coworkers in the Canadian study (Barrett & St. Pierre, 2011) as had 8% of Australian victimized women (Meyer, 2010). One in 10 Swiss women and 1 in 9 British women had disclosed to colleagues (Killias et al., 2005; Walby & Allen, 2004). These are lower rates than disclosures to family and friends in the same studies but are not trivial figures. A pattern of more disclosure to friends than coworkers was also found by Brabeck and Guzmán; 53% had sought help from friends and 15% from coworkers (Brabeck & Guzmán, 2008). In the sample of women whose cases had gone to court, most (92%) had friends that knew about the abuse, and nearly two out three (64%) had a coworker or classmate who knew (Belknap et al., 2009). Just as with family members, most friends, coworkers, and classmates (>80%) were supportive when they found out.

Disclosing to coworkers was even more common in another study, reported by two of three women (67%) (Swanberg et al., 2006). Swanberg and colleagues may have obtained a higher rate of coworker disclosure because they included many possible reasons for disclosure that may have helped remind women of all of the protective steps they have taken. It is one of the most detailed studies on reaching out to coworkers and does a great job of elucidating all of the things that a woman can do to get help in the workplace. The reasons for disclosing to colleagues and supervisors ranged from seeking support or advice (45%) to explaining absences or performance problems (37%) to explaining the perpetrator's behavior (25%). In the Swanberg et al. study, colleagues came through with many forms of support, including a "listening ear" (90%), scheduling flexibility (73%), and helping to come up with a security plan for the workplace (44%).

CHARACTERISTICS ASSOCIATED WITH DIFFERENT TYPES OF HELP-SEEKING

Understanding who reaches out to their social networks and under what circumstances is important for improving the response to survivors of violence. Understanding these patterns could help identify ways to encourage further protective strategies, help loved ones understand how they can be most helpful when a family member or friend has been victimized, and suggest modifications for interventions so professionals are better at providing support when informal networks cannot meet the needs of survivors. It is also important to be cautious, however, that small differences in informal help-seeking are not used to stigmatize or pathologize some subgroups of women. In this regard, there is considerable room for improvement in this research, which all too often assesses the association of static factors such as race or immigration status with help-seeking. Too often, variables such as race are used simply as social address markers. More nuanced analyses that consider the intersection of variables such as socioeconomic status with race are needed. It would be even better if "race" were unpacked in such a way that more explicit measures of the experiences of prejudice and unequal treatment were measured. This is especially important when thinking about protective strategies involving employers or human service agencies. Prejudice still exists at many social service agencies (Donnelly et al., 1999; Hamby, 2004). The field would benefit by focusing instead on malleable or situational factors. In particular, it would be useful to focus on situational characteristics to better understand coping choices and more useful to focus on modifiable factors to improve prevention and intervention. Here and elsewhere, I have focused on findings that seem most relevant to those goals.

As with other forms of help-seeking, characteristics of the situation and characteristics of the victim both influence which type of protective strategy survivors will choose. In the Canadian study, both formal and informal help-seeking were done more often by women experiencing violence so severe they thought they were in danger for their lives (Barrett & St. Pierre, 2011). Severity of violence was also correlated with disclosure in a study of court-involved victimized women (Belknap et al., 2009). Both higher severity and higher frequency of violence were associated with more disclosure in British Crime Survey data (Walby & Allen, 2004). More religiously active women were less likely than others to approach family, friends, and coworkers (Barrett & St. Pierre, 2011).

REACHING OUT TO OTHER VICTIMIZED WOMEN

Get out to talk to other people that [are] going through domestic violence. Hearing somebody else tell their story lets you know you are not alone.

Another category of reaching out for social support involves joining support groups or visiting websites for survivors. Especially in this age of social media, it is more possible than ever before to talk with people who have had experiences similar to one's own. Although some of these support groups are housed in shelters or otherwise offered as part of a professional organization's programming, some are more informal. Even those that are offered by shelters are more about peer-to-peer interaction, in many cases, than they are about professional counseling. As a percentage of the total population of victimized women, these support groups appear to be used less often than the more-routine accessing of family, friends, and coworkers, but it is important to recognize the full universe of possibilities. The proliferation of survivor websites is another understudied phenomenon. One study found that many women (31%) had spoken with other battered women for support and advice (Brabeck & Guzmán,

2008). Similarly, in the VIGOR study, 32% of the women identified attending a support group as one of their most important options.

CONCLUSION

The evidence on reaching out for social support of all types shows that women *routinely* access their social networks when they have experienced violence in relationships. One underappreciated implication of these findings is that they also provide a compelling refutation of the assumptions that women deny and minimize their problems. They can hardly be in denial about something they have, on average, told more than three people about (Sullivan et al., 2010). Not seeing the situation the same way that a researcher or an advocate sees a situation should not be taken as *de facto* evidence of psychopathology. Seeking social support is an important and flexible protective strategy that needs more explicit recognition in risk management and safety planning. Seeking social support is a good protective strategy to include in the VIGOR or other frameworks for complex problems. Seeking social support can be combined with many other types of protective strategies and can help improve outcomes almost no matter how other efforts turn out. Families and friends will be part of women's lives long after shelter stays have ended and court cases are over and they ought to be more explicitly incorporated into more interventions.

9

Turning to Spiritual and Religious Resources

A young, pregnant mother came to see me once. In addition to being pregnant, she had a toddler—a little boy about 3 years old. She was a victim of domestic violence, although the violence she had experienced was less severe than that experienced by many women who seek help for violence and had not endangered her pregnancy. Nonetheless, we did a dangerousness assessment and safety planning. I told her, as I told most survivors at the time, that I was concerned for her safety, the safety of her unborn child, and even her life. She told me that she was from a fundamentalist church (which one is not important). Her church did not believe in divorce and she and her entire family were committed members of this church. So divorce or even separation was out of the question. She wanted to know, given those circumstances, what I could offer in way of assistance.

What I mostly offered was a critique of her religious values. Sad, but true. I suggested to her that I was certain that valuing the sanctity of marriage and even a general injunction against divorce could not possibly mean that she should place her and her children's lives in danger. Living in rural areas and mostly in the southern United States, I have had numerous opportunities to practice this speech. I think I am pretty good at it, to the extent there is a "good" way to tell someone that their religion is okay as far as it goes but that they need to rethink a few tenets here and there. Although I did not think of it this way at the time and I did not phrase it in these terms, my suggestions often essentially amounted to a recommendation that survivors adopt humanistic and, if necessary, more secular values that are more like mine and virtually every other practicing psychologist I know. This particular woman assured me that her church's tenets about the sanctity of marriage did not have any subclauses or exceptions. I did mention a few other things she could do, all taken straight from the lists of the standard safety plans that we have discussed throughout this book. Get her papers together, pack a bag, hide the knives. Other suggestions included making a signal for her neighbors to call the police if she needed help, such as lowering the shades of a certain window. She looked a little mystified. These suggestions were not, in retrospect, answers to any questions that she had actually asked. She had asked how she could make her life better with her husband given that her entire church and family would reject her if she left him, even for a short period. Still, as was so often the case, she thanked me politely for my time before heading back to her life.

I did see her one more time. She came by a couple of weeks later (still pregnant) to tell me that she had given a lot of thought to what I had said and that she had decided that it was, in fact, possible that her life was in danger. She had not questioned her religious values or adopted a secular world view. She did not want my help. She wanted me to know that she had come up with a response on her own. She chose a protective strategy that fit with her personal values and the values of her family and community. She had gone to see a lawyer and put her affairs in order, so that if anything did happen to her, her children would be well cared for and financially stable (her family had more resources than many who seek help in the current service environment). She had purchased life insurance and named her children (including the unborn one) as beneficiaries. She had drawn up a will. She had been quite active in the short time since I had seen her. She felt strongly that it would be better for her children, in the long run, if they knew their mother had stood by her principles and brought no shame on the family by "giving up" on a marriage. She had a large extended family and felt confident her children would be well looked after no matter what happened to her. She declined the offer to schedule a return appointment and excused herself.

I was flabbergasted after she left. Drawn up a will? That was her idea of a safety plan? I seriously pondered whether I could get her committed for being a danger to herself (a reaction I now regret). I only reluctantly decided that there was no precedent for putting one's affairs in order as grounds for commitment and that it probably would not go over with a judge. I heard later from a local colleague that the woman reported that I "hadn't told her anything" during our two sessions. At the time, I was rather miffed by that because we spent a couple of hours going over dangerousness assessments and safety planning materials, as well as getting her "history." Not to mention all my great advice about how to improve her religious values.

If you have read this far you can probably already guess that I see the matter somewhat differently now. As reviewed in the sections on separation violence and the other risks in Chapters 3 through 5, leaving would not have necessarily increased her safety. It is probably not really true that she was in any imminent, meaningful way, "in danger for her life." She did not die. She did not need to be committed. I think her response was actually rather inventive and even proactive. Her affairs are now in better order than most people I know, including many providers and researchers. Many, many people—including, not coincidentally, Jesus, but also a great many of the most revered people in any cultural or spiritual tradition—have put their lives on the line rather than sacrifice their values. In almost any other scenario, even if a person could save themselves, we admire those who refuse to compromise their values in the face of extreme adversity. Almost everyone will have their values tested, perhaps not in extreme circumstances (for the more fortunate and privileged among us) but often and in many situations. I admire that woman for sticking up to the "expert doctor" and not making a choice that had unacceptable costs to her. I admire her even more and also thank her for being one of the few to come back and offer me a chance to learn about the complexities of her life situation and how she was taking active steps to carefully balance an array of risks, goals, and values that was right for her. She invested time and money and enlisted expert legal assistance to cope with her situation in a way that was acceptable to her. She gave me the opportunity to learn about the limits created by my own humanist and secular values and the paradigm through which I viewed all cases of domestic violence.

THE PROFESSIONAL DISMISSAL OF SPIRITUAL
AND RELIGIOUS VALUES

There are certainly benefits to secular approaches to human services. I am not suggesting that every social agency adopt a manifestly religious point of view. It is important that all people, of any faith or no faith at all, feel comfortable approaching social agencies for help. This is especially true of government agencies or institutions that fulfill public health roles. This includes not only most public organizations but also some privately owned agencies, such as some hospitals. I do not think providers should impose their own religious beliefs on the people that they serve. I also recognize that religious participation is declining in many countries and around the world; now one in six people report no religious affiliation (Pew Research Center, 2012). Nonetheless, this leaves the other five of six people in the world affiliated with a religion and, intentionally or not, providers and agencies often impose secular approaches to dealing with victimization (and a host of other problems). As a result, providers and agencies can miss opportunities to help survivors access the help and the strength to persevere.

One of the worst sins that human services professionals commit is looking down on people with strong religious faith and looking down on church-related ministries. This is true regarding faith-based organizations from the most common religious tradition in the world, Christianity (Pew Research Center, 2012), and in some cases even more true of mosque-based, synagogue-based, or faith-based institutions from other religious traditions. Although there are individual providers and agencies that avoid condescension, the message from the field as a whole is one of intolerance and irrelevance. Maybe in some secular utopian future, needs are cared for without the trappings of religious dogma, and maybe that would be a good thing. Speaking as someone who is not involved in an organized religion (I identify as Unitarian but seldom go to church), I nonetheless find it incomprehensible how little respect the field offers faith-based help and religious people.

Churches are some of the most generous social institutions around. Regular members of many religious congregations can count on substantial help from the church through all kinds of trouble. Churches will pay people's utility bills when they face financial crises. They will help people get needed repairs for their homes. They will arrange transportation for congregants who need to get to the doctor. For members who are in the hospital, not only will the clergy visit but also many churches will organize (formally or informally) a visiting schedule so people have a steady stream of company in the sterile hospital environment. When church members give birth to a child, especially a first child, churches commonly organize meal deliveries to ease the transition home, with different families taking the responsibility to provide a home-cooked meal each night for a week or two. More routinely, many churches regularly organize social and community events that often cost nothing to attend.

The generosity of many religious organizations even extends beyond the members of their immediate congregations. In places I have lived, I have known churches that would help pay the utility bills of clients of the domestic violence agency in town, even when those women were not members of the congregation. This was especially common among larger and older churches with a big base of supporters. No questions, no "hope to see you on Sunday" or other proselytizing, just generosity. In one town, the utility's heating assistance fund usually got tapped out long before winter was over. Further, the utility's assistance program came with all kinds of paperwork, documentation requirements, and long waiting lists. In sharp contrast, people in need could just carry their bill to many kind and willing clergy. The food banks of many communities are organized and run by religious organizations. Many religious organizations are actively involved in efforts to reduce violence. Jewish Women International, for example, is a leader in the anti-domestic violence movement. Clergy and congregants will help people get a truck to move their belongings and find a couple of strong young people to carry it for them. Many religious organizations will help people in need regardless of their immigration status, in some places even in defiance of the law as acts of civil disobedience. They will help immigrants apply for documented status. They will teach people to read and write English (even if their native language is English). They will help people regardless of their HIV status, history of severe mental illness, or struggles with addiction. Help for children is readily attainable too, including everything from school supplies to winter coats to free, safe youth programming. So many churches exemplify the values of the Good Samaritan. I have never known any social agency to provide the kind of immediate, practical, no-strings-attached support that can be found at many religious organizations. Further, unlike many social agencies, providers, and advocates, many religious leaders are willing to help without any preliminary screening or interview where they demand to know whether a woman is "serious" about leaving. Over the 20-plus years that I have been involved in human services, access to the assistance of social service agencies of all types has only gotten harder and harder to obtain, with more forms, more documentation, longer waiting lists, and shorter periods of service eligibility. In contrast, access to the assistance of religious institutions is much the same as it has been for many, many years.

Yet many psychologists, researchers, and others involved in social and human services are openly hostile to religion and to religious values. Formal safety planning documents seldom include a recommendation to seek assistance from religious organizations or religious leaders. Jill Davies' Advocacy Beyond Leaving is a notable exception (Davies, 2009), but even this document primarily lists "religious institutions" as an area to consider and does not include any specifics on what sort of help a woman might seek from a church, synagogue, or mosque. Advocates tell horror story after horror story about clergy who are opposed to divorce. Yes, I know a few horror stories, more than a few. Still, one seldom hears the other stories about clergy and others who are motivated by religious faith to do good work. The field could also tell stories about the support religious organizations provide that can carry on for months or even years, long after a woman has "maxed out" on what the local shelter can or will provide. Unlike some shelters, churches can be far more forgiving about the ups and downs of coping with violence, and do not demand firm commitments during middle-of-the-night crises.

PRAYER, RELIGION, AND SPIRITUALITY IN THE LITERATURE ON BATTERED WOMEN

The research literature is frequently disparaging of methods of coping that are grounded in spirituality or religion (Hamby & Gray-Little, 2007). Banyard and Graham-Bermann (1993) have noted that most coping questionnaires take a very "top-down" approach to classifying good and bad coping. If someone reports avoiding a problem, that is universally deemed poor coping, without investigating whether, given the particulars of that situation, that may be the best approach available at the time. Even worse, coping paradigms have been largely based on the typical coping strategies of dominant culture, White Americans. In the early days of coping research, when many core ideas such as "passive" or "emotion-focused" coping were developed, the research was even more narrowly restricted to the coping strategies of White American men (Banyard & Graham-Bermann, 1993). Questionnaires can set the framework for research on a topic to a surprising degree. In the stress and coping literature, prayer and other spiritual strategies have frequently been categorized as "passive" or "avoidant" coping (Edwards, Moric, Husfeldt, Buvanendran, & Ivankovich, 2005; Snow-Turek, Norris, & Tan, 1996; Rosenstiel & Keefe, 1983). These are seen as less desirable than "active" or "problem-focused" coping. This view of coping persists despite the emergence of a separate body of research that shows that religiosity can have protective effects for many psychological problems. For example, a recent 10-year-long prospective study found that youth who reported greater religion and spirituality (but not church attendance *per se*) at age 10 years were less likely to be depressed at age 20 years and that this effect was strongest for the youth who were deemed at highest risk because they had a parent with major depression (L. Miller et al., 2012). The research on battered women also shows that religion and spirituality can have positive effects. Table 9.1 lists some spiritual and concrete sources of support available from faith-based practices and organizations, and the sections below elaborate the role these serve for some women.

PRAYER AND FAITH AS PROTECTIVE STRATEGIES

"I believe in a higher power."
"It was knowing I had two small children to care for and my faith in Jesus Christ that helped keep me strong."
"I am good, honest, hard-working person with strong faith in God."

Prayer and other spiritual ceremonies and resources, despite negative labeling by the psychological community, can be great sources of strength for victimized women of many cultural and ethnic backgrounds (Hamby & Gray-Little, 2007; Potter, 2007). Just as using social support is the norm, so is relying on prayer and personal faith, which is reported by clear majorities of victimized women. More than 90% of battered women report that faith in God or spirituality was an important source of strength and coping in two studies (Gillum, Sullivan, & Bybee, 2006; Hage, 2006). El-Khoury et al. (2004) similarly found that 88% used prayer to find strength and guidance. Another study found that 71% said that maintaining a relationship with God helped them survive the abuse (Brabeck & Guzmán, 2008). Maintaining a relationship with God was also reported to be the most helpful of all coping strategies examined in that study. In the VIGOR 1 study, religious faith was one of the most commonly mentioned strengths that women volunteered (46% of the sample) (Hamby & Clark, 2011). Survivors' ability to rely on their church community was also reported by almost half (49%) of the women as one of their strengths and major resources.

Table 9.1 THE FREE TYPES OF SUPPORT WOMEN CAN OFTEN OBTAIN FROM
FAITH-BASED PRACTICES AND ORGANIZATIONS

Strength and perseverance from prayer and faith in God or a higher power
Comfort from inspirational stories in religious texts
Hope for the future from practicing prayer and other religious practices
Strength from confidence one can rely on one's religious community
Social support from other members of the congregation
Social support from religious leaders
Pastoral counseling from religious leaders
Free social activities
Help paying utility bills
Help with home repair
Transportation
Support during illness
Support following birth of child
Donations of food, clothing, furniture, and other necessities
Help with immigration status
Literacy and English as a second language classes
School supplies, winter coats, and other essentials for children
Free activities for children

Note: As noted in the text, I offer these examples based on the research literature, my experience seeking resources for battered women, and from the experiences of women I have known. Not everyone will find support from accessing faith-based protective strategies, but it should be a valued alternative for those who do.

PASTORAL COUNSELING AS A PROTECTIVE STRATEGY

"I'll talk to a preacher that I know."

Talking to a spiritual advisor is an important form of help-seeking used by 12% of women in one national Canadian study (Barrett & St. Pierre, 2011) and 16% in a sample of Mexican-origin women (Brabeck & Guzmán, 2008). Approximately one in four women indicated their religious leader knew about the abuse in four help-seeking samples (23%, 25%, 26%, and 27%, respectively, in Belknap et al., 2009; Cattaneo, Stuewig, Goodman, Kaltman, & Dutton, 2007; El-Khoury et al., 2004; Goodman et al., 2003). The VIGOR study obtained a slightly higher rate of 30% of victimized women having sought help from their pastor or church (Hamby & Clark, 2011). According to Belknap and colleagues, women rated religious leaders highly, with 89% saying their religious leaders were supportive and 72% reporting they were "very supportive" (Belknap et al., 2009). Goodman and colleagues (2003) found that more than half (54%) of the help-seeking women in their study described the strategy of seeking assistance from clergy to be "helpful," which may be a more stringent criterion than just "supportive."

A study by Cattaneo and colleagues (2007) offers some particularly striking insights about the role and importance of clergy to many victimized women. They have longitudinal data on help-seeking patterns (unfortunately still all too rare in domestic violence research). Interestingly, seeking the help of clergy turned out to be the most consistently used strategy over four follow-up assessments taking place in the year following the time of women's initial help-seeking and recruitment into the study. Turning to clergy was the most commonly used strategy at the 6, 9, and 12-month assessments (Cattaneo et al., 2007), although legal and shelter sources had been accessed much more frequently at the time of the initial interview. This is consistent with the idea that churches or other faith-based organizations might be equipped to offer longer term and more consistent support than many human service agencies. As discussed in Chapter 4, many shelters, for example, have 30-day (or even shorter) limits on stays.

So often, the field has focused on the negative feedback that people receive from clergy (see Chapters 4 and 5). But there are also more positive stories about the kinds of social support that women can obtain. The Belknap et al. and Goodman and colleagues studies cited above suggests that many women find their clergy very supportive. Qualitative research has found that women who wonder whether divorce is a failure to uphold their religious principles have been comforted by ministers who have told them that it was their partner who "spiritually" broke the covenant of marriage through his violent and abusive behavior (Nash & Hesterberg, 2009). Some ministers have devoted considerable energy to thinking through challenging verses, such as those found in Ephesians 5 of the Bible (and discussed in more detail in Chapters 4 and 5) (Miles, n.d.-b).

Many faith-based ethicists have addressed the complex and varying messages that can be found in the texts of many religions (Mashhour, 2005). For example, many Christian ethicists believe that the message of nonviolence and love is the most important message of the Bible (e.g., Farley, 2008; McLennan, 2010; Thornton, 2009). Christian scholars and ministers from a variety of religious denominations view the Bible in its historical and cultural context and point out that inconsistent messages can be found throughout the text (D. Ott, Presbyterian minister, personal communication, June 18, 2012). From this viewpoint, passages such as Ephesians 5 are seen, at least in part, as a product of an ancient patriarchal society. Not all Christian churches interpret Ephesians 5 as contemporary relationship advice and many Christian scholars believe there is ample evidence in the Bible to suggest that there were philosophical struggles over the issue of the indissolubility of marriage at the time the Bible was written (Farley, 2008). Another strategy that some ministers take is to suggest to women that they read the rest of that chapter in Ephesians, which outlines the husband's duty to honor and love the wife as his own body and as Christ loves the church (Ott, personal communication, June 18, 2012). Bible interpretation is a controversial area, and a consensus is unlikely to emerge soon for it or other religious texts. For the purpose of this book, the important point is that the domestic violence field tends to focus on the views of just one segment of the Christian community or conservative segments of other religious traditions, but these views do not represent the entire Christian or the entire faith-based community.

CULTURE, RELIGION, AND SPIRITUALITY

Attitudes about prayer and other religious and spiritual practices are not just driven by the secular stance of most social sciences and human services; they are also to a great extent influenced by other majority culture U.S. values. The dominant U.S. culture and, to some extent, other similar Western cultures are individualistic, fast-paced, oriented toward the nuclear family, tolerant of divorce, and heavily influenced by the medical model, among other characteristics. Although the "melting pot" approach of U.S. culture has helped make it one of the most multicultural countries on the planet, the predominance of the dominant culture contributes to a one-size-fits-all zeitgeist that will not work for all victimized women (Hamby, 2000). For example, in one study, Japan-born respondents were less likely to use "active" coping strategies and perceived them to be less effective than U.S.-born women of Japanese descent (Yoshihama, 2002). Culturally specific spiritual practices play an important role in the process of healing and protection, as exemplified by the statement of this American Indian woman from the Seattle area:

> "... That helped me a lot,.... smudging [ritual purifying with the smoke of sacred herbs such as sage] and just doing a lot of different things about being strong and protecting myself, you know. The Native person can teach me how to protect myself in a Native way, like smudging, and not cutting my hair, and just leaving it on the ground so someone can stomp on it! And you know, just things like that, little things. And the music, powwow music was a big healing for my heart and made my heart strong again." (Senturia, Sullivan, Cixke, & Shiu-Thorton, 2000, pp. 114–115)

Spiritual practices are often reported more frequently by women of color in research on battered women, including African-American women (El-Khoury et al., 2004) and Muslim women (Hassouneh-Phillips, 2001, 2003). This is consistent with other research on the use of prayer as a coping strategy, which often finds that European Americans use prayer as a coping strategy, on average, less than other U.S. ethnic groups (e.g., Edwards et al., 2005). Spiritual and religious practices can differ across ethnic and racial groups in other ways as well. Religious involvement was more closely associated with social support for African-American women than it was for Caucasian women in one study, for example (Gillum et al., 2006). Still, spiritual practices are important to all racial, ethnic and cultural groups and some research has found that more involvement with religious institutions was associated with less depression and better quality of life across ethnic groups (Gillum et al., 2006).

A NUANCED APPROACH

A complete model of the role of religious and spiritual practices in coping will take into account both positive and negative aspects of religiosity. A study of American Muslim women found that the effects of so-called "passive" religious strategies varied. Many women derived strength from prayer and meditation, but many of their partners also tried to use scripture to enhance their power and control over the women (Hassouneh-Phillips, 2001, 2003). Hage (2006) also described how some women benefited from spiritual practices but were also simultaneously hampered by the rules and traditions of organized religions, which may discourage divorce for any reason, even battering. Nash and Hesterberg (2009) also described a complex interplay between positive and negative aspects of spirituality and religion. Recognizing that prayer and other faith-based practices have protective and positive elements does not require ignoring the adverse effects that can also occur. Many protective strategies can vary in their effect. Sometimes calling the police is helpful, sometimes that creates more problems on top of the violence. The complexities of coping are not limited to dealing with violence, either. Seeking medical treatment is often helpful for a wide array of problems but can also fail for reasons ranging from errors by health-care professionals to abuse of the medical system by drug-seeking patients. Simplistic checklists that always treat a given behavior as "active" or "passive" or good or bad are building error into research and scholarship on coping because there are few, if any, actions that will always have the same effect for every person in every situation.

THE INTERCONNECTION OF RELIGIOSITY AND SPIRITUALITY WITH OTHER PROTECTIVE STRATEGIES

Perhaps not surprisingly, spirituality influences women's choice of services. As with other areas, we need more information on this than is currently available. A high percentage of research on religiosity and spirituality among battered women has been qualitative. Qualitative research is limited in its ability to look at the association of religious and spiritual coping with other protective strategies. A few quantitative studies have examined these questions. Not surprisingly, women who reported participating in religious activities were more than five times as likely to turn to a spiritual advisor as less religious women in the nationally representative Canadian study mentioned earlier (Barrett & St. Pierre, 2011). A smaller, shelter-based study also found that more religious women are more likely to use faith-based services than women who describe themselves as less religious (Fowler, Faulkner, Learman, & Runnels, 2011). More religious women were also less likely to use shelter-based services (Fowler et al., 2011). Unfortunately, however, the comparison in that study was rather imprecise. All of the women were recruited from a shelter, so in that respect they were all users of shelter-based services. Response categories such as "some of the time" and "all of the time" were not defined and may have meant different things for faith-based versus shelter services. Could a week in a shelter be "some of the time?" It would take a lot of faith-based services to add up to a similar number of hours of service. In the same study, women who had experienced higher levels of violence were less satisfied with faith-based services than women who had experienced lower levels of violence. This finding needs replicating. This result could, as Fowler and colleagues suggest, indicate a need for faith-based services to become better equipped to deal with severe violence. This finding could also be something fairly unique to the location or sample of their study. Still, this is one of the few studies that attempted to examine who chooses faith-based services and how those compare to other services. In that respect, it points the way for much-needed future research.

CONCLUSION

Perseverance, endurance, strength. These traits are needed to survive domestic violence and many more of life's adversities. Faith in a set of enduring spiritual principles can and does help many, many victimized women find the will to go on, no matter what they face. For some women, this is the protective strategy that makes all of the other protective strategies possible. For advocates, providers, researchers, and other violence professionals, there are many goals that must be delicately balanced. It is important that women of all faiths, or no faith, feel welcome and able to approach any agency for help. In this regard, the secular approach of most agencies and most providers is beneficial. However, it is also important not to esteem one's own secular, ecumenical point of view above the more specifically faith-based or creed-based views of one's clients. Nonreligious coping and coping that is not grounded in a specific religious viewpoint is not better or inherently more active. Even more essentially, the vast resources and support networks offered by the religious community should not be ignored or avoided simply because they are faith-based organizations. These are significant resources despite the fact that some religious people and some religious organizations do not support victimized women. No class of provider or agency can pass that test. There are unsupportive individuals in any large group of people. More needs to be done to craft ways of supporting women's spirituality and working with them when they choose religious-based protective strategies. As with seeking social support, faith-based forms of coping need more explicit incorporation into risk management and safety planning. As with most of the protective strategies we have examined so far, faith-based protective strategies can be combined into a multistrategy plan that addresses multiple priorities.

10

Using Formal Services

Once, years ago, a colleague and I gave a talk on domestic violence for parents' night at a local school. We were there in our official capacity as advocates and counselors. It was pretty standard "DV 101" material, as insiders in the field call the basics on domestic violence, including fairly standard advice on leaving and safety planning. Among other well-known information, we presented the power and control wheel (Pence & Paymar, 1993). The power and control wheel presents eight ways that batterers routinely control their victims in addition to resorting to violence, such as economic abuse. The talk was reasonably well received. There were a lot of questions, but they were mostly along the lines of "I've known situations…" or "I have a friend…" and none of it got too personal. A few people approached us after the talk but more to discuss violence as a general issue and not for personal help-seeking. That was pretty much the end of it as far as I knew, but several months later a woman approached my colleague in a store and told her that our presentation had a profound effect on her. She had not previously thought of the monitoring and control issues as so closely connected to the periodic violence in her relationship. It turned out she started making plans the night of that presentation—mostly financial plans—and within 6 months had moved to an apartment and gotten a divorce. She was already much happier and she just wanted to say thank you. I would, in turn, like to thank her for alerting me to impacts that are often unseen.

UNDER-RECOGNIZED ASPECTS OF DOMESTIC VIOLENCE ADVOCACY

The last chapter described some of the impressive services offered by faith-based organizations that are often lost in the critique of those religious leaders or religious institutions that are not supportive of women's right to safety. Although domestic violence advocates do not receive as much direct criticism in the field, there are many ways in which their work goes underappreciated. Some of the advocates I have known are among the most heroic and amazing women I have ever met. They routinely put their own safety at risk to try and help others, with little financial reward and sometimes under incredibly stressful conditions. Much of what advocates do is hard to measure—more invisibility in the lives of battered women. Domestic violence agencies and advocates touch lives in ways that do not make it into annual reports. One of the most important impacts is shifting social norms and reaching people who may not be direct clients, in the traditional sense of how that is counted in patient care. They help people who never appear on their doorstep. In the 1960s and 1970s the women's movement often spoke of consciousness raising but the impact of efforts to make domestic violence a less taboo topic has received little formal study, beyond the generally apparent impact of the many increases in services. Once a basic research frame gets established, most subsequent studies tend to be heavily influenced by that framework. There are literally thousands of data points on how many women who have experienced domestic violence have gone to shelter and, as far as I am aware, none on how many women went to a public forum on domestic violence to learn more about the problem of violence. There are no studies of how many women made changes in their lives as a consequence of researching or learning about domestic violence on their own initiative.

Although it is hard to say with any certainty how many lives have been saved from the shelter movement, there is no question that the number of intimate partner homicides has fallen substantially since the shelter movement first started in the early 1970s. In the United States in 1976, there were 1,587 recorded cases of intimate partner femicide. By 2005, that number had fallen to 1,181, a drop of about 25% (Fox & Zawitz, 2010). Of course, at the same time the population of the United States also increased substantially, so in that sense it is even a larger drop. Perhaps surprisingly, the number of male victims has fallen even more rapidly than the number of female victims. From 1976 to 2005, the number of intimate partner "androcides" (killing of men) fell from 1,304 to 329, a 75% drop (Fox & Zawitz, 2010). Some people think this is because shelters have provided a way out to women who might otherwise have been driven to desperate acts. Some data also suggest nonfatal domestic violence has also dropped (Truman, 2011). Estimates also suggest the social movement against domestic violence has saved billions from reduced health-care expenses and time lost from work, among other savings (Clark, Biddle, & Martin, 2002).

The advocacy movement's relentless drive to put domestic violence on the public's and media's agendas deserves most of the credit for creating the social and legal changes that are associated with the decreases in both lethal and nonlethal domestic violence that we have seen in the last 40 years (Fox & Zawitz, 2010; Truman, 2011). It is hard to remember how recently, in social change terms, a little "smacking around" was seen as a normal part of married life. A few decades ago, a running joke on the show *The Honeymooners* involved Ralph Kramden threatening to hit his wife, Alice Kramden, so hard it would send her all the way to the moon. In *I Love Lucy*, it was amusing that Ricky Ricardo refused to let his wife Lucy work outside the home. Social norms have changed dramatically since then (Hamby & Gray-Little, 2000). These are just a few examples of important positive outcomes from the advocacy movement that are not captured in surveys of help-seeking among survivors.

Researchers spend more time studying victimized women's interactions with other violence professionals. As a result, there are a lot of data on protective strategies such as calling the police and going to shelter in comparison to some of the other protective strategies we have studied. Seeking formal services is an important component of many women's protective strategies. Despite the stigma of help-seeking and the financial obstacles involved (Logan et al., 2004), many women access many health, mental health, and legal services in their efforts to deal with the problem of violence. Exploring this topic will be another opportunity to reframe common perceptions, because sometimes it is assumed that all victimized women should seek formal services and that those who do not are being passive or are in denial. The implicit assumption is that domestic violence is one type of life problem that can never be handled on one's own.

This conclusion is flawed, however. Rates of help-seeking among domestic violence victimized women are similar to or higher than those of people experiencing other problems. For example, in one nationally representative Canadian survey, only 28% of those meeting criteria for a psychological disorder such as depression or alcohol abuse had ever sought treatment (Bland et al., 1997). Similarly, a large European study found 26% of those with a psychiatric disorder had sought treatment (The ESEMeD MHEDEA investigators et al., 2004). Data from the United States suggests somewhat higher rates of help-seeking (41%) for people with psychological disorders, but still more than half of people with a diagnosable mental illness receive no treatment at all. Further, people most commonly seek formal help from their general practitioner and not from specialized mental health services. Rates of help-seeking to psychiatrists was only 12% and to other mental health providers was 16% in the U.S. study (P. Wang et al., 2005). Although it is widely thought that many psychological and other life problems would benefit from more formal interventions (Kazdin & Blase, 2011), lack of seeking formal services should be recognized as common. Regarding mental illness, professionals recognize that low rates of help-seeking result from a wide range of factors such as access. Lack of help-seeking is not thought to be solely or primarily caused by the passivity or cognitive distortions of the person needing help, as is commonly stated in the domestic violence field. Help-seeking patterns are not only influenced by obstacles such as access or cost either. A woman's personal resources, social support networks, or faith-based community may provide her with all she needs to adequately address the problem of partner violence. A recent longitudinal showed that approximately half of women who recovered from post-traumatic stress disorder did so without any formal mental health services (Cougle, Resnick, & Kilpatrick, 2013). Still, there is no doubt that there are many situations when professional assistance is needed, and so the data on accessing formal services is essential to understanding the spectrum of protective strategies. Although the limitations of some services are well known and have already been discussed in Chapter 4, many women decide formal services are worth trying, and fairly large numbers have used one or more traditional services for victims of violence.

USING "CLASSIC" LEGAL AND ANTI-DOMESTIC VIOLENCE SERVICES

Seeking help from formal social service and human service agencies is not at all unusual. In one representative survey of Canadians, two-thirds (66%) reported using at least one type of formal social or human service (Barrett & St. Pierre, 2011). Formal services include activities such as contact with domestic violence programs, law enforcement, mental health providers, other health-care providers, or other treatment programs. A range of professional services are described below and listed in Table 10.1.

Going to a Domestic Violence Shelter

"The shelter is a great place. It gives women hope for their future."
"Through talking to the staff and talking to other ladies at shelter I felt like I was not alone, that I did have options."

Table 10.1 PROTECTION THROUGH ACCESSING FORMAL SERVICES

Going to a domestic violence shelter
Other domestic violence program services
Information from direct contact with program staff
Information from Internet searches on domestic violence agency websites
Referral
Transportation
Children's programming
Court accompaniment
Calling the police
Seeking help from victim assistance programs
Obtaining a restraining order/order of protection
Mental health services
Healthcare
12-step programs such as Al-Anon
Other social services
Support groups

Just as with the other protective strategies we have described, there are more to shelter services than are just suggested by the simple rates of who has sought shelter. "Shelter" is not limited to just housing and women reach out to these agencies for all kinds of help. Most shelters are open 24 hours a day, 7 days a week not only for housing but also for crisis intervention. Many will send advocates to emergency rooms, courts, and some even accompany police. They will often go to where a victim is and provide transportation to the shelter. In addition to providing housing, shelters will provide essentials ranging from diapers to shampoo. They often have donated clothing and furniture that they will give to women who are trying to set up new housing or just need clothes. Many shelters also have programs for children to help them cope with exposure to violence and upheaval caused by violence.

Access to shelters or other domestic violence services is not as universal as sometimes believed. Fewer than half of U.S. counties have shelters, and those shelters that exist are often full. A recent national survey on shelter services found that, in a single day, there were more than 6,000 unmet requests for shelter or transitional housing (National Network to End Domestic Violence, 2012). Further, as outlined in Chapter 4, some shelters have policies that, although often originally designed to protect residents, result in some battered women being excluded from shelter or not wanting to use shelter services. These include excluding boys older than age 12 years (or even younger), excluding women who are actively using drugs or alcohol to cope with abuse, or requiring residents to participate in other interventions such as parent training. Often operating with very limited resources, shelters may struggle to offer culturally relevant services, particularly to battered women who are the most marginalized, including undocumented immigrants; women of color; people with disabilities; lesbian, gay, bisexual, and transgender survivors; and battered women charged with crimes. From an even broader perspective, some have criticized shelters for setting up the expectation that it is women who should leave (Neptune, personal communication, 2000). Why should the victims have to vacate the residence? This is a remnant of a more patriarchal era when women were often not equal owners of shared property.

Statistics about how many victimized women use shelter services as part of their protective efforts are less available than one might expect, especially given the huge social investment in these services. Available data show that many women and children use shelters. In 2011, just on a single day, more than 11,000 adults and 12,000 children resided in emergency shelter at domestic violence agencies in the United States. Another 12,000 adults or children were in transitional housing (National Network to End Domestic Violence, 2012). Although this certainly represents a lot of service, these figures do not indicate what percentage of victimized women seek housing services. In one nationally representative community survey (Tjaden & Thoennes, 2000a), 4% of women who left their partner went to a safe house or homeless shelter (frequencies calculated at the online archives of the Inter-University Consortium for Political and Social Research, http://www.icpsr.umich.edu/). In a Canadian nationally representative survey, 11% of victimized women had contacted an emergency shelter or housing program (Barrett & St. Pierre, 2011). In a nationally representative Australian study, only 2.6% of help-seeking women had stayed in a shelter (Meyer, 2010). In a study of women whose cases had reached the criminal justice system, about one-third (31%) reported that a shelter worker knew about the abuse (Belknap et al., 2009). Although it is not clear if that many had stayed in shelter, this figure shows a high level of help-seeking. It is possible that referrals from the police or in-court victim advocates may have made these women more aware of how to access shelter services. One of the higher rates of shelter use was found in a Swiss study. When they looked only at cases of more severe violence, they found that one in five women (21%) had used shelter services (Killias et al., 2005). Although not used by all victimized women, emergency shelters are an important strategy, especially for the most severely abused women with the fewest financial and social resources.

Other Domestic Violence Program Services

Most domestic violence programs offer a variety of services in addition to shelter, and some offer advocacy but do not have shelter facilities. Unfortunately, data are largely lacking on the percentage of victimized women who seek these services. Some figures are available for the number of agencies who provide various services in the United States from the National Network to End Domestic Violence, who track more than 30 forms of shelter services (2012). Individual support and advocacy is most commonly offered, reported by virtually all programs (98%). The next most commonly reported service was children's support or advocacy (79%). More than half also assist with transportation (53%). Approximately half (53%) of agencies provide legal advocacy and court accompaniment. Other kinds of advocacy related to housing and public benefits such as TANF were also provided by about half of agencies. About one in four programs offered financial skills training and almost one in four offered some kind of job training or employment assistance.

Data collected by the state of North Carolina indicate that the most commonly offered domestic violence-related services in that state are information about domestic violence and referral to other organizations (North Carolina Council for Women, 2007). Their data indicate that information and referral are provided to about four times as many people as shelter services were. In 2006 to 2007, domestic violence programs provided shelter to approximately 12,000 people (6,500 adults and 5,500 children). Information was provided more than 95,000 times and referrals more than 75,000 times to approximately 48,000 clients. Transportation, court accompaniment, and counseling were also all provided more frequently than shelter. The Canadian study mentioned above gave a figure of 11% for contacting an emergency shelter but also said that 17% had contacted a crisis line or crisis center, 16% had contacted a community center, and 11% had contacted a women's center (Barrett & St. Pierre, 2011). In many communities, these services may all be offered from a centralized location and suggest that nonshelter domestic violence services are utilized by many survivors.

Interpreting service data is complex because many of these services were probably provided to women while they were in shelter and because a single shelter "service" can comprise as much as a 90-day stay, whereas most of these other services take place over much briefer periods. Further, not every domestic violence program has the resources to offer shelter (approximately one in four do not; National Network to End Domestic Violence, 2012). As noted earlier, data also indicate that shelters are often full and substantial needs for shelter are not meant (National Network to End Domestic Violence, 2012). Shelters might be used more if they were more widely available. Finally, data that come from programs, not victims, do not tell what percentage of victimized women is using these services as part of their protective strategies. Still, data suggest that a variety of advocacy services are used by large numbers of women and children exposed to violence.

Calling the Police

"Well-trained police in hometown"

Substantial numbers of women, especially those who have experienced the most severe battering, call the police. This is the case even though it is widely known that the police response may have limited effectiveness in preventing future violence, may increase the risk of retaliatory violence or other punishment by their partners, may put a victim at risk of being arrested herself, and, in some communities, may expose victimized women or their partners to violence perpetrated by police (Hirschel & Buzawa, 2002; Martin, 1997; Ritchie, 2006). Further, law enforcement involvement can also be risky for women who may be worried about involvement from child protective services or immigration enforcement.

Studies of women who have had contact with shelters or social services indicate that between 32% and 78% have also called the police (Brabeck & Guzmán, 2008; Bui, 2003; Campbell et al., 1998; Krishnan, Hilbert, & VanLeeuwen, 2001; Magen et al., 2001; Rounsaville, 1978; C. E. Rusbult & J.M Martz, 1995; Wright & Johnson, 2009). A sample of women who had either had a domestic violence case at the district court or gone to a shelter found that 85% had called the police (Goodman et al., 2003), although this high number probably partly results from recruitment through the criminal justice system. A similar but less well-recognized tactic is threatening to call the police, which has been reported by some women (Campbell et al., 1998).

Nationally representative samples also find high rates of calling the police. In the National Crime Victimization Survey (a very large community sample), 53% of women reported their intimate partner victimizations to police between 1993 and 1998 (Rennison & Welchans, 2000). Reporting also rose slightly during that time period. In the National Survey of Children's Exposure to Violence, law enforcement contact was common in families whose children had been exposed to violence (Finkelhor et al., 2011). More than half of cases (52%) of a parent getting "beaten" were known to authorities, and one in four (25%) incidents involving parents arguing and breaking objects were known to police. The presence of children may make law enforcement contact more likely, because in other nationally representative community surveys, the rates of reporting to the police are lower. It could also be because the typical violence reported in some surveys is more minor and infrequent. Surveys vary in whether they tend to capture more or less severe violence (Hamby, 2009a). Those that capture more severe violence tend to find more police reporting. A nationally representative U.S. survey found that 21% of victimized women had contacted the police (27% of all victimizations were reported, but not always by the victim; Tjaden & Thoennes, 1998). In a Canadian survey, the rate was 30% (Barrett & St. Pierre, 2011) and in an Australian survey, 19% (Meyer, 2010). The Swiss version of the International Violence Against Women Survey (IVAWS) found that more than one in four women experiencing domestic violence (28%) had called the police and a similar percentage (29%) had used a victim assistance program (Killias et al., 2005). Overall, IVAWS has found lower rates of police reporting in many countries. Poland had a relatively high rate, also exceeding 20% of incidents (H. Johnson et al., 2008). This may be because, in many countries, domestic violence is still not seen as something appropriately dealt with by law enforcement or law enforcement may be less helpful.

Factors associated with calling the police. Although the rates of reporting are lower in community surveys, more severe forms of violence are more likely to be reported to the police. In one survey, women who sustained severe violence were more than four times as likely to call the police as women who sustained minor violence (14% vs. 3%; Kaufman Kantor & Straus, 1990). Similarly, one study found that by far the strongest predictor of help-seeking was whether a woman feared for her life, which increased reports to police and all other types of help-seeking (Barrett & St. Pierre, 2011). Increasing severity of violence was the strongest correlate of virtually all kinds of help-seeking (both from formal institutions and from family and friends) in another sample as well (Belknap et al., 2009). Importantly, these data rebut the idea that more severely victimized women are in greater denial.

Not all groups are equally likely to turn to police, in an indication that race, immigration status, and age are also associated with this type of help-seeking. Groups that historically have problematic relationships with the police often have good reasons not to call the police, which may lead to more problems than it solves (Crenshaw, 1991). Consequently, it is not surprising that research shows members of many oppressed groups appear to be less likely to call the police. Immigrants were less likely to call the police in a Canadian national survey than other victimized women (Barrett & St. Pierre, 2011). Bui (2003) estimates, using data from Houston, Texas, that Vietnamese immigrants are five times less likely to call the police than other ethnic groups in that city. Fear of problems with immigration authorities (whether or not women are documented) and fears of racial or ethnic discrimination by law enforcement may prevent some victimized women from contacting police or other authorities (Bui, 2003). On the other hand, not all studies have found ethnic or racial differences. One study found similar rates of police reporting for Latina and non-Latina women (Krishnan et al., 2001).

Age is another factor that affects reporting patterns. In NatSCEV, dating violence victimizations involving youth aged 12 to 17 years were less likely to lead to police contact than victimizations involving youths' parents. Only 3.6% of physical teen dating violence was known to police. Teen dating violence was more likely to be reported to school authorities—14% of cases had been reported to teachers or other school staff in NatSCEV (Finkelhor et al., 2011). This is in contrast to police involvement rates ranging from 25% to 52%, depending on the type of assault, for interparental violence. This was consistent with reporting patterns for other types of victimizations that largely involve peer-on-peer assaults in the NatSCEV dataset and suggests that the public may perceive that different social agencies are better suited to responding to violence, depending on the ages of the victims and perpetrators.

Obtaining a Restraining Order/Order of Protection

Orders of protection, which are also sometimes called "restraining orders" and referred to as "OPs" or similar acronyms, are court orders intended to separate a perpetrator and a victim in cases where there has been repeated unwanted contact and usually repeated victimization. Outside of domestic violence cases, another familiar use of orders of protection would be to stop celebrity stalkers. They are similar in principle to orders for convicted sex offenders to keep a certain distance from schools or other places where children congregate. In cases of domestic violence, sometimes a minimum set distance, such as 500 feet, is also prescribed. More general "no contact" orders are also supposed to prevent phone calls, e-mails, and other contact. Orders of protection can also include orders for a perpetrator to move out of the home of a survivor. Thanks to the Violence Against Women Act, any U.S. jurisdiction that is in compliance with federal law will offer OPs to women with no court costs and will recognize the authority of an OP granted in any other U.S. jurisdiction. Temporary OPs are now granted more or less routinely in most parts of the United States and can be obtained on an emergency basis on nights, weekends, and holidays. Permanent OPs usually require appearing before a judge and giving the defendant the right to appeal. They have become a cornerstone of domestic violence victim services in most parts of the United States, Europe, and elsewhere.

Maintaining OPs over a period of time is associated with decreased risks of at least some types of violence (physical is reduced more than psychological or sexual), although OPs do not eliminate violence for all women who have and maintain them (Holt, Kernic, Lumley, Wolf, & Rivara, 2002; Holt, Kernic, Wolf, & Rivara, 2003). One study found that all women who had applied for an OP had decreased violence at follow-up, regardless of whether the OP was granted or not (McFarlane et al., 2004). This speaks to the possibility that applying for these OPs is part of a larger protective endeavor on the part of women and these other factors may be contributing to women's increased safety along with or perhaps even instead of the OP itself.

Despite some evidence of effectiveness, OPs do have their limits. As any advocate and many survivors can attest, they are only pieces of paper. They are not magic force fields and they will not stop or even slow down a perpetrator who has no regard for the law. They work best for perpetrators who are motivated to comply with the law and stay out of jail. Batterers with criminal histories, for example, are much more likely to violate orders of protection (Goldfarb, 2008). Truly antisocial or delusional perpetrators may even become more agitated if they are served with these documents. One study found that approximately one in four women reported that their partners had violated their OPs, but even more notably, the mean number of violations was more than nine (Shannon et al., 2007). Once a perpetrator realizes it is just a piece of paper, an OP is scarcely a barrier to contact at all. More than one woman with an order of protection in place has been assaulted and even killed. Other problems exist regarding restraining orders, including lack of legal representation in civil protection order hearings for low-income women. The most commonly mentioned problem is limited enforcement of protection orders. It has often been reported that police do not always intervene when a batterer initiates contact despite the presence of an OP (Goldfarb, 2008). As with virtually every protective strategy, the eventual goal should not be to get 100% of victimized women to pursue OPs. The research does show that many women try OPs as one protective strategy, especially women who have sustained more serious violence. The rate of women seeking restraining orders varies widely, even in help-seeking samples. Among many factors, this variation probably results from differences in policies across legal jurisdictions and sometimes even from one judge to the next. The rate has ranged from more than 78% of women in one study (Strube & Barbour, 1984) to 18% in another (Magen et al., 2001). A study of immigrant women who had sought advocacy services found that 68% had filed a protection order (Dutton, Ammar, Orloff, & Terrell, 2007). A study of a rural sample of victimized women found 23% had sought an order of protection (Krishnan et al., 2001). The National Violence Against Women Survey, a community survey, found that 17% of women attained a temporary restraining order.

Factors associated with obtaining an order of protection. Obtaining an order of protection is more likely with more frequent contact with police and medical personnel (Durfee & Messing, 2012; Wright & Johnson, 2009), suggesting that professionals may be informing victimized women about this option. This is one way professionals can support victimized women's protective strategies. Nurius and colleagues (Nurius, Macy, Nwabuzor, & Holt, 2011) found that although rates of obtaining both permanent and temporary restraining orders were generally high, they also varied considerably according to resources and vulnerability of victimized women. More vulnerable and resource-poor women had higher rates of seeking restraining orders (63%–74%), whereas women with more resources did so at somewhat lower rates (39%–67%). In one sample (Krishnan et al., 2001), Latinas (27%) were twice as likely to seek a restraining order as other women (13%). This could be because non-Latinas were experiencing less severe violence and were dealing with different derivative losses and cascading effects or because they felt they had other avenues for dealing with the problem.

Violations of orders of protection. As mentioned above, orders of protection do not deter all perpetrators. Thus, the use of this strategy may be affected by knowledge that restraining orders are often violated—in the NVAWS, for example, half the women (51%) said their partner violated the restraining order (Tjaden & Thoennes, 1998).

Another study found approximately one in four women had a partner who violated an order (Shannon et al., 2007). In an immigrant sample, 37% felt an order of protection would increase their danger (M. A. Dutton et al., 2007). Women may know from their own experience or that of others that restraining order violations are common. As with other protective strategies, deciding not to use any particular strategy can represent a considered assessment of whether or not it would be protective.

Use of Traditional Health, Mental Health and Social Services

Police and shelters may be most associated in the public eye with the professional response to domestic violence but the health and mental health communities are also approached by many survivors. Large numbers of women seek help from psychologists, social workers, physicians, drug and alcohol abuse treatment providers, community health centers, and other health and social service providers. These providers offer another forum for talking about multiple risks and working out solutions and can also help address the emotional after-effects of trauma. Because many of these providers do not focus primarily on domestic violence, they may be considered less stigmatizing to approach by some and may be more amenable to addressing a wider range of risks. Significant impediments to using these services exist, including financial costs, concerns about confidentiality, and access to providers with training in partner violence (Logan et al., 2004). Still, they are used fairly frequently. Several studies have found the percentage of battered women who sought counseling to range from 9% to 44% (Barrett & St. Pierre, 2011; Belknap et al., 2009; Brabeck & Guzmán, 2008; Cattaneo et al., 2007; El-Khoury et al., 2004; Krishnan et al., 2001; Magen et al., 2001; Saunders, 1994). In Belknap and colleagues' study (2009), counselors were rated as most supportive among all types of services assessed, with 94% of counselors described as supportive and 80% as "very supportive." Johnson and Zlotnick (2007) found that 40% of women staying in shelters had received mental health treatment just in the last 6 months. Although they found that number low with respect to the number experiencing significant symptoms of psychological distress, it is a substantial portion of that population. As noted at the beginning of the chapter, these rates of help-seeking are comparable to the rates of help-seeking for psychological disorders in the general population. Although the findings may suggest a need for more services for battered women, these data indicate that survivors' seeking of mental health services is equal to or greater than the general population of people experiencing clinically significant psychological distress.

Other types of health and mental health services are also commonly assessed. Saunders (1994) found that more than one in five (21%) had participated in a 12-step program, and Cattaneo and colleagues (2007) found that more than one in four (26%) had sought substance abuse counseling. Seeking help from a physician or nurse has been reported by 20% to 45% of women in several nonrepresentative studies (Belknap et al., 2009; Brabeck & Guzmán, 2008; Cattaneo et al., 2007; Goodman et al., 2003; Krishnan et al., 2001; Magen et al., 2001). Seeking help from medical personnel was reported by 24% to 32% of victimized women in representative studies in Canada and Switzerland (Barrett & St. Pierre, 2011; Killias et al., 2005). These relatively high rates may result from the wider range of incomes found in nationally representative samples. Further, health-care utilization might be lower in U.S. shelter samples because, unlike shelter services, healthcare is not freely available to all in the United States. Another study found that approximately one in four women (24%) had participated in a support group (Johnson & Zlotnick, 2007). Perhaps because of overcrowding at domestic violence shelters, that same study found that one in five had at some time also lived in a homeless (non-domestic violence) shelter (Johnson & Zlotnick, 2007). Sometimes women try to obtain services for their partner too. In addition to seeking couples therapy, as discussed in Chapter 7, two studies found that substantial numbers of women had encouraged their partner to seek counseling—approximately half of women (47%) in Goodman and colleagues' project (2003) and two of three (67%) in Brabeck and Guzmán's study (2008).

Factors associated with use of health and mental services. There may be ethnic or cultural differences in the use of these services. Two studies found European American women were more likely to seek mental health counseling than African-American women (El-Khoury, et al., 2004; Johnson & Zlotnick, 2007). European American women were also more likely to be taking psychotropic medication than African-American women in Johnson and Zlotnick's study. The Canadian national survey found that women who described themselves as members of a visible minority were less likely to seek medical or mental health services (Barrett & St. Pierre, 2011). Although some of these differences may result from differing cultural attitudes about psychotherapy, access is also likely an issue (Logan et al., 2004). In Canada, rural women were less likely to seek mental health services but more likely to see a doctor or nurse about their victimization, possibly because of better access to general healthcare than mental healthcare in some rural areas (Barrett & St. Pierre, 2011). Women with health insurance, not surprisingly, are more likely to seek mental health services than women without health insurance (Johnson & Zlotnick, 2007). As noted above, costs associated with healthcare might also affect utilization and could explain relatively low utilization in U.S. samples.

It is also important to recognize situational factors. Being in fear for one's life was associated with increasing contact with mental health and medical personnel in the Canadian survey (Barrett & St. Pierre, 2011). One study found that women who had experienced other types of trauma (such as rape, robbery, and accident) in addition to domestic violence were more likely to seek help of all kinds, including being more likely to seek mental health services (Johnson & Zlotnick, 2007).

The Effects of Interagency Cooperation and Coordination

More sophisticated statistical techniques are slowly promoting an increase in the study of the impacts of human service policies on women and their communities. Coordinated community responses to domestic violence are one important innovation in domestic violence services (Shepard & Pence, 1999). Some of the benefits include improving referral pathways and sharing information about best practices across agencies. In some communities, relationships among different human services agencies can be tense, and coordinated community responses provide mechanisms to create stronger collaborative relationships and improve the consistency of messages given to victimized women in different agencies in the same community. Research is starting to show how efforts to better respond to victimized women are being felt across social institutions and across communities. For example, Javdani, Allen, Todd, and Anderson (2011) have examined the impact of coordinating community councils on judicial referrals to domestic violence shelters and issuance of protective orders. They examined how the rates of referrals and protective orders varied across 21 judicial circuits (districts) in the United States over the course of 15 years with and without coordinating councils. This is a complicated statistical analysis because referrals and protective orders are clustered within judicial circuits and likely are correlated with other characteristics of those circuits. These researchers found a general increasing trend in the number of protection orders given over the 15-year period, but more specifically this trend occurred only in geographic regions that had established coordinating councils. Even more strikingly, the amount of time that the council had been in existence was associated with the rate of protective orders issued in the judicial circuits. This study is a good example of ways in which social change could be better documented. A similar study on sexual assault response teams also found arrests were more likely when these teams were in place (Nugent-Borakove et al., 2006). More research on the effects of agency coordination could help broaden support for social services as well as help guide future policy reform. Although the focus of this book is on the strategies of women who have been victimized, it is important to recognize how larger institutional factors affect victimized women's choices. It may not make sense to seek a protection order if you live in a court district where it is widely known that they are difficult to obtain. Women might incur the losses of time to pursue a court case, stigma of publicly seeking help, and risks of getting arrested themselves and at the end of all that have no benefit to show for it. Under those circumstances, it would be rational not to seek help. As a field, we need to do more to make sure that a rational decision is to seek professional help.

CONCLUSION

Use of professional services is an important part of many women's array of protective strategies. Although not used by all women, they are used by substantial numbers of women. Women who have been victimized engage in formal help-seeking at rates that are similar to or higher than the help-seeking for various psychological and mental health problems. This is further evidence that battered women do not have unusually passive coping strategies but, rather, that they approach life problems in much the same way as people with other types of problems. This broader context is essential for appreciating women's strengths. As can be seen from the services reviewed, many professional services focus fairly narrowly on the risk of physical danger. Although an important part of any comprehensive risk management plan, expanding professional services with a more explicit goal of helping survivors to address other risks too might increase their usefulness and their effectiveness This could eventually lead to even greater numbers of women making use of these important services.

11

Invisible Strategies

One woman I met took $20 bills, sometimes less, and sewed them into the hems of old clothes hanging in the back of her closet. Even if her batterer thought to check the pockets of those unworn clothes, which seems unlikely, what are the chances he would feel every single hem for some folded paper? Even if he felt a bill, he would not necessarily think it was money but perhaps some sort of basting or other mysterious substance found in the hem of women's clothes. Pure genius. I wish I had thought of this or many of the other great ideas women have shared with me but they are yet more things that I have learned from women who have been victimized. This is one example of an invisible strategy. What are "invisible strategies?" These are the many protective actions that women employ that seldom get researched, studied, or written about by scholars or advocates.

A few moments consideration will show that there are many "invisible" strategies to address domestic violence. As already pointed out in previous chapters, many global categories of protective strategies, such as "social support" and "going to a shelter" are often spoken of and studied as unitary concepts or single actions but are really complex, multifaceted phenomena that can involve many different protective steps. The way each woman approaches people and resources varies tremendously and is usually based on the consideration of numerous contextual factors. Like the strategies discussed in previous chapters, these protective strategies also reflect the complex and multifaceted approach most women take to coping with violence. These strategies, however, do not readily fit into the main areas that have so far been the focus of most research. Some of them could easily become entire subject areas in their own right. For example, all of the ways in which women take proactive steps to work on the financial aspects of coping with violence could be its own research domain. Dealing with finances requires an approach that is just as multifaceted as dealing with any other aspect of the challenges presented by a violent partner, ranging from saving money to organizing one's affairs. Other strategies represent emerging areas, such as the many steps needed to protect one's identity and digital presence in today's modern world.

Why are these strategies invisible? There are several reasons. One reason, not widely known by the general public, is that research, practice, and policy can all be remarkably conservative enterprises that do not support change or innovation. This is especially unfortunate for science, which now experiences many institutional pressures to be cautious (Hamby, 2012). The framing of the problem of domestic violence is still very much influenced by the way wife-beating emerged as a public issue back in the 1970s. Not only has this contributed to an endless rehashing of questions like "Why do they stay?" and discussions of the little-supported "cycle of violence" (Walker, 1979), but the conservatism of the field has also meant that there are dozens of very similar studies on trauma symptoms, child abuse histories among victims, and a fairly limited set of other variables. Shelters for battered women have changed in some ways, but the basic structure of emphasizing short-term emergency housing has not. Safety planning has barely changed in 20 years. Meanwhile, alternatives have been little explored.

The evidence base for domestic violence is limited in other ways. One, already mentioned, is that research tends to be very analytical and reductionist, so a great deal of research examines one strategy at a time or treats strategies as lists of unconnected actions. As a consequence, we have relatively little information about common combinations of strategies or the typical numbers of strategies that women try. Another major limitation is that research has most often focused on the most severely battered women who have gone to battered women's shelters or are involved with the criminal justice system. In many cases, shelter clients are the women with the fewest resources who are in the worst circumstances, and they do not represent the entire population of victimized women who might benefit from help. Many, many women leave abusive, maltreating partners without ever visiting a shelter, speaking with an anti-domestic violence advocate, or disclosing the violence to a civil or criminal court, and we know very little about them or their protective strategies. Another limitation of most existing research is that it is cross-sectional, or, in other words, women are only interviewed at a single point in time. This creates two major limitations. One, as a result we know almost nothing about the onset of violence. All too often, only women who are seeking help for multiple incidents of serious violence are included in our research. Two, it is very hard to see how women's strategies change over time.

These issues are not unique to scholarship on battered women. Many institutional forces contribute to the narrow and repetitive scope of much research (Hamby & Grych, 2013). It is easier to get published and especially to get grant funding if a research project is only incrementally different than what has come before and if the questionnaires included in the project are ones that are familiar to reviewers. Many service grants place many requirements and restrictions on the activities of advocacy programs, law enforcement, and other recipients. These requirements and restrictions can quickly become institutionalized and create obstacles to innovation. In addition, people often try to protect their turf and this can also create inertia.

Even if people are interested in breaking the mold, it is not easy to do so. Information overload is a widespread phenomenon—hardly limited to domestic violence or other problems—but still one that is largely unsolved (Hamby & Grych, 2013). It is impossible for a single person to keep up with all of the newly published articles or new program initiatives, even if a person stopped doing everything else. There are few filtering mechanisms to identify the best, most important, or most groundbreaking articles or program initiatives. Knowledge integration and knowledge synthesis are lacking (Hamby, 2012).

Sometimes these strategies serve people's other agendas, whether or not they realize it. This includes the under-recognized motivations of many professionals in the field, who are not immune to the pressures to create social distance between themselves and those who are perceived to be lower functioning than they are (Hamby & Gray-Little, 2007). Feeling good about oneself by looking down on others is an age-old tradition. As described in Chapter 1, condescending comments are common in discourse about battered women. Published scholarship describes them with phrases such as "compliant zombies" (T. Mills, 1985). Within the last year, I have heard battered women described publicly in professional conferences as "compromised" and described as "confused about what love means." Ignoring information that does not fit with your preconceptions is an age-old tradition too, and many people are not interested in seeing battered women as someone like themselves who are in a bad situation.

Sometimes people might think they are helping battered women by focusing on the most pathetic aspects of their existence. They may see that as the best way to ensure sympathy or charity. At one of the very first conferences on domestic violence I attended, in 1995, Angela Browne gave a talk suggesting that battered women had inner strength despite issues of dependency or substance abuse. In my notes, some examples of strengths she gave were loyalty, compassion, and the ability to affiliate. The audience response, including responses from some extremely well-known feminist researchers, was that they "didn't like the term *strengths*" because they felt this would lead to a decrease in services. Around that time, there was considerable defensiveness about whether the National Violence Against Women Survey indicated a drop in rates (Tjaden & Thoennes, 2000a). The drop in domestic violence rates remains a controversial issue. There indeed may be individual judges, physicians, bosses, ministers, or family members who will only deign to help if they think a woman is helpless. Proposed diagnoses such as "battered woman's syndrome" (Walker, 1984) may be aimed at engendering sympathy. However, these oversimplifications, even if they can be expedient, in the long run are harmful to women who have been battered and do them a disservice. As a result of these and other forces, there are many, many invisible strategies that have been long neglected or ignored by the research and advocacy communities. It would be hard to describe them all. But here are some that have been important in the lives of women I have known.

MONEY

"I know we shouldn't keep secrets but it is good to have a little money of your own."

Recommendations for many protective strategies are routinely talked about as if these choices can be made independently of one's personal resources. However, real women know that every choice is bound up with money. The path to creating viable alternatives requires money. As discussed in Chapter 4, in most parts of the United States establishing a new permanent living situation requires several thousand dollars. I had another client who once stood up to me and my traditional recommendations. She was a health-care provider, and she was strong and tough. She wanted to leave but she wanted to save some money first. I tried to talk her out of it by suggesting she could leave first and save money later. She had a job and a car, and I suggested she could stay in a domestic violence shelter (although the only two shelters within realistic driving distance of her job would have added considerably to her commute and had maximum 30-day stay limits). She disagreed with that plan. She had worked out her budget and she knew she needed about 6 months to save up and get on steady footing in a new place. And that is what she did.

Survivors do all kinds of things to start building a financial base (Campbell et al., 1998). At the time of writing this book, almost all U.S. savings accounts are paying negligible interest rates that are usually less than 1% (Carrns, 2012). Thus, in contrast to years past, hiding money is not a bad alternative to a bank account. For survivors of violence, for whom privacy is often of the utmost importance when they are strategizing about how to better protect themselves, hiding money also solves the problem of having to deal with paper statements, tax forms, e-mails, or other evidence of a separate bank account. There are other creative methods for dealing with the challenges of a paper (or digital) trail. If survivors have a trusted family member or friend, they can use that address (physical or e-mail) to receive bank information. Sometimes women create alternate Gmail, Hotmail, or other free e-mail accounts and only check them from safe locations, such as a friend's house or a public library.

Women also find creative ways to get some money together so they can afford their coping strategies. One favorite way of getting some cash together in otherwise-hard-to-get sums is to coordinate protective actions with tax return season. Many families receive fairly substantial sums of cash with their tax return and that can create protective opportunities not only for leaving but also for going back to school, pursuing professional counseling, or other opportunities that might lead to a better future. Other financial windfalls can come from events such as the sale of a home or the settlement of a lawsuit. It can be helpful to consider the timing of these events and not rush into actions that would be substantially easier if one were to only wait a few weeks or months. I have also known women to wait until something such as the refinancing of a home comes through, although that was more common before the housing market crashed circa 2008. In the past few years, refinancing a home has become more difficult, and this may be a less viable strategy in many housing markets now. I encourage women not to be shy about borrowing money from family or friends or asking for other tangible help. Few people enjoy asking to borrow money, but sometimes a little encouragement can be helpful. Other resourceful ways that women get money include pawning or selling items. Applying for "welfare" or other public support can also be a means of obtaining funds to protect oneself from violence (D. Davis, 2006). Financial management can also involve disentangling one's finances from one's partner by avoiding joint purchases or even foregoing child support (Campbell et al., 1998).

All of these examples show that women understand that most options require money. They also show that many victimized women understand, better than some professionals, that it takes time to implement many protective strategies and that the problem of victimization and its derivative losses are not going to be solved over the course of a short interview in an emergency room in the middle of the night. Perhaps that is another reason that financial strategies have been so invisible in the domestic violence literature; they do not fit with the conventional narrative that this is something to be dealt with on a short-term emergency basis. There are not very many choices that can be implemented without money, however. Sometimes it is challenging to siphon off any extra money at all. Even saving relatively small sums such as $20 to $50 in cash can make further protective strategies easier. Even in a shelter, it is difficult to get by with absolutely no money at all. This is especially true for women who are there with children who are used to getting occasional treats or being able to buy something in a store. If the focus of services for battered women moved away from short-term crisis intervention to greater consideration of longer term strategizing, then suggestions such as saving even small sums would likely become more commonplace. We do women a disservice by failing to prioritize this as an essential step toward planning for a safe and happy future.

Research on saving money. There have been a few efforts to examine protective strategies related to money. One study found that many women (32%) reported saving money (Brabeck & Guzmán, 2008). Two U.S. studies have found that approximately two of three women reported hiding money or valuables (Goodman et al., 2003; McFarlane et al., 2002). A Chinese study found that only 17% of victimized women had hidden money at intake, although that increased to 78% when it was suggested as a safety strategy (Tiwari et al., 2012). Unfortunately, none of these studies have explored what "saving" or "hiding" meant or investigated how much money was involved. Some research has shown that women who have experienced violence benefit from financial education courses that are made available to them, with resulting increases in financial knowledge and financial self-efficacy (Sanders, Weaver, & Schnabel, 2007). Financial education courses are becoming more common but are still offered by only one in four domestic violence programs (National Network to End Domestic Violence, 2012). Offering financial education courses more widely could be one way of improving choices for battered women, especially low-income women.

One innovative effort (Sanders, 2010) offered a combined program that included matching funds for saving money and financial education. Matched withdrawals from this program could be used for specific purposes, including purchasing or repairing a home, acquiring career-enhancing education, purchasing an automobile, supporting a small business, and retirement (they could also take out their own deposits for any purpose). The median savings in the first trial of this program was $1,500 per woman over a median 16-month period of time, an impressive sum. The most common purpose of a matched withdrawal was to purchase a car, with 33% of withdrawals going toward that goal (Sanders, 2010). More than one in four (28%) participants used the money for educational expenses. Covering small business and home repair expenses were also fairly common (17% and 16%, respectively). This promising program offers an approach to concretely improving women's situations and letting them take control of their own protection.

ORGANIZING OTHER AFFAIRS

There are other steps that women often take to get ready to make changes in their life situation that are related to finances but worth discussing as separate strategies. These include working on transportation needs. For example, a vehicle may need repairs, a current vehicle inspection sticker, license plates, or insurance. They may need one or more additional car seats. They may need to purchase a vehicle, as so many women did in the above study on the matching funds savings program (Sanders, 2010). There are few places in the United States and many places in the world where it is practical to function without a car. Women also often apply the steps recommended in many safety plans. These include collecting their social security cards, birth certificates, and other documents for themselves and their children and storing them in a convenient and safe place. They make copies of prescriptions and other important medical information. These copies can be safely left with family or friends, put in a safe deposit box, or even kept at their office. Collecting documents is another recommendation that, despite its presence in almost every major safety plan, is seldom studied empirically, but Lisa Goodman and her colleagues found that almost half (44%) of a sample of women had hidden important papers and that the majority of those who did (78%) found it to be a helpful strategy (Goodman et al., 2003). Another U.S. study found that most women kept a variety of important documents and information available

(McFarlane et al., 2002). In the Chinese study asking about similar documents and information, the rates were much lower at baseline (20% or lower for everything but access to important telephone numbers) but increased substantially for both the intervention and "control" groups, suggesting that just mentioning these ideas was enough to generate an increase in protective strategies for women (Tiwari et al., 2012). There are also steps such as preparing a will or speaking to someone about taking custody or guardianship of one's children, should it ever become necessary, as the woman described in Chapter 9 did.

Other things that fall into the general category of organizing one's affairs include steps such as packing up valuables and moving them to a safe location. Sometimes this is to protect financial interests by ensuring that items with cash value, such as jewelry and silver, are in a safe location. This can also include protecting irreplaceable sentimental items such as photos, heirlooms, and souvenirs. Batterers sometimes intentionally destroy things of personal sentimental value to the victim. A valuable service that shelters could offer is setting up a relationship with a bank to offer safe deposit boxes to women needing places to store things for protection. This might also be a way for shelters to extend their services so that they are more relevant to victimized women who are less economically disadvantaged and may not need free housing but could benefit from other assistance as they cope with victimization.

At a more mundane level, organizing one's affairs can also refer to steps such as organizing and clearing out one's things in anticipation of a move. People almost always underestimate how much stuff they have and how long it will take to pack it up. A woman who is considering leaving can anticipate that it might be hard to pack once the batterer knows she is leaving. The police are not going to be able to spend days supervising a household move, but in some jurisdictions police will accompany a woman to her home to safely claim some of her possessions. Those possessions should ideally be easy to grab and ready to go. Note this is another invisible strategy—steps women take to claim some of their belongings after relationship termination.

EDUCATION AND JOB TRAINING

> *"I have everything to look forward to—college, everything else is positive. Got my college course, [daughter] is doing really well, she is going to be in full-time nursery. This I have done myself. I have come a long way."* (Bostock, Plumpton, & Pratt, 2009, p.106)

Furthering one's education or getting more specific job training are also essential steps for increasing one's coping options for many women. Contrary to popular stereotypes, some battered women are professionals with well-established careers. Many others, especially younger victimized women, make long-term plans to create more personal resources and economic independence. Going back to school or work has been mentioned as a key step by some women (Bostock et al., 2009). In the VIGOR 2 study I added an opportunity for women to identify personal goals. Finding a job or getting a better job was identified by three of four women and was the most common goal in the study. The second most common goal was getting more education, reported by more than half (63%) of the women who participated in VIGOR 2.

CYBERPROTECTION

Cyberstalking and cyberbullying are becoming increasingly recognized issues. The public is routinely told to be cautious about online and electronic privacy and security and to be vigilant against the risk of identity theft. Yet we know almost nothing about the steps taken by survivors to protect their online security and privacy. It might be difficult for some reading this book to even imagine a battered woman with computer skills or owning a computer, because our stereotypes for these women are so powerful and pervasive and do not include attributes such as computer skills. As described in Chapter 3, many forms of technology now available can assist batterers with stalking and identity theft. In response, many battered women now engage in protective strategies that focus on technological safety and privacy.

People are getting wiser to technology-based dangers, and survivors of violence are no exception to this. For example, Facebook has added more privacy options in response to various outcries about privacy and the need to be able to negotiate different kinds of relationships. Facebook also makes it easy to start an entirely new profile, which can be made unsearchable. Once unsearchable, only people invited by the profile owner can find these profiles. Similarly, Twitter and Flickr and other accounts can be changed. Passwords can be changed. People can post more cautiously or stop posting at all. You can "defriend" your partner/ex-partner, although if you have mutual friends he may still be able to see some information about you. In Facebook, it is also now possible to "detag" your name from other people's posted photos of you. Although you cannot easily remove a picture posted by someone else (unless you file a complaint), detagging photos makes it harder for someone else to find you in those pictures (Hamby, Clark et al., 2011). This can be especially useful if you still have mutual friends with a partner or ex-partner, because he may still have full access to their postings. These are not uncommon options considered by battered women, despite the lack of attention to them.

OTHER TYPES OF IDENTITY THEFT PROTECTION

Other disruptive things that batterers can do electronically are legion. They can tell utility companies that you are "moving" and get your lights or water turned off (one in five victimized women had experienced that in one study; Anderson et al., 2003). They can run up debt on joint credit cards or overdraft joint bank accounts. They can change passwords and close accounts, especially joint accounts, without permission. They can access and delete messages on voicemail systems. As a consequence, victimized women have developed many protection strategies. They change passwords before batterers can. They create new e-mail accounts that the batterer does not know and link their utility, credit card, and other business accounts to the new e-mail. They get new phones. They use pay-as-you-go phones. They subscribe to identity protection services that will alert you any time someone makes a credit inquiry or applies for a credit account in your name. In the VIGOR 1 study, almost one in five women (19%) volunteered they had taken steps to increase their technological privacy or avoid identity theft, including changing passwords, switching phone numbers, and making Facebook profiles more private. Many women (41%) who had engaged in cyberprotection reported taking more than one step.

ACTIVISM

Many survivors become active in the anti-violence movement and this can also be part of the path to protection (Bostock et al., 2009). Sometimes survivors are motivated to participate in research studies to help future victimized women. One study provided an explicit opportunity to survivors to develop suggestions for improving services (Brabeck & Guzmán, 2008). Suggestions for making domestic violence shelters more useful included no exit dates, longer stays, greater confidentiality, privacy, more space, more hotlines, and more alternative housing when the shelter was full (like hotels) (Brabeck & Guzmán, 2008). Women also had suggestions for law enforcement, including offering more information about shelters, providing safe refuge, arresting the abuser and not the victim, punishing offenders more severely, and more strictly enforcing protective orders. In the VIGOR studies, women volunteered many ideas, including developing a Spanish version of the VIGOR and adapting it so that it could be used with sexual assault survivors. Both of these are now in the planning stages. It might be worth noting that although it had also occurred to me to develop a Spanish version of the VIGOR, I had not thought of doing one for rape survivors until a survivor suggested it to me. As these few examples suggest, survivors are knowledgeable and sophisticated critics of the system.

WELLNESS ACTIVITIES

Because coping with battering is like coping with a lot of other negative life events, many activities that help people feel better in general help for battering too. A few that have been mentioned in the literature include reading, walking, and gardening (Bostock et al., 2009). As these examples suggest, common strategies for coping with stress can also help with the particular stressor of violence in a relationship. There is no reason why the field should focus only on protective coping strategies that are unique to violence.

RETURNING TO BATTERER OR WITHDRAWING ORDER OF PROTECTION

Yes, returning to batterers and withdrawing orders of protection are supposed to be bad things. However, everything must be considered in context. No action is protective in and of itself, and sometimes returning to the batterer or withdrawing criminal justice actions may be the safest choices (Davies, 2009; Davies et al., 1998). If the separation violence is worse than staying violence, then it might be protective to return, especially at any given moment.

RECOGNIZING PERSONAL STRENGTHS

The dominant narrative about passive, confused, and helpless women is so powerful that people seldom even consider the possibility of strengths. When I created the VIGOR, part of the reason that I included categories of personal and psychological strengths was to increase the chance that all women would have something to list. Many people who do not have much still have their health or their youth and those are strengths that can also help someone build towards a better future. Even I was surprised about how affirmatively some women described their personal characteristics.

I am strong, I have great faith and I'm a good mom.
I am relatively a calm person and feel that has helped me ultimately get through this.
You have to believe in yourself or nobody will.
I have the faith and courage, wisdom and knowledge to carry on.

THE FLUIDITY OF COPING

We need to know how violence emerges in relationships and how coping strategies change over time. The limited existing evidence suggests that abuse typically arises not as an overnight shift but as a slow escalation of what may have started out as more minor problems. The line between "unhappy," "high conflict," and "abusive" is probably not as clear-cut as many people imagine. We know very little about the early decision-making and coping processes of women when they are first exposed to violence.

There is that day, that first time, when a romantic partner indulges his aggressive impulses. The field pushes people toward thinking of battering as a "master status"—as the organizing feature about that person's identity and certainly their relationship. However, the path that women walk is more complex. As anyone who has been in a long-term marriage or committed relationship can attest, people's lives tend to be organized around these partnerships. Perhaps a couple has children together, or a home, or pets. Disagreements arise occasionally—how could it be otherwise when two adults have so many decisions to make together? Perhaps sometimes they argue heatedly. (I have personally always doubted the 25% or so of American couples who claim, in national surveys, that they have never shouted at their partner in a single argument over the entire course of their relationship. Two or 3%, maybe. 25%? Seems unlikely.) Many couples face difficult periods when they experience more stressful life events than usual. Whatever the reason, in some of these relationships, one time an argument gets even more heated than usual, and one partner grabs or pushes the other. The existing evidence suggests the first aggressive act likely was not an actual "hit." In addition to grabs and pushes, throwing things is also common.

What would most people do in this situation? Pack their bags and walk out the door? Although that is the response of some, it seems an unlikely decision for many people. If they disclose the violence, probably many family and friends would commiserate but at the same time also avow that "things would work out" and perhaps even make excuses for the violent man. It should not be surprising when women do what they usually do when they encounter a relationship problem: They work on it. Take it out of the framework of some extraordinary, unique problem that is unlike anything else and consider it as one of any number of relationship problems a couple might have. It seems likely that the first time is experienced as an aberration that would lead relatively few people to redefine their entire relationship and their entire life. The question then becomes, how does that change? How many acts of violence does it take then? Two? Three? To put this in research terms, we know almost nothing about the onset of intimate partner violence or the personal experience of transitioning from being in a nonviolent relationship to a violent one. We do not understand how the process of coping with violence as an aberration changes to coping with violence as an ongoing problem.

The very small amount of longitudinal research that has been conducted on protective strategies has only looked at women who have, by the time they are enrolled in the research study, experienced multiple violent incidents. This research suggests that women's strategies do change over time, as they try first one and then another resource (not necessarily receiving much useful help at any). One important study of help-seeking women found that calling the police was initially the most common help-seeking strategy, but their strategies varied over the course of a year. Three months after the initial interview, women said the most common thing they had done since the first interview was talk to a hotline or shelter (Cattaneo et al., 2007). Although calling the police and talking to a shelter/hotline remained among the most-used sources of help throughout the follow-up period, talking to clergy was the most commonly reported strategy at 6, 9, and 12 months after their initial recruitment into the study (Cattaneo et al., 2007). Further, in general, the use of most strategies declined over time. Unfortunately, the reasons for this were not explored. It could be that they were already receiving those services, had already made use of them, had dealt with the violence to their satisfaction, or did not find the services helpful. Still, all kinds of help-seeking persisted. This study is just one example of ways that we could learn more about the fluidity of women's protective strategies over time.

OTHER INVISIBLE STRATEGIES

There are an almost endless number of protective strategies that could be adopted. Some, despite their lack of attention in the literature, are quite common. For example, one common short-term response is discussing the violence with one's partner. This was reported as one of the most immediate responses to an incident by 29% of women in one study (Hamby & Gray-Little, 1997). Shockingly, in one study, one in three women had disguised themselves to get away from the abuser (Brabeck & Guzmán, 2008). Some of the other protective strategies reported in the Brabeck & Guzmán include: staying optimistic, focusing on good times, forgiving, maintaining hope, using humor to cope.

The VIGOR studies provide a unique opportunity to generate protective strategies. My students, Sarah Clark and Lauren Croasdaile, and my research assistant, Melissa Hurd, have worked with me to develop a list of all of the strategies that were suggested by those women. Many strategies were mentioned many times. Almost half, for example, mentioned seeking counseling or getting a new job. In terms of fully fleshing out the entire universe of strategies, however, one of the most useful results of these studies is just seeing the entire list. Those women generated more than 140 unique strategies in our reading of their responses. These are listed in Table 11.1. Although some of them are similar to ones identified earlier from the review of the literature, I think it is worth seeing the entire list (Hamby, 2013b).

Table 11.1 147 PROTECTIVE STRATEGIES IDENTIFIED BY PARTICIPANTS IN THE VIGOR STUDIES

Housing
Go to shelter
Stay in their own home/fortunate because lease is in their name (can ask partner to leave)
Get a roommate
Stay with family
Stay with friends
Put children in safe housing
Apply for subsidized or public housing (such as Section 8)
Move to another house or apartment, buy or rent new housing
Stay in a hotel
Seek assistance with getting a down payment for a new home
Stay and fight
Financial and employment related
Keep current job
Seek new full-time or part-time work
Get a second job
Get job training
Establish a retirement account
Pay down debt
Save money
Develop a budget
Sell or pawn extra items
Borrow money
Declare bankruptcy
Open new account and/or get separate bank accounts
Apply for "welfare" (TANF, food stamps, or other public assistance)
Save to buy a car
Use only cash
Change insurance
Apply for Medicaid
Continue education (apply for college funding such as Pell Grant)
Take GED exam (earn certificate of high school equivalency)
Stash money with family or otherwise hide money from partner
Have family help with finances
Get financial help from friends at work
Pay his bills so easier to divide property
Apply for disability (SSDI)
Keep bank statements and other financial records
Put all financial assets in own name (remove spouse's name)
Apply for church assistance

(continued)

Table 11.1 (Continued)

Learn from past financial mistakes
Vocational rehabilitation
Cook own meals (eat out less)
Legal and law enforcement
Call the police
Notify police/sheriff if Protection/Restraining order not being followed
Ask police to drive by home frequently
Don't be afraid to reach out to police/sheriff for help
Apply for Orders of Protection/Restraining order
Obtain a divorce or separation
Petition for custody of children
Petition for child support
Pursue alimony
Seek help from Legal Aid
Get a private attorney or lawyer
Get a gun permit
Report partner's abuse to child protective services
Document all abuse (save texts, phone messages, pictures)
Make sure keep all identifying documents in possession (for example, birth certificates, social security cards, passports, and driver's licenses)
Social and Personal
Rely on support of friends
Make new acquaintances, expand social circle
Rely on family as social support
Attend church more frequently
Visit with pastor, minister, reverend, or other religious figure
Rely on God as a counselor
Pray
Seek a new relationship
Seek a trusting relationship
Exercise
Spend time outside with children
Keep a journal
Stay clean (no drugs or alcohol)
Share testimony/share story (tell other people their story to help others)
Get social support and advice from advocates at shelter
Take a vacation
Believe in yourself
Look to your children for strength
A new look, a new outlook
Don't look back
Stop thinking he will change

Table 11.1 (CONTINUED)

Stay committed to school
Find a hobby
Focus on self and children
Volunteer in community
Volunteer at children's school
Help others
Community resources
Seek domestic violence advocate or social worker
Rely on church community
Research domestic violence resources available in area
Look for all types of help can obtain from the community
Use food bank
Use Goodwill or Habitat for Humanity or other thrift stores
Find daycare for children
Join Al-Anon (group for family and friends of alcoholics)
Use community resources to obtain food, clothing and help with prescriptions
Go to parks or other free community recreation with children
Live near a police station
Participate in single mom programs
Participate in meal program
Look for job training
Develop safety plan with social services
Take a self-defense class or firearm safety class
Campus ministry
Seek counseling/therapy
Seek psychotropic medication
Seek information about domestic violence
Seek community mental health services
Seek therapy with partner
Attend support groups
Cyber protection/guarding against identity theft
Get a private phone number
Have two phones (don't give second number to partner)
Increase Facebook privacy
Avoid Facebook/ do not use social media
Change MySpace account
Change password for phone
Change password for email
Keep personal information private (in general)
Get a PO Box instead of having mail sent to home
Put a lock on mail box

(continued)

Table 11.1 (CONTINUED)

Change accounts
Change passwords on various accounts
Increase internet security (general)
Don't use a computer
Only use computer at work to access personal information
Other Safety Steps
Leave town (relocate)
Hide—stay away from abuser and hide
Get a gun
Keep knife under mattress
Get mace
Get a dog
Change locks and/or add new or stronger locks to home (dead bolts)
Avoid unnecessary alone contact with spouse or use a mediator for necessary contact
Change routines to avoid abuser
Never go out alone—always bring a friend or family member
Home security/alarm system
Carry cell phone at all times
Be more cautious, be more aware of surroundings
Create a safety plan and share with kids
Change last name
Get a prepaid phone
Alert neighborhood/community watch
Install outdoor lights all around the house
Use a rotary phone (always on, no caller id)
Use a daycare with security cameras installed
Provide daycares and childcare workers with a list of safe people who can pick up your kids
Use code words
Continue promoting strong, healthy relationships with family, friends, and boyfriend
Become acquainted with law enforcement officers
Request record checks for potential romantic interests
Change vehicle (so partner won't recognize)

Note: These are options generated by women in the VIGOR studies. As with other protective strategies in this book, this list is not intended as an endorsement of any particular strategy for any particular person. As a psychologist, I would not personally recommend getting a gun or keeping a knife under the mattress, for example. Those options and others, though, do show how much battered women are doing to protect themselves and how much consideration they are giving to the possibilities for protection. It is an impressive list longer than any other existing safety plan.

ALL WOMEN ARE NOT THE SAME: INVISIBILITY OF SUBTYPES

Different Approaches to Protection

So far we have been talking about these issues mainly from the perspective of group averages or trends or else from the individual level in stories about specific women. But there is another way of looking at protective strategies that has also largely been invisible in existing literature. A person-centered perspective is an approach that looks for whether there are meaningful subtypes among the general population of battered women. Although there are many possibilities for such subtypes, for the purposes of emphasizing protective strategies, it is useful to think about differences in the ways that different women might approach the task of protecting themselves and their loved ones.

Risk-Based Coping Strategies

With Bernadette Gray-Little, I have proposed a risk-based model of coping strategies that better accounts for the wide range of coping responses in women's responses to partner violence (Hamby & Gray-Little, 2007). Unlike many coping models that divide coping into dichotomous categories, such as problem-focused versus emotion-focused (Folkman & Lazarus, 1991), we propose that coping strategies can best be understood as a continuum. Our model (*see* Fig. 11.1) is inspired by typologies of common strategies for financial investment (Bajtelsmit & Bernasek, 1996; Embrey & Fox, 1997). It represents a continuum of approaches that victimized women might adopt and is based on a model from the world of finance. One key advantage offered by this model is that the full range of coping choices is destigmatized—no one strategy is automatically deemed superior for every person. Consciously choosing models from outside the realm of victimization or mental health is another way to depathologize victimized women and their coping responses. This model provides a concrete analogy for how we might re-frame our perceptions of victim's coping choices.

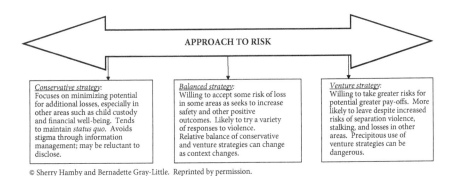

© Sherry Hamby and Bernadette Gray-Little. Reprinted by permission.

Figure 11.1.   A Continuum of Risk-Based Coping Strategies for Partner Violence Victimization.

The Conservative Strategy

In finance, a conservative strategy emphasizes low-risk investments and embodies a preference for assets with guaranteed returns, such as savings accounts or certificates of deposit. The conservative strategy minimizes or even virtually eliminates the risk of losing money. In exchange for low risk, however, investors accept a relatively low rate of return on their investments. The conservative strategy is a better descriptor for strategies that might otherwise be labeled as passive. People who take a conservative coping approach tend to focus on minimizing risk of further losses in the many areas described in Chapters 3 through 5, such as the loss of financial well-being, homelessness, or loss of custody of their children. Conservative "copers" also may be trying to reduce the risk of separation violence, stalking, or harm to animals. Thus, conservative copers may be more likely to choose ways of addressing violence, such as discussing it with their partners or seeking counseling, which do not involve leaving the relationship or making other large changes in their situation. They may also try to minimize the risk of stigma by using information management. The chief information management strategy used by those trying to avoid stigma is nondisclosure (C. Miller & Kaiser, 2001). This is a conscious coping choice, not a cognitive distortion (Hamby & Gray-Little, 2007).

In the financial world, personal characteristics such as low net worth are associated with a greater tendency to use a conservative strategy (Embrey & Fox, 1997). Such findings provide another parallel to the situation of battered women, who may be seen as passive copers but only when others fail to include contextual elements, such as lack of financial resources. Leaving takes considerable economic and social resources. Thousands of dollars are required, for example, to secure and furnish a new home and file for divorce, as detailed in Chapter 4. Other protective strategies, such as counseling, can also require significant financial resources. Likewise, it is difficult to make major life changes without social support. Women without these resources may adopt a conservative strategy because they do not have the resources to choose other strategies, or because they stand to lose the few resources they do possess if their strategies do not work as they plan.

The Venture Strategy

At the other end of the continuum is the "venture" strategy (Hamby & Gray-Little, 2007). In the investing world, this strategy is frequently referred to as an "aggressive" strategy. Because this might suggest a focus on women's use of violence, which is not the only or even a necessary element of this approach, the term "venture" is used for this model. The term "venture" is designed to capture the higher element of risk that is the central component of this strategy. Confronting the perpetrator and leaving, especially in the midst of a crisis, are examples of what are, statistically, high-risk strategies. Some venture risks pertain directly to increased risks of further violence and stalking following separation, both of which are well documented (e.g., Tjaden & Thoennes, 1998). As discussed in Chapter 3, leaving is also associated with threats by the batterer to harm children, pets, and women's family members (Amanor-Boadu et al., 2012). Some victimized women face other significant and even life-threatening risks, such as the risk of deportation for some immigrants. Because many battered women face a daunting array of such risks, an overemphasis on venture strategies may be dangerous.

The Balanced Strategy

Many financial advisors recommend a strategy between the two extremes of conservative and venture—a balanced strategy. In finance, a balanced strategy refers to the creation of a diversified portfolio of investments that represent varying degrees of risk. The recommended balance of low- and high-risk investments varies with an individual's personal situation. A young or wealthy person can afford to take greater risks than people approaching retirement age with modest assets. The balanced strategy probably characterizes most women who have been battered. As has been described throughout this book, existing evidence indicates that most women are trying numerous protective responses to violence, including some that are typically labeled "active" and some that are typically labeled "passive." Rather than trying to characterize victim's coping as *either* active *or* passive, it would be better to recognize that a smart overall strategy includes elements of both. That is likely to be the best way to simultaneously minimize harms and maximize potential gains (Hamby & Gray-Little, 2007). This philosophy is shared by the MCDM approach. Financial planning is another complex challenge that shares features with victimization, like the other examples of complex problems discussed in Chapter 2.

A recent latent class analysis provided some support for the typology outlined above (Zanville & Cattaneo, 2012). These authors found that higher risk led to more use of all kinds of coping strategies, consistent with findings reported elsewhere in this book. The choice of "public" versus "private" coping did not vary across high- and low-risk groups. They found that women in the "venture" group were experiencing the worst violence and hence engaging in the most coping strategies, compared to women in the "conservative" or "balanced" groups. Their study indicates that there is need for more appreciation of heterogeneity among victimized women in research on domestic violence. Their analyses, which were based on an existing dataset, had limited measures of nonphysical risks, suggesting another avenue for further research that might help better explain coping choices among differently situated women.

CONCLUSION

The many and varied strategies used by victimized women, including all of the invisible strategies, offer great promise and hope that much more can be done to help women who are seeking suggestions about how to cope with victimization by their partner. Domestic violence is a winnable battle. It is a problem that can be handled when it does occur. These strategies may also offer promise for helping to prevent violence before it occurs by making women less vulnerable to victimization in their own homes. These many invisible strategies show the innovativeness and inventiveness with which many women approach the problem of victimization. This type of creative and broad thinking is an essential component of MCDM and other approaches to solving complex problems.

12

Bringing a More Holistic Approach to Services and Tools for Intervention

A holistic, multiple-criteria-based approach can inform and serve as a base for domestic violence services that are more person- and family-centered. An important function of any framework is to guide practice in the field. The accumulated data demonstrating battered women's range of risks and their numerous protective strategies provide strong evidence that intervention should be organized around the full context of individuals' and their families' experiences, not narrowly focused on physical attacks. The research and clinical material discussed in previous chapters provides new urgency to calls to meet women where they are—in the midst of multiple protective efforts. This chapter addresses the ways in which knowledge of battered women's risks and protective strategies can guide assessment and intervention. More comprehensive approaches can include formal use of the VIGOR framework or other multiple-criteria decision-making frameworks. This chapter also describes approaches developed by others that are consistent with these goals.

Limiting dangerousness assessments and safety plans to physical violence leads agencies to miss the opportunity to understand and intervene in the array of factors with which women cope. The true mission of most shelters and other agencies that serve domestic violence victims is to ensure the welfare of women, children, and families. It is not making women leave. A "band-aid" approach to helping people who have experienced victimization falls well short of that true mission. Here are a few possibilities for improving intervention for domestic violence.

IMPROVING SERVICES WITH MORE HOLISTIC APPROACHES

I was telling someone about the topic of this book, and her reply was, "If we don't tell them to leave then what are we supposed to do?" We lack a definitive answer to that question because of 40 years overly focused on divorce and relationship termination as the solution. So I cannot offer firm answers, only some ideas, as much as possible informed by existing science, that are worth trying.

1. Make assessment of multiple risks the norm and build these into the tools providers use. The most fundamental implication of the data on risks and protective strategies is that, as was argued in Chapter 2, "dangerousness assessment" needs to become "risk assessment" and "safety planning" needs to become "risk management." Our services should recognize the full spectrum of risks and coping responses that routinely apply when domestic violence occurs. As also argued elsewhere in the book, we need formal tools that incorporate the full spectrum of risks so every advocate does not have to rediscover these issues and even novice advocates can systematically take a comprehensive approach. See the section below under the heading *"Approaches to Services that are Consistent with a Holistic Approach"* for some specific examples of how to go about doing this.

2. *Refer and assess across the spectrum of human services.* The general public cannot be held responsible for understanding our complicated social service systems. It is difficult to seek help and people should not feel turned away or discouraged when they do. As with other social institutions that serve survivors of violence, the domestic violence field needs to adopt the principles of the "No wrong door" movement (Center for Substance Abuse Treatment, 2000; Sacks & Ries, 2005). Rather than turning away victimized women who have inadvertently found their way to the wrong service agency, applying the "no wrong door" philosophy to victimization involves offering sufficient help with referrals and coordination so that help-seeking itself is not unintentionally discouraged. Although time constraints may prevent conducting a complete assessment and developing a management plan in every contact, even law enforcement and emergency department personnel can refer people to holistic, person-centered services. An overly narrow focus on the presenting problem does not capture the reality of many people in need of help. More carefully designed feedback and help developing an alternative plan that meets the clients' needs and desires could better steer clients to suitable services (Hamby & Grych, 2013).

3. *Explicitly address risks to all family members.* Too many services focus on a single family member, rather than the whole family, as "the" client. My colleagues and I have argued elsewhere that a more family-centered approach is important for improving services to child witnesses and to promoting the safety and well-being of everyone in the family (Hamby et al., 2010; Hamby & Grych, 2013). For domestic violence survivors, this includes more formally incorporating their needs into child protection assessments. It does not make sense to order a parent to follow a treatment plan without considering whether this might endanger the parent because of separation violence. According to some data, the majority of intimate partner femicides occur in couples who have had at least one separation in the past year (Campbell, Glass, Sharps, Laughon, & Bloom, 2007). All of the coercive forces—threats and otherwise—a parent is facing should be assessed and systematically addressed.

In some child protection agencies, virtually every parent is given the same "treatment" plan—leave now or lose your kids, without any serious consideration given to the safest way to handle the risks that are facing a particular family. The derivative losses and cascading effects of different interventions need greater consideration too, including the cascading negative effects of foster care placement (Viner & Taylor,

2005). CPS recommendations often assume the non-offending parent can freely choose her actions, but this may not be the case. I know from my own experience that it is easy to view a case quite differently depending on whether you are in the role of child advocate or parent advocate. Although some efforts toward more balanced approaches have been made, the child protection system still often treats parents as adversaries and this needs further improvement (Sirotkin & Fecko, 2008). Fear of child protective services involvement was reported by nearly one in five women (18%) in the VIGOR 1 study. It is unfortunate, to say the least, that families in need are fearful of social service agencies. A more family-centered approach could potentially improve this.

Likewise, the high degree of co-occurrence among forms of family violence (Hamby et al., 2010) indicates that screening for child victimization in domestic violence agencies should be more widely implemented. Dangerousness assessments and safety planning should explicitly include risks to children to help parents develop plans that respond to those risks, using the VIGOR, the Davies guide, or other protocols. Many shelters house similar numbers of children as adults. The most recent census of shelter residents indicated that slightly more children than adults were housed in 2011 (National Network to End Domestic Violence, 2012). (This happens because many women have more than one child.) The same data, however, indicate that approximately one in five (21%) U.S. domestic violence programs do not provide children's support or advocacy. Only one in three (32%) offer advocacy related to child protective services; only one in four (24%) offer any kind of child care or daycare support while women engage in protective strategies; and only one in six offer counseling to children by a licensed practitioner (National Network to End Domestic Violence, 2012). Children should not reside in a social service program without having their needs addressed (Hamby & Grych, 2013).

4. Evaluate the merits of different approaches to screening and assessment. Much more outcome research needs to be conducted on services to domestic violence victims. None of the safety plans in widespread use are evidence based. Not one. Recent evaluations of screening for domestic violence in health-care settings have not shown benefits of screening, although these trials provide further evidence that domestic violence tends to decrease over time with or without intervention (Nelson, Bougatsos, & Blazina, 2012). Further, different risk assessment and risk management tools should be explicitly compared to each other to identify the ones that perform best, not just whether some tool performs better than no intervention at all. More research also needs to be done to determine how to help people who do not seek formal assistance through law enforcement or shelters, or who approach such institutions but are not served beyond an initial contact. The study by DeBoer and colleagues provides a good example of how important this is. As described earlier, they found that about one-third of couples who were refused conjoint therapy because of domestic violence levels that exceeded the criteria for one program simply went and sought couples therapy elsewhere (DeBoer et al., 2012). Unfortunately, 2 years later, rates of violence were still high for couples who both had and had not sought treatment elsewhere. Regardless of whether a woman or a couple can be served in a particular program, more needs to be done to identify appropriate services for people when they seek treatment.

5. *Consider other intervention models.* We know that home visitation programs are one of the most promising methods of preventing child maltreatment (Olds, 2006). Some coaching/mentoring programs that share similar principles have been tried with domestic violence (Smyth, Goodman, & Glenn, 2006). These may have some potential. I visited one woman once or twice a week for several months. Her husband did not seem to like it—he always left as soon as I showed up—but he tolerated it for a while. Some days I felt rather like one of those treehuggers who chain themselves to trees they are trying to save from the ax but it worked well until he finally prevailed upon her to tell me to stop coming by. Although home visits may not be a complete solution in and of themselves, they could be one approach to reducing violence. One benefit of home visits is that many professionals can do them, including clergy and law enforcement. Home visits by advocates could be added to diversion and probation agreements. I do not know how effective this would be on a broad scale, but given how ineffective most interventions are now, even over similar relatively short-term time frames, interventions that have been successful for other types of violence are certainly worth considering.

CHALLENGES IN MAKING SERVICES MORE HOLISTIC AND PROTECTIVE-FOCUSED

There are many challenges in making substantial changes in service delivery. A couple of examples are provided here along with some suggestions for addressing them.

1. *Changing institutional culture.* The culture of a given agency, "how we do things around here," embodies the collected wisdom of the agency staff and can be a valuable source of insights that cannot be found in a book. However, as John Grych and I have argued elsewhere, long-established cultures also can create inertia that makes change difficult as new evidence and insights are accumulated (Hamby & Grych, 2013). Regarding domestic violence, we know much more about battering and women's responses to it now than we did 20 or even 10 years ago. Incorporating this new knowledge into existing organizational procedures will involve some growing pains. However, there are models that offer new approaches to working with women who have experienced domestic violence, a few of which are described below. People have been working to develop processes, such as the sanctuary model (Bloom, 2010), which can help organizations move more smoothly and swiftly to more client-centered models. These models focus on the process of organizational change itself and work collaboratively toward new intervention models. This helps take the burden off of individual providers to exert heroic efforts to try and single-handedly create systemic change.

2. *"Failure to protect" and mandatory reporting for exposure to domestic violence.* Domestic violence and child abuse often co-occur in the same family (Hamby et al., 2010). Rather than promoting holistic services for families, one unfortunate way that the intersections among types of violence has been dealt with is by use of child protection policies such as "failure to protect," which

involves charging a victimized, nonoffending parent as neglectful because of their victimization (Hamby & Grych, 2013). "Failure to protect" charges and child protection intervention for exposure to domestic violence are non-evidence-based practices that have never been evaluated and may have harmful effects, especially if they lead to unnecessary removal of children from their parents or discourage help-seeking by nonoffending parents. They are also problematic because they can send the message that exposure to violence is somehow the fault of victims, rather than perpetrators. The adverse consequences of common child protection interventions need greater consideration. Ordering parents to separate may put children at increased risk for some victimizations, including homicide and custodial interference. Removing children from their parents is traumatic to children and should only be used as a last resort. Common child protection interventions, such as foster placement and court interventions, have many adverse effects themselves (Viner & Taylor, 2005) and are not the solution for reducing violence against children. There is no evidence suggesting that witnessing violence warrants extreme interventions.

A more holistic, family-centered approach should guide family violence investigations. Good model policies exist that specifically address exposure to domestic violence and cases of multiple victims in one family—perhaps most notably the Greenbook, a guide for family court judges (Schechter & Edleson, 1999). The Greenbook recommends that, especially in cases of low or moderate severity, children be kept with nonoffending parents and services be made available without opening a child protection investigation. Mandatory reporting is one reason that such an adversarial approach has developed between social service providers and families. Many countries, including other wealthy, industrialized stable democracies such as Germany, the United Kingdom, and New Zealand (Mathews & Kenny, 2008), use some version of a voluntary reporting system for dealing with cases of child maltreatment. Mandatory reporting was implemented before the importance of evidence-based practice was recognized, and the merits of different variations of mandatory reporting policies would be worth investigating in formal, scientific evaluations. There is far more evidence in support of collaborative efforts such as early home visitation, which helps children in violent families and prevents considerable amounts of maltreatment (Olds, 2006).

APPROACHES TO SERVICES THAT ARE CONSISTENT WITH A HOLISTIC APPROACH

Several existing interventions either implicitly or explicitly adopt a holistic philosophy. Although not intended to be an exhaustive list, I offer a few descriptions of services or program philosophies that best exemplify comprehensive, holistic approaches for addressing domestic violence. Unlike more piecemeal approaches or more narrowly focused programs, these approaches offer ideas about how to better work with women's own protective efforts as they cope with battering. These approaches can be used alone in or in conjunction with more "traditional" dangerousness assessment and safety planning tools that focus more specifically on threats of future physical violence. As emphasized throughout the book, domestic violence is a complex problem and is best addressed with a multifaceted approach.

WOMAN-DEFINED ADVOCACY

Davies and her colleagues have advocated for two important improvements to standard domestic violence interventions (Davies, 2009; Davies, Lyon, & Monti-Catania, 1998). First, they suggest linking safety planning to a comprehensive risk assessment, and second, they suggest incorporating other risks in addition to the risk of violence into safety planning. Their approach includes assessing risk to children. Davies and colleagues suggest three sources that can help create options: the advocate, the battered women, or another agency or system. As a result of these improvements, woman-defined advocacy assesses more resources and options than most safety plans. One especially distinctive feature of the women-defined advocacy approach is the explicit emphasis on options and priorities that would lead a woman to remain in contact with her partner (Davies, 2009; Davies et al., 1998). They suggest that various "life-generated risks," such as poverty or court-ordered visitation with the couple's children, might indicate that staying or remaining in contact with her partner may be the best available option. Davies' document, *Advocacy Beyond Leaving* (Davies, 2009), which is freely available on the Internet at the Futures Without Violence website (www.futureswithoutviolence.org), provides an interview guide for advocates that prompts them to cover a wide range of issues, including life-generated risks, and even offers sample questions.

STRATEGIC SAFETY PLANNING

Lindhorst and colleagues (Lindhorst, Macy, & Nurius, 2005) have also developed an intervention model that is congruent with risk-based coping. They recognize that there may be legitimate higher priorities for some women, such as not losing custody of their children. The risk of losing one's children is just one potential consequence that may be more harmful than the harm caused by the perpetrator's physical assaults. Other harms may include escalating danger following separation and economic problems. Lindhorst and colleagues recognize that women may engage in coping efforts that can seem perplexing if one focuses exclusively on the expectation that they will leave but make sense when one recognizes that many women are juggling complex environmental situations and are attempting to minimize multiple harms. They recommend that traditional safety planning, which focuses almost entirely on ways to establish or maintain separation from a partner, be revised to strategically address the potential for multiple harms. Their four-step model includes assessing for multiple harms, identifying environmental resources and barriers, recognizing changes in appraisal and coping over time, and developing social capital (Lindhorst et al., 2005). The model explicitly recognizes that advocating that a woman leave may not always be appropriate, depending on what else is at risk for a woman.

RELATIONSHIP-CENTERED ADVOCACY

Goodman and Epstein (2008) have called for a "survivor-centered approach" to advocacy. Focusing especially on the needs of low-income women, they also provide a cogent critique of existing institutional frameworks. Goodman and Epstein suggest a number of reforms for mental health, justice, and other systems. For advocacy, they recommend reaching out to members of a battered woman's social network and developing short-term financial assistance programs. These "bridge funds," as they call short-term financial aid, can include one-time cash assistance programs from state or nonprofit agencies. Companies can also provide bridge funds by making pay advances or vacation time payouts for victimized women in crisis. They also suggest doing more to address housing issues for battered women (Goodman & Epstein, 2008).

More recently, Weintraub and Goodman (2010) have reported some preliminary qualitative results of their efforts to develop relationship-centered advocacy for victimized women. Relationship-centered advocacy reframes the association between advocate and victim as an "advocate–partner" relationship and endeavors to build collaborative methods of addressing the needs of help-seeking women. Perhaps the most important principle identified in early efforts to implement this model was staying with women's priorities, which is very consistent with the holistic approach advocated in this book. Their model also helps to counter the social distancing often found among social and health service providers. Working from this perspective, advocates recognize that they have shared identities and experiences with help-seekers rather than focusing primarily on aspects of their lives that are different from women who have experienced victimization.

COMPUTERIZED SAFETY DECISION AID

Another recent innovation in risk management is the development of a computerized version by Glass and colleagues (2010). Their safety decision aid incorporates many components that are consistent with the VIGOR framework. For example, it is one of the few instruments that allows women to weight their own priorities. In this case, a fixed set of possible priorities are offered: affordable housing, childcare and employment (apparently integrated), feelings for partner, desire for confidentiality and privacy, safety, and children's well-being (for those who have children). This aid then asks each woman to compare the importance across all possible pairs of these priorities to devise a rank ordering of priorities. The Safety Decision Aid incorporates the Danger Assessment (Campbell, 2005). Their priority weights are then used to help guide women to resources that "most closely match their safety priorities" (Glass et al., 2010, p. 1958). Unfortunately, existing published data on this method do not indicate how well the referrals matched women's own views of their needs or whether it improved outcomes, but this is a promising approach.

COORDINATED COMMUNITY RESPONSES

There has been a move toward greater integration in a number of different domains related to violence research, advocacy, and practice. This broader perspective on coping with violence can be seen as part of this larger trend. On the advocacy and practice sides, there have been movements such as coordinated community response teams for domestic violence (Shepard & Pence, 1999) and the National Domestic Violence Fatality Review Initiative (http://www.ndvfri.org/). There have been similar efforts for sexual assault, child abuse, and elder abuse (Hamby & Grych, 2013). These efforts bring together stakeholders from different agencies who work with victimized women and get them to work together in ways that minimize institutional obstacles to services, such as those reviewed in Chapter 4. In teams that focus on family violence, they often involve representatives from domestic violence agencies, child protective services, community mental health centers, law enforcement, and hospital emergency departments. They can also include representatives from victim assistance programs, legal aid, and housing and welfare offices. There is no set formula and the particular professionals involved in any one locale depend on the way institutions are set up in that jurisdiction and the vagaries of local politics and who will talk to whom. As mentioned in Chapter 10, these can have positive effects on the institutional results of women's formal help-seeking. One example is the Full-Frame Approach (Smyth et al., 2006). These authors identify an overemphasis on specialization across a wide range of interventions, especially those primarily offered to marginalized groups. The Full-Frame Approach is not limited to the problem of domestic violence, but domestic violence is well suited to it (Goodman et al., 2009). The Full-Frame Approach focuses more on systems than individual advocacy. The approach emphasizes analyzing the interplay among different needs, recognizing the centrality of social relationships, and empowering victimized women by putting them in control of the process of framing their concerns and problems (Smyth et al., 2006).

All of these efforts at coordination recognize that violence touches people's lives in many ways and that, therefore, violence often means that people will interact with many different institutions. Many of these efforts are also more victim-centered. Their genesis was inspired by a desire to be more victim-friendly and to at least avoid secondary traumatization of victimized women by further institutional mistreatment on top of what they experienced by batterers. All of these values are consistent with those espoused in this book. There are, however, also some differences between these movements and the present thesis. Although these movements are aimed at creating kinder, gentler institutions, they still, by their very natures, focus on institutional responses to violence and so in some cases still do not go far enough to recognize that sometimes institutions are not needed when someone experiences violence and that victimized women are already doing a lot for themselves. At their best, these movements recognize that institutions can create problems resulting from lack of interagency coordination and mixed messages that create obstacles to safety. At their worst, they can just become better, more coordinated agents of control that can be harder to work around if the recommendations they make do not work for a particular victim.

THE VICTIM INVENTORY OF GOALS, OPTIONS, AND RISKS (VIGOR)

The Victim Inventory of Goals, Options and Risks (VIGOR) shares some elements with woman-defined advocacy (Davies et al., 1998) and strategic safety planning (Lindhorst et al., 2005), such as inclusion of risks besides physical danger and recognition that contact with partners may be inevitable or even the best option for some women. The broader view of risks and priorities is also similar to the computerized decision safety aid (Glass et al., 2010). The VIGOR shares elements with relationship-centered advocacy in that it emphasizes women's own priorities and that women who have been victimized should not be thought about exclusively in terms of their victimization (Goodman & Epstein, 2008).

The VIGOR also differs from these approaches in several respects. First, the VIGOR explicitly adopts the principles of the multiple-criteria decision-making process (MCDM; *see* Chapter 2). Second, in addition to the development of principles for advocacy, the VIGOR is a specific tool that can be used for risk assessment and risk management. The VIGOR is more structured than some of these approaches, because it asks women to consider a number of domains in a semistructured format, but less structured than the computerized decision safety aid, which requires paired comparisons of predefined priorities. Third, the VIGOR has some quantitative data on its perceived helpfulness and how women responded to the different steps of the framework. As described in Chapter 2, MCDM is a well-established method that is frequently used in environmental sciences, engineering, and related fields (Hajkowicz, 2008) but also offers considerable promise as a method for helping people who have experienced domestic violence (Hamby & Clark, 2011). In MCDM, the existence of numerous important and potentially conflicting objectives is explicitly recognized.

As noted in Chapter 2, an even more important advantage of the MCDM framework is that, unlike other approaches such as cost–benefit analysis, MCDM allows for the inclusion of objectives that are not easily assigned a quantitative figure such as costs in dollars. For example, it is popular in environmental science because it can include objectives such as maintaining a pristine natural environment. This latter feature makes it particularly well-suited to addressing the situations of many victimized women, because the value of intangibles such as custody of one's children can be included in the risk assessment and risk management process. The VIGOR applies MCDM principles in a simplified format that does not require special algorithms or formulas and tailors them for the special case of domestic violence. Rather than a generic checklist of safety precautions, the VIGOR produces a personalized plan that links coping responses to specific risks.

The VIGOR was developed through extensive work in consultation with advocates, students, and pilot testing with two groups of women who have experienced domestic violence. I also want to acknowledge the work of Sarah Clark, who helped me revise this assessment tool and spent many hours coding pilot data (Hamby & Clark, 2011). The VIGOR was developed based on my advocacy experiences with victims and especially the frustrations many victimized women reported regarding the typical dangerousness assessment and safety planning approach. After more than 40 years of services for battered women, it is time for alternative approaches to be explored. I believe in the collected wisdom of advocates and survivors and that this wisdom has been insufficiently reflected in the tools available to advocates and women. Six other experienced advocates from across the United States reviewed the VIGOR and provided extensive feedback. Then, as described earlier in the book, two pilot studies with women who have been victims of battering were conducted and their feedback was solicited. Numerous revisions were made after each of these stages. Finally, students in an undergraduate research seminar helped further streamline and simplify the wording. They were particularly helpful in identifying language that, intentionally or not, suggested the VIGOR was for low-income women. This is a work in progress and I welcome feedback from survivors, advocates, providers, researchers, and anyone else who is interested in the safety of victims of violence.

The quotes that have appeared in many chapters are from these women's analyses of their situations. In addition to these quotes, in ratings of the VIGOR in the first pilot study, 79% of the sample said that they thought the VIGOR would be helpful to most people and 74% said that it was more help than whatever safety planning they had done before. For the second VIGOR study, I made numerous revisions with the input of the students acknowledged above, and these figures were higher in VIGOR 2: 92% of the women in that study said they thought the VIGOR would be helpful to most people, and 86% said it was an improvement over their past experiences with safety planning (Hamby, 2013b). These are notable figures because these women had engaged in formal help-seeking from domestic violence and other agencies prior to completing the VIGOR. Some of them commented on how it was helpful to them:

> "This was a great help to me just in writing these things down, 'seeing' it on paper aided me in recognizing my accomplishments and what I yet need to do!"
> "Helped me see different options I may have."
> "I liked thinking about my strengths."
> "I liked having to think and acknowledge my strengths and options—made me hopeful."

Using the VIGOR

The first step in MCDM is to structure the problem by identifying goals and criteria. In the VIGOR, there is a section for women to identify goals and also one to identify risks. See the Appendix for the full instrument. In the goals section, they are encouraged to think about where they would like to be in 6 months, what they think is their ideal living situation, and whether they have other goals such as going back to work or school. The next step is to identify risks, and several suggested categories are provided. Personal safety is at the top of the list because that is one of the most important—if not the main—reason that many battered women seek help. Next on the list are risks to others' safety and well-being, including children, family, pets, friends, and others. All of the other risk categories that we have been discussing in this book are included: financial, legal, social, and psychological. There is also a place for "other" risks. All of these are open-ended categories, not checklists, to enable a woman to personalize them to her situation and put them in her own words. Some examples are provided to help stimulate thinking, but these examples have been carefully chosen, reviewed, and pilot-tested to help broaden thinking, not limit or narrow the scope of the problems or the solutions. Some sort of prioritizing of goals and risks is required in the MCDM process. Although this can involve complicated weighting, scoring, or rank ordering, I have found that most women find it helpful to just identify the most important three or four issues they are facing. These then become the "multiple criteria" part of the MCDM process. For an initial risk assessment, it is hard to incorporate more than three or four issues without resorting to mathematical formulas and computerized algorithms.

In traditional MCDM, it is possible to move directly to identifying options. In many systems, identifying viable options implicitly includes recognizing resources and abilities. For working with individuals, however, I have found it helpful to separate these processes and have women first identify their strengths and resources. Many of the women who have so far used the VIGOR have commented that they appreciated this section the most, because sometimes in dealing with the crisis of battering, a focus on strengths can get lost. As far as I am aware, it is also one of the most unique aspects of the VIGOR, because few, if any, other approaches for helping women cope with domestic violence provide an explicit recognition of their strengths.

Strengths and resources are also organized into sections that again map onto many of the issues we have discussed. This section leads with personal and psychological resources, including faith. Housing resources are listed separately as that is usually a key issue. Financial and legal resources are additional categories. Social and community resources include any person or organization, such as a church, that women can rely on in times of trouble. We have also included a section on privacy and protection that mostly focuses on identity protection and ways to make one's home more secure. See the appendix for how these are defined in the VIGOR. My colleagues, students, and I spent many hours crafting these definitions and examples in such a way that they would not limit women's responses. The wide range of responses given to all sections suggests we were successful in that goal.

The third step is identifying options. These revisit many of the same categories. There are housing options, financial options, and legal options. There are social and psychological options. There are community options. There are also privacy and protection options. At all of these stages, there are also opportunities to add further options that do not fall under any of the categories listed. Some of the examples provided here refer to "traditional" advocacy services such as shelters, orders of protection, and support groups. Newer services such as couples counseling and less violence-focused options such as job training are also listed as examples that go beyond these traditional ones. We need to expand our toolkit. A better appreciation of risks will help focus on other needs—financial planning, job training, coping with a stigmatized identity, talking with family members or clergy. I recommend using Table 11.1, which includes more than 140 possibilities, to help generate options.

Importantly, the field also needs to rethink the time frame required to cope with victimization. Once you start thinking about coping this way, it becomes immediately apparent that many options cannot be realistically implemented in the 30 or 60 or 90 days that women are allowed to stay in shelter. Nonetheless, pursuing options with a longer time horizon, such as saving sufficient money to pursue more costly options, may be essential to obtaining better outcomes.

The last step is the key to the MCDM process. In conventional MCDM analyses, each option is rated on how it performs relative to each criterion. In the best case scenario, one option will emerge that has "strict dominance." In the strict dominance case, one option is better than all of the others on at least one criterion and possibly more, and it is as good as all of the other choices on other criteria. When strict dominance is lacking, then the option or options are chosen that help the most overall, taking all of the different criteria into consideration, even if it is not the number one best choice for some criteria. In many cases, it will be possible to implement more than one option and further improve the final outcome. Of course, this is commonly true for coping with battering, where one can certainly seek both housing and social support, for example, at the same time.

In our preliminary research, this fourth step has been the most challenging to adapt to a non-engineering, non-science application. We have worked extensively to adapt this section in a way that will make sense to the general public, advocates, health-care professionals, law enforcement, and others who want to help battered women but may not have extensive mathematical or statistical training. In our current version, Stage 4 is called "Reflecting on Your Choices." There is a place for victimized women to restate their biggest or most important risks. In the last stage, they can then put this all together and choose the combination of options it makes the most sense for them to pursue right now. They can also identify other steps that might need to happen and resources they will need to implement their plans. The result will not be a generic, one-size-fits-all checklist of safety precautions but a personalized plan that links coping responses to specific prioritized risks. Fleeing on an emergency basis with few belongings and possibly not even with your children will not minimize most risks faced by typical battered women. It is unlikely that strategy will have "strict dominance" for many women.

The VIGOR framework offers three distinct improvements over existing practice. One important outcome is that the VIGOR framework can potentially improve our response to the most disadvantaged women as we try to help them address multiple needs. Even more importantly, the VIGOR offers a way to reframe what may look like poor coping or denial through the recognition that some victimized women may be prioritizing other goals and risks in addition to or more highly than their own personal safety. Finally, it is no secret that most of our domestic violence programs are, intentionally or not, aimed at the most disadvantaged women. The MCDM-based VIGOR framework, unlike shelters and many other domestic violence services, is just as appropriate for women of considerable financial or other resources as it is for women with few resources. Currently, we are neglecting all of the accountants, teachers, health-care professionals, professors, and others who also experience domestic violence and may feel that shelter-based services are not meant for them. Advocacy should not be just about free shelter, and we need to work to make the broader population aware that the domestic violence field has more to offer than free short-term housing.

CONCLUSION

New directions are needed to make prevention and interventions of all kinds more effective. Although many types of evidence are urgently needed to make more informed programming decisions, the field also underutilizes existing data that already provide a picture of the array of battered women's protective strategies. Building on women's numerous protective efforts can lead to more coordinated, person-centered services that have the potential to advance the field and reduce the burden of domestic violence on individuals and families everywhere. Although some suggestions enumerated here would entail fairly large system reform, others can be done simply by broadening the focus of existing services and by taking a more intentional approach to addressing multiple forms of violence. The VIGOR and several other holistic approaches are available and can be implemented more widely. The efforts described in this chapter offer some ideas that will hopefully be built on further in future work.

13

Conclusion: Recognizing Protective Strategies Can Create Progress

In these last few pages, I would like to suggest some broader implications of a shift to a more strengths-based paradigm. There are implications of recognizing the full spectrum of risks, the full spectrum of protective strategies and recommendations to help avoid further over-reliance on a deficit-focused perspective. Despite what has often been an overly deficit-focused approach in the field, these suggestions build on many important accomplishments of past efforts to address the problem of domestic violence. Much has been achieved in the last 50 years. Domestic violence is now recognized as a major and widespread social problem that has costs that extend to families, communities, and the broader society (Clark et al., 2002). Despite the lingering influence of stereotypes, we understand much more about domestic violence and other forms of family violence than we did even 10 or 20 years ago.

Most research cited in this book represents progress in the field as we continue to move beyond stereotypes of battered women and expand our scope to encompass the many factors in women's lives that should inform any serious study of domestic violence. Still, the goal is to continue moving forward. Greater appreciation of battered women's protective strategies can serve as the foundation for a more holistic and family-centered approach to domestic violence. Systemic change is needed. These changes should not depend on noble individuals going above and beyond their existing responsibilities, although there are many who do just that. To forge lasting change, we need to create incentives and institutional frameworks that help the field as a whole become more holistic and strengths-focused.

The most important and fundamental message is that services for battered women need to be more respectful. When the Red Cross opens a shelter for victims of natural disasters, they manage to respond to people in crisis without subtle and not-so-subtle messages of disparagement. No one says, "What were you thinking, living so close to the water?" or "Don't you know tornadoes are common in the plain states?" There is probably some optimal geographic location in any country for minimizing exposure to natural disasters, but that is not the only factor influencing where people live. No one thinks it should be. Similarly, we need to recognize the numerous influences on people's decisions not only about where they live but also with whom they live. As mentioned in many places throughout the book, we need to stop thinking of battering as some kind of problem that is unlike any other faced by women, men, and families.

Battering shares elements with many other types of adverse events, including natural disasters, other crimes, and other relationship problems. Recognizing that battering is one of many complicated but common life problems is the first step on the path to stopping the unique disparagement of battered women. How can that translate into being more respectful of battered women? In the language of science, more respect can be "operationalized" in several concrete ways.

TRAIN AND EDUCATE

One larger implication of the holistic view of victimized women's lives is that advocates would benefit from a broader background in intervention. Advocates should have more than a few hours or few days of on-the-job training. A more thorough training in the psychology of marriage and families would be advantageous. It does not take away from the heroism of the women who invented the shelter system and domestic violence advocacy to suggest that not everyone comes to this work with the natural helping instincts and dedication to social action that they showed. A few hours or even a few weeks are not sufficient to turn someone into a skilled social service provider, much less one equipped to deal with a challenging and even dangerous caseload. Going over traditional safety planning, dangerousness assessment, and other advocacy basics does not provide the skills to develop the contextualized picture that will best serve battered women. Frustrations with one's clients are part and parcel of any social or health service, but in most fields these frustrations have not been institutionalized as "theories" of passive coping, denial, learned helplessness, or traumatic bonding—to name just a few. More training might also help address problems with burnout and high turnover among advocates that are also major issues in this field.

SUFFICIENT AND CONSISTENT FUNDING

An undertrained workforce is directly related to the chronic underfunding of services for battered women. Domestic violence advocates are paid less than almost all other social service providers. Many of them work for nonprofit agencies that are usually operated on shoestring budgets and even those are often on uncertain, year-to-year, grant-cycle-to-grant-cycle footing. As a result, services are seldom provided by licensed practitioners such as social workers or psychologists or nurses. Many domestic violence advocates are "natural helpers" who have developed formidable helping skills over the course of their own life experiences (Waller & Patterson, 2002). I recognize and applaud those who stay with the work for 3 or 4 years and learn many of the skills needed the hard way. Still, even people who are temperamentally suited to this work would benefit from formal training. The lack of innovation in services for battered women may partly result from the relatively uneducated and young work force who provide the lion's share of these services. Although many of these people could provide cogent critiques of the system, they do not have the professional voice with which to do so. Like the young woman from the victim's assistance program I mentioned in Chapter 1, they are not trained to question the existing bureaucracy and have not been taught elsewhere how to do that. Trained providers cost money. Trained providers are not going to work for salaries that are often in the low $20,000s (USD) and offer few, if any, benefits and little social prestige. If we, as a society, were really committed to women's safety, then we would find a way to make sure that these services are financially supported.

INTEGRATE AND COORDINATE DOMESTIC VIOLENCE SERVICES WITH OTHER SERVICES

One piece of the solution to the funding problem could be integration and coordination. This is also a potential avenue for improving services. Our compartmentalized approach to battering leads to many unfortunate outcomes. Offering just housing to children—or worse, offering housing only to a limited age and gender range of children—is not sufficient. Children who are actually residing in a social service should be getting their needs sufficiently assessed and addressed. Many of them will have needs that go well beyond housing and a weekly counseling group.

Shelters, however, are not the only services that need a less compartmentalized approach. Too many physicians and other health providers still ask what family violence has to do with medicine (Rhodes et al., 2006). Answer: Everything. It is impossible to look after the health and well-being of women and children without assessing their safety. The health care system needs to pay more attention to the social context of people's physical well-being, and this includes more attention to victimization. Unfortunately, resistance to domestic violence screening is still widespread (Rhodes et al., 2006). In my experience, even when screening is performed, questions are often asked in a way that does not promote disclosure ("You're not experiencing any violence are you?"). Resistance to screening is often discussed as a problem with health-care providers, but this is a systemic problem, too. There would probably be less resistance among health-care providers if there were better systems in place to support "yes" answers when patients are asked if they have been victimized. This will require substantial institutional change, but envisioning is the first step to enacting.

RESEARCH AND INVESTIGATE

As has already been noted in several places throughout the book, we have only skimmed the surface of what can be learned about battered women's protective strategies. Almost every topic in this book would benefit from further study. In addition to still simply needing good data on the basic patterns of protective strategies, we also need more work on understanding who chooses what protective strategies and how they go about making those choices. In other words, we need more research on the mechanisms underlying these patterns. This research should focus on the situational and malleable factors (such as all of the protective strategies discussed in this book) that can inform intervention and prevention and not on static and historical factors that neither women nor the providers who want to help them can change (this latter group includes factors such as age, race, and childhood history of violence). There are many opportunities for new research. A good start would be to at least allow for the possibility of protective strategies and other strengths to be identified by including them in research protocols. I hope this book helps spur further research.

A DIVERSITY OF VOICES

Many of the women who have opened my eyes to the problems with the dominant deficit-focused paradigm were women of color who are not members of the dominant European American culture in the United States. Most of them are also not members of the "academy," the research community that supports the scientific study of social problems yet also institutionalizes and bureaucratizes it. For example, Elizabeth Neptune, a Passamaquoddy tribal member with many years of experience in community health care, was the first person I heard give a cogent critique of the expectation that battered women should leave while criminal perpetrators get to stay in the comfort of their own homes. I was immersed in the paradigm and her comments initially took me by surprise. The paradigm has scarcely budged since the era when married women had few property rights. Lack of property rights and the lack of legal response to most cases of domestic violence helped create the idea of shelter for women. Shelter was once literally fleeing from the law and potential charges of "abandonment." Women were not entitled to anything else; they were not even really entitled to shelter. We changed the legal situation. Women, even married women, can now have credit in their own name and are entitled to half of a couple's assets in most cases. The law enforcement response to domestic violence has changed dramatically—in most respects for the better.

Yet no one from the advocacy movement revisited what these changes might mean for services. The jobs, offices, and professional identities of so many advocates are tied to the shelter system. One cannot help but wonder whether those circumstances might have affected the lack of review. We need a wide range of voices, especially outside voices, to keep fresh perspectives. Standpoint theory explains how those who are situated outside of a system can more readily "see" the system (Hamby, 2000; Hartsock, 1998). Although it is possible for insiders to acquire at least some of these insights, for insiders this must be a more conscious effort to maintain awareness and sensitivity to these issues. The domestic violence field needs to be much more inclusive. The movement against domestic violence needs to include not only more women of color but also more men. The field also needs to better represent the perspectives of those who are involved in domestic violence as both victims and batterers (surely at least some batterers would like to be less involved in violence). Voices from all different professions need to be better heard as well. I believe the problem of domestic violence is a winnable battle, but we are not going to solve the problem of domestic violence without everyone at the table.

BE MORE DEVELOPMENTALLY ATTUNED

A more developmental approach might help refine our recommendations. Most domestic violence is perpetrated by adolescents and young adults with relatively little relationship experience. Contrary to stereotypes, some (if not many) of these individuals will not go on to become the stereotyped image of the chronic batterer (Jasinski, 2001). Many might respond to a broader array of interventions than single-gender group treatment and criminal justice penalties. In this regard, the pattern for domestic violence is similar to that for other types of offending, because many individuals who are violent in youth do not remain persistent offenders (Moffitt, 1993). In some cases, victimized women who wish to pursue couples therapy may be choosing a reasonable protective strategy (McCollum, 2012; O'Leary et al., 1999; Stith & McCollum, 2011). Understanding how and when violence has emerged in a particular relationship could help provide women with more specific guidance about how to protect themselves, rather than one-size-fits-all recommendations as currently embodied in most safety plans.

PATHWAYS TO PREVENTION

The ultimate goal of all of these efforts is to reduce domestic violence. A holistic, strengths-based paradigm can inform prevention as well as intervention. It is no secret that many of our efforts to prevent domestic violence (often in the form of dating violence prevention) have met with only modest success (Foshee, Bauman, Helms, Koch, & Linder, 1998; Hamby, 2006; Taylor, Stein, Woods, & Mumford, 2011). Teens in a dating violence prevention project in Switzerland did a great job describing the need for a more strengths-based approach (Hamby, Nix, De Puy, & Monnier, 2012):

> "I would present more things like: help young people understand how to function in a relationship, what they can do to succeed in romantic relationships...Don't put abuse in the center, put the emphasis on the positive. It's more thrilling to say how I will succeed in a relationship than how I will fight against abuse."
> "We talk about problems, now we want solutions!"

Curricula on "red flags" and "warning signs" do not approach youth where they are. This is another way that our work needs to become more developmentally attuned. Youth feel invincible. This feeling of invincibility is a developmentally normative process, not something that can—or should—be thwarted with a few classroom sessions about life's dangers. The best evidence we have right now is that classroom curricula are not very effective. In addition to focusing on strengths, another idea that may hold some promise is better patrolling of potential "hotspots"—school cafeterias, buses, hallways, and other places traditionally providing less supervision (Taylor et al., 2011).

MEN

I have written a great deal about women and women's lives in this book. I would like to say a few words about men, because it is inconceivable to imagine any effective solutions to violence that do not include men. Much of the book has focused on the need to counteract oversimplified stereotypes that make it harder for survivors to seek help. However, people who have been victimized are not the only ones who have been plagued by stereotypes. People who have committed violence are also treated as if their involvement in violence is the only important thing about them and I still often hear providers and researchers of all types insist that once a perpetrator, always a perpetrator. That attitude is inherently untherapeutic. How can people in human services professions disavow the possibility for change?

However, I have been guilty myself of eyeing those with a history of perpetration suspiciously. Although I have long thought of myself as someone who was relatively open-minded on this topic, recently I became aware that I had more work to do on this issue and have re-assessed my thinking on perpetrators again. One experience that particularly impressed me occurred at a recent conference. One day the speaker was someone with a history of perpetration. As is often the case, other speakers had referred to their personal histories, including prior victimization and their personal flaws. Although I know that perpetration and victimization are often intertwined, I had been listening to the talks about victimization without thinking much about the perpetration side. So I was as surprised as anyone when this man got up and started talking. He told his story, which definitely emphasized that what he did was wrong. However, he also said that he had changed. It is not the first time I have seen a reformed perpetrator at one of these events. Usually, however, the "perps" are paraded out, say some version of "I'm a bad person, but now I realize that and please don't turn out like me" and get escorted off stage and sometimes even literally back to prison. In typical dominant-paradigm fashion, the follow-up discussion and analysis usually underscores "us versus them" and "bad guys and good guys" stereotypes that promise that these people are completely unlike us. This was different. This man was treated like a peer and a colleague by the presenters and staff. I thought that this seemed like a very bad idea at the time. I found myself staring at him, looking for any kind of "tell" that might betray an underlying evil. Once I think he even caught me staring at him this way. I sort of begrudgingly tried to stop staring and act nonchalant after that, but I mostly kept my distance and was glad I did not have to interact with him directly.

At the same time, along what was for a long time a completely parallel and separate track in my mind, I was incredibly impressed by men's involvement in this program. There are so few men at so many events focused on reducing violence—especially those that focus on victimization. This program was different. There were substantial numbers of men in attendance and they seemed to be really involved and engaged. The staff there told me it didn't start off this way—it started off with few men, like most other violence prevention.

For months after, I told many people how amazed I was by the involvement of men there and that it was such a mystery about how this organization accomplished that. Then one day I told someone both of these stories in the same conversation and I suddenly realized that these were not two stories, they were one. Now I believe that staff's acceptance of that former perpetrator is one of the main reasons, if not the main reason, that the other men are there. I believe that my initial response was wrong and was (still!) influenced by either–or stereotypes about victimization and perpetration. I believe the frank, yet non-blaming, discussion about how perpetration and victimization gets entwined for some is how they were reaching segments of the population who normally would never get involved in the anti-violence movement. Virtually all members of the population experience involvement in violence, whether it is family violence or peer victimization or witnessing violence or conventional crime, at some level and in some role at some time in their lives. Unlike some of the arguments that have been made for thinking about how victimization and perpetration are entwined, I do not think that painting survivors as dysfunctional and violent is accurate or helpful. Many victimized people do not perpetrate violence, and there are large gender differences in perpetrator–victim patterns, with men who experienced childhood exposure to violence far more likely than victimized women to go on to become offenders

(Hamby & Grych, 2013). The point is not to find new ways to extend deficit-based paradigms to victims or perpetrators. We need approaches to violence that do not disparage and condemn people for their involvement in violence, no matter the role, and that incorporate a committed belief in the possibility of change.

These are just a few possibilities. It is likely that many of them would be more difficult to implement widely than they are to describe. Nonetheless, greater recognition of protective strategies can lead to more holistic, person-centered, and strengths-focused approaches to domestic violence research and intervention. These types of reforms are essential to improving our response to the problem of violence.

FINAL THOUGHTS

A lot of people look at the efforts of battered women and see a glass half empty—too few efforts, executed too late after the violence begins. The data, however, better support the view that most women are making many efforts to protect themselves, protect their children, and to find ways to improve their situation. These are not half-hearted coping responses, they are comprehensive marshaling of available resources. It is impressive, given that most safety plans have only 10 or 20 suggestions, that the women in the VIGOR studies thought of more than 140 protective options. This makes the list of options developed by these survivors longer than any other existing safety plan. This is all the more impressive because the list comes from a group of women who are not socially or economically privileged. Women who have been victimized make sophisticated and creative analyses of their situations and we all have much to learn by listening more carefully to what they have to say.

It also makes sense that not all women will use all of the strategies that are potentially available. For example, a woman with financial resources is probably more likely to move directly into another home or apartment, rather than staying in a shelter. The typical battered woman is constantly assessing her risk of danger and trying different protective strategies in response. That may be the only thing that is "typical" about battered women as a group. As women see how different strategies work under varying conditions, they continue to strategize and adapt. We need to know much more than we do about when and why women choose particular strategies and much more about all of the various strategies that women choose. A balanced overall strategy that operates on several fronts—not just focusing on safety but also acknowledging all of the risks that women face—is almost certainly what most women do. Advocates, providers, and scholars all need to work harder to step back and see the full world victims live in. This will best help women maximize gains and minimize losses across all the domains of their lives. The story of battered women is not a story of empty efforts. It is a story of perseverance, endurance, strength, and protection.

The VIGOR
The Victim Inventory of Goals, Options, & Risks

An Aid to Help Survivors of Violence Assess Their Risk and Decide How to Cope

Developed by Sherry Hamby, Ph.D. & Sarah Clark
sherry.hamby@sewanee.edu

The VIGOR helps you to develop a personalized plan for coping with violence and other life problems and can be used multiple times as your situation changes.

Of course, some problems are outside any one person's individual control. Especially, your partner's behavior is outside of your control. The outcomes of these steps cannot be guaranteed.

Domestic violence advocates know a lot about the options and resources in their own communities. They are based in domestic violence agencies and shelters. You might find it helpful to complete the VIGOR with an advocate, who can provide you with detailed information about the resources in your home town. The National Domestic Violence Hotline at **1-800-799-SAFE (7233) (or 1-800-787-3224 for TTY) will help you find the nearest advocate.**

Identify Goals

Where would you like to be 6 months from now? What hopes do you have for yourself or your family? List your goals.
1. 2. 3. 4.

Identify Risks

First, think about the different problems you are currently dealing with. Most people who have been hurt by a partner face the risk of future physical danger. Other life areas need to be considered, too. They may not all apply to you; for example, not everyone has pets. The idea is to make a list that is unique to **you**.

Risk Category	Your Actual & Possible Risks (describe)
Personal Safety **Physical, verbal, sexual safety & well-being**	

Others' Safety/Well-being
    Children[**]
    Family
    Pets
    Friends, others	

Financial risks **Money issues related to work, school,** **moving, legal fees, bills, insurance, debt, etc.**	
Legal risks **Concerns about police, divorce, child** **protection, immigration, other legal actions**	
Social risks **Ways that your relationships with family,** **friends, co-workers, etc., might be affected**	
Psychological risks **Feelings you might have about your situation,** **emotional risks like stress or sadness**	
Other risks **Anything not covered by above categories**	

List your biggest or most important risks:
1. 2. 3. 4.

[**] Note: If you tell about a child in danger from abuse, advocates must contact child protective services in most areas.

Identify Strengths and Resources

You may have more resources than you thought, or you may get some ideas about what you need in order to meet your goals.

Resource Category	Your Actual or Possible Resources (describe)
Personal & Psychological Ways in which you are strong and can keep safe. Include all kinds of strength, such as courage & faith	
Housing resources Access to safe place to live (own a home, name on a lease, affordable housing, etc)	
Financial resources Sources of income or other financial support	
Legal resources Documents, legal help, or other things that can help you deal with courts & agencies	
Social & community resources People you can rely on in times of trouble. Include family, friends, AA or other 12-step programs, religious groups, or other organizations too.	
Privacy & protection Ability to increase privacy settings on computer, phone, or make home more secure.	
Other resources Things that can help you that are not included above.	

Identify Options

Thinking about your resources, start to identify your options and choices about what to do. Many choices can be used together. At this point, just put down all of the possibilities you might be willing to do.

Option Category	Existing & Potential Options (describe)
Housing options Stay with family or friends, rent apartment or other new housing, go to shelter, stay with partner	
Financial options Open bank account, get job training, apply for job, start saving money, borrow money, sell items to raise money	
Legal options Apply for order of protection/ restraining order, file for divorce, seek full custody of children, crime victims compensation	
Social options Join community group, talk to supportive friends/family, speak to religious leaders	
Psychological options Join support group, individual or couples counseling, exercise, journal	
Community options Work with advocate, job training, employment agency, apply for public assistance (TANF, food stamps, Medicaid, Medicare, state health insurance for children, etc.)	
Privacy & protection Change privacy settings on social networking sites, change locks, change phone numbers & passwords, get prepaid phone	
Other options	

Reflecting on Your Choices

You have identified your goals, risks, and options. Now, consider what you think are your best choices to create the best plan for you. **Remember, you can change your choices later if you want.**

List your biggest or most important risks (from page 2)

Write one thing you can do here:
This choice helps with the following risks (describe):
This choice doesn't help with these risks (describe):
Do I need anything I don't have right now in order to do this? How can I get what I need to do this?

Something else you can do:
This choice helps with the following risks (describe):
This choice doesn't help with these risks (describe):
Do I need anything I don't have right now in order to do this? How can I get what I need to do this?

Something else you can do:
This choice helps with the following risks (describe):
This choice doesn't help with these risks (describe):
Do I need anything I don't have right now in order to do this? How can I get what I need to do this?

You can add more steps you want to take on the back if you want

Adams, J., & White, M. (2005). Why don't stage-based activity promotion interventions work? *Health Education Research, 20*(2), 237–243.

Albadvi, A., Chaharsooghi, S. K., & Esfahanipour, A. (2007). Decision making in stock trading: An application of PROMETHEE. *European Journal of Operational Research, 177*(2), 673–683. doi: 10.1016/j.ejor.2005.11.022

Alexander, P. C., & Morris, E. (2008). Stages of change in batterers and their response to treatment. *Violence and Victims, 23*(4), 476–492. doi: 10.1891/0886-6708.23.4.476

Amanor-Boadu, Y., Messing, J. T., Stith, S. M., Anderson, J. R., O'Sullivan, C. S., & Campbell, J. C. (2012). Immigrant and nonimmigrant women: Factors that predict leaving an abusive relationship. *Violence Against Women, 18*(5), 611–633. doi: 10.1177/1077801212453139

American Psychiatric Association. (2013). *Diagnostic and statistical manual of mental disorders DSM-5 Fifth edition.* Washington, D.C.: Author.

Anderson, M., Gillig, P., Sitaker, M., McCloskey, K., Malloy, K., & Grigsby, N. (2003). "Why doesn't she just leave?": A descriptive study of victim reported impediments to her safety. *Journal of Family Violence, 18*(3), 151–155. doi: 10.1023/a:1023564404773

Araji, S. (2012). Domestic violence, contested custody, and the courts: A review of findings from five studies with accompanying documentary. *Sociological Perspectives, 55*(1), 3–15.

Araz, C., Selim, H., & Ozkarahan, I. (2007). A fuzzy multi-objective covering-based vehicle location model for emergency services. *Computers & Operations Research, 34*(3), 705–726. doi: 10.1016/j.cor.2005.03.021

Archer, J. (2000). Sex differences in aggression between heterosexual partners: A meta-analytic review. *Psychological Bulletin, 126*, 651–680.

Arquette, M., Cole, M., Cook, K., LaFrance, B., Peters, M., Ransom, J., . . . Stairs, A. (2002). Holistic risk-based environmental decision making: A Native perspective. *Environmental Health Perspectives, 110*(Suppl 2), 259–264.

Ascione, F. R. (1998). Battered women's reports of their partners' and their children's cruelty to animals. *Journal of Emotional Abuse, 1*(1), 119–133.

Ascione, F. R., Weber, C. V., & Wood, D. S. (1997a). The abuse of animals and domestic violence: A national survey of shelters for women who are abused. *Society and Animals, 5*(3), 205–218.

Ascione, F. R., Weber, C. V., & Wood, D. S. (1997b). *Animal welfare and domestic violence: Final report.* Logan, Utah: Geraldine R. Dodge Foundation.

Bajtelsmit, V., & Bernasek, A. (1996). Why do women invest differently than men? *Financial Counseling and Planning, 7*, 1–10.

Baker, E. H., Sanchez, L. A., Nock, S. L., & Wright, J. D. (2009). Covenant marriage and the sanctification of gendered marital roles. *Journal of Family Issues, 30*(2), 147–178. doi: 10.1177/0192513x08324109

Banyard, V., & Graham-Bermann, S. (1993). Can women cope: A gender analysis of theories of coping with stress. *Psychology of Women Quarterly, 17*(3), 303–318.

Barrett, B. J., & St. Pierre, M. (2011). Variations in women's help seeking in response to intimate partner violence: Findings from a Canadian population-based study. *Violence Against Women, 17*(1), 47–70. doi: 10.1177/1077801210394273

Belknap, J., Melton, H. C., Denney, J. T., Fleury-Steiner, R. E., & Sullivan, C. M. (2009). The levels and roles of social and institutional support reported by survivors of intimate partner abuse. *Feminist Criminology, 4*(4), 377–402. doi: 10.1177/1557085109344942

Bell, M., Goodman, L., & Dutton, M. (2007). The dynamics of staying and leaving: Implications for battered women's emotional well-being and experiences of violence at the end of a year. *Journal of Family Violence, 22*(6), 413–428. doi: 10.1007/s10896-007-9096-9

Bible, A. (2011). *Issues to consider when facilitating groups with battered women in jail or prison.* Philadelphia, PA: National Clearinghouse for the Defense of Battered Women.

Bies, W., & Zacharia, L. (2007). Medical tourism: Outsourcing surgery. *Mathematical and Computer Modelling, 46*(7–8), 1144–1159. doi: 10.1016/j.mcm.2007.03.027

Black, M., Basile, K., Breiding, M., Smith, S., Walters, M., Merrick, M.,…Stevens, M. (2011). *The National Intimate and Sexual Violence Survey: 2010 Summary Report.* Atlanta, GA: Centers for Disease Control and Prevention.

Bland, R. C., Newman, S. C., & Orn, H. (1997). Help-seeking for psychiatric disorders. *Canadian Journal of Psychiatry, 42*(9), 935–942.

Bloom, S. (2010). Organizational stress as a barrier to trauma-informed service delivery. In M. Becker & B. Levin (Eds.), *A public health perspective of women's mental health* (pp. 295–311). New York: Springer.

Blumberg, S. J., & Luke, J. V. (2010). *Wireless substitution: Early release of estimates from the National Health Interview Survey, July–December 2009.* Atlanta, GA: National Center for Health Statistics.

Bostock, J., Plumpton, M., & Pratt, R. (2009). Domestic violence against women: Understanding social processes and women's experiences. *Journal of Community & Applied Social Psychology, 19*(2), 95–110. doi: 10.1002/casp.985

Brabeck, K. M., & Guzmán, M. R. (2008). Frequency and perceived effectiveness of strategies to survive abuse employed by battered Mexican-origin women. *Violence Against Women, 14*(11), 1274–1294. doi: 10.1177/1077801208325087

Braun, C., Stangler, T., Narveson, J., & Pettingell, S. (2009). Animal-assisted therapy as a pain relief intervention for children. *Complementary Therapies in Clinical Practice, 15*(2), 105–109. doi: 10.1016/j.ctcp.2009.02.008

Brooks, J., Hair, E., & Zaslow, M. (2001). *Welfare reform's impact on adolescents: Early warning signs.* Washington, D.C.: Child Trends.

Brown, L. S. (2010). *Feminist therapy.* Washington, D.C.: American Psychological Association.

Browne, A. (1989). *When battered women kill.* New York: Free Press.

Browne, A., Saloman, A., & Bassuk, S. S. (1999). The impact of recent partner violence on poor women's capacity to maintain work. *Violence Against Women, 5*(4), 393–426.

Browne, A., Salomon, A., & Bassuk, S. (1999). The impact of recent partner violence on poor women's capacity to maintain work. *Violence Against Women, 5*(4), 393–426.

Bryan, P. E. (1999). Women's freedom to contract at divorce: A mask for contextual coercion. *Buffalo Law Review, 47*(3), 1153–1273.

Buel, S. (1999). Fifty obstacles to leaving, a.k.a., why abuse victims stay. *The Colorado Lawyer, 28*(10), 19–28.

Bui, H. N. (2003). Help-seeking behavior among abused immigrant women. *Violence against Women, 9*(2), 207–239.

Burke, J. G., Mahoney, P., Gielen, A., McDonnell, K. A., & O'Campo, P. (2009). Defining appropriate stages of change for intimate partner violence survivors. *Violence and Victims, 24*(1), 36–51. doi: 10.1891/0886-6708.24.1.36

Burkitt, K. H., & Larkin, G. L. (2008). The Transtheoretical Model in intimate partner violence victimization: Stage changes over time. *Violence and Victims, 23*(4), 411–431. doi: 10.1891/0886-6708.23.4.411

Cammarota, J. (2011). Blindsided by the avatar: White saviors and allies out of Hollywood and in education. *Review of Education, Pedagogy, and Cultural Studies, 33*(3), 242–259. doi: 10.1080/10714413.2011.585287

Campbell, J. C. (2001). Safety planning based on lethality assessment for partners of batterers in intervention programs. *Journal of Aggression, Maltreatment & Trauma, 5*(2), 129–143. doi: 10.1300/J146v05n02_08

Campbell, J. C. (2005). Danger assessment. Retrieved May 13, 2009, from http://www.dangerassessment.org/WebApplication1/pages/da/

Campbell, J. C., Glass, N., Sharps, P., Laughon, K., & Bloom, T. (2007). Intimate partner homicide: Review and implications for research and policy. *Trauma, Violence and Abuse, 8*(3), 246–269.

Campbell, J. C., Rose, L., Kub, J., & Nedd, D. (1998). Voices of strength and resistance. *Journal of Interpersonal Violence, 13*(6), 743–762. doi: 10.1177/088626098013006005

Carlisle-Frank, P., Frank, J. M., & Nielsen, L. (2004). Selective battering of the family pet. *Anthrozoös, 17*(1), 26–42.

Carrns, A. (2012, January 18). Those incredible shrinking savings account rates, *New York Times*. Retrieved from http://bucks.blogs.nytimes.com/2012/01/18/those-incredible-shrinking-savings-account-rates/

Cascardi, M., & Vivian, D. (1995). Context for specific episodes of marital violence: Gender and severity of violence differences. *Journal of Family Violence, 10*(3), 265–293.

Cattaneo, L. B., DeLoveh, H. L. M., & Zweig, J. M. (2008). Sexual assault within intimate partner violence: Impact on helpseeking in a national sample. *Journal of Prevention & Intervention in the Community, 36*(1-2), 137–153. doi: 10.1080/10852350802022415

Cattaneo, L. B., Stuewig, J., Goodman, L. A., Kaltman, S., & Dutton, M. A. (2007). Longitudinal helpseeking patterns among victims of intimate partner violence: The relationship between legal and extralegal services. *American Journal of Orthopsychiatry, 77*(3), 467–477. doi: 10.1037/0002-9432.77.3.467

Cavanagh, K. (2003). Understanding women's responses to domestic violence. *Qualitative Social Work, 2*(3), 229–249.

Cavanagh, K., Dobash, R. E., Dobash, R. P., & Lewis, R. (2001). "Remedial work": Men's strategic responses to their violence against intimate female partners. *Sociology, 35*(3), 695–714. doi: 10.1177/s0038038501000359

Center for Substance Abuse Treatment. (2000). *Improving substance abuse treatment: The national treatment plan initiative.* Washington, D.C.: U.S. Department of Health and Human Services.

Chang, J. C., Dado, D., Hawker, L., Cluss, P. A., Buranosky, R., Slagel, L., ... Scholle, S. H. (2010). Understanding turning points in intimate partner violence: Factors and circumstances leading women victims toward change. *Journal of Women's Health (15409996)*, *19*(2), 251–259. doi: 10.1089/jwh.2009.1568

Chen, Y.-W., Wang, C.-H., & Lin, S.-J. (2008). A multi-objective geographic information system for route selection of nuclear waste transport. *Omega*, *36*(3), 363–372. doi: 10.1016/j.omega.2006.04.018

Clark, K. A., Biddle, A. K., & Martin, S. L. (2002). A cost-benefit analysis of the Violence Against Women Act of 1994. *Violence Against Women*, *8*(4), 417–428. doi: 10.1177/10778010222183143

Cougle, J., Resnick, H., & Kilpatrick, D. (2013). Factors associated with chronicity in posttraumatic stress disorder: A prospective analysis of a national sample of women. *Psychological Trauma*, *5*(1), 43–49.

Crenshaw, K. (1991). Mapping the margins: Intersectionality, identity politics, and violence against women of color. *Stanford Law Review*, *43*(6), 1241–1299.

Crocker, J. (1999). Social stigma and self-esteem: Situational construction of self-worth. *Journal of Experimental Social Psychology*, *5*, 89–107.

Cromwell, P., Olson, J., & D'Aunn, W. (1991). How residential burglars choose targets: An ethnographic analysis. *Security Journal*, *2*(4), 195–199.

Crowley, D., & Selvadurai, N. (2009). Foursquare. New York, NY. Retrieved, June 22, 2013, from https://foursquare.com/

Cruz, J. M. (2003). "Why doesn't he just leave?": Gay male domestic violence and the reasons victims stay. *Journal of Men's Studies*, *11*(3), 309–323.

Cuevas, C., Finkelhor, D., Turner, H., & Ormrod, R. (2007). Juvenile delinquency and victimization: A theoretical typology. *Journal of Interpersonal Violence*, *22*(12), 1581–1602.

Davies, J. (2008). *When battered women stay....advocacy beyond leaving*. Harrisburg, PA: National Resource Center on Domestic Violence.

Davies, J. (2009). *Advocacy beyond leaving: Helping battered women in contact with current or former partners*. San Francisco, CA: Family Violence Prevention Fund.

Davies, J., Lyon, E., & Monti-Catania, D. (1998). *Safety planning with battered women: Complex lives/difficult choices*. Thousand Oaks, CA: Sage.

Davis, D. (2006). *Battered black women and welfare reform: Between a rock and a hard place*. Albany, NY: SUNY Press.

Davis, R. E. (2002). "The strongest women": Exploration of the inner resources of abused women. *Qualitative Health Research*, *12*(9), 1248–1263.

DeBoer, K. M., Rowe, L. S., Frousakis, N. N., Dimidjian, S., & Christensen, A. (2012). Couples excluded from a therapy trial due to intimate partner violence: Subsequent treatment-seeking and occurrence of IPV. *Psychology of Violence*, *2*(1), 28–39. doi: 10.1037/a0026175

DeCourcey, M., Russell, A. C., & Keister, K. J. (2010). Animal-assisted therapy: Evaluation and implementation of a complementary therapy to improve the psychological and physiological health of critically ill patients. *Dimensions of Critical Care Nursing*, *29*(5), 211–214 210.1097/DCC.1090b1013e3181e1096c1071a.

Donnelly, D. A., Cook, K. J., & Wilson, L. A. (1999). Provision and exclusion: The dual face of services to battered women in three Deep South states. *Violence Against Women*, *5*(7), 710–741.

Doss, B., Simpson, L., & Christensen, A. (2004). Why do couples seek marital therapy? *Professional Psychology: Research and Practice*, *35*, 608–614.

Downs, W. R., Rindels, B., & Atkinson, C. (2007). Women's use of physical and nonphysical self-defense strategies during incidents of partner violence. *Violence Against Women, 13*(1), 28–45. doi: 10.1177/1077801206294807

Dragiewicz, M. (2011). *Equality with a vengeance: Men's rights groups, battered women, and antifeminist backlash.* Boston: Northeastern University Press.

Drown, D. (1986). *Attributions for violence in relationships: Do battered women blame themselves?* (Psy.D.), Virginia Consortium in Clinical Psychology. Unpublished dissertation.

Dunham, K., & Senn, C. Y. (2000). Minimizing negative experiences - Women's disclosure of partner abuse. *Journal of Interpersonal Violence, 15*(3), 251–261.

Durfee, A., & Messing, J. T. (2012). Characteristics related to protection order use among victims of intimate partner violence. *Violence Against Women, 18*(6), 701–710. doi: 10.1177/1077801212454256

Dutton, D. G. (1995). *The domestic assault of women: Psychological and criminal justice perspectives.* Vancouver, Canada: UBC Press.

Dutton, M. A., Ammar, N., Orloff, L., & Terrell, D. (2007). *Use and outcomes of protection orders by battered immigrant women.* Washington, D.C.: U.S. Department of Justice.

Edleson, J. L. (1999). The overlap between child maltreatment and woman battering. *Violence Against Women, 5*(2), 134–154.

Edwards, R. R., Moric, M., Husfeldt, B., Buvanendran, A., & Ivankovich, O. (2005). Ethnic similarities and differences in the chronic pain experience: A comparison of African American, Hispanic, and White Patients. *Pain Medicine, 6*(1), 88–98. doi: 10.1111/j.1526-4637.2005.05007.x

Ehrensaft, M. K., & Vivian, D. (1996). Spouses' reasons for not reporting existing marital aggression as a marital problem. *Journal of Family Psychology, 10*(4), 443–453. doi: 10.1037/0893-3200.10.4.443

El-Khoury, M., Dutton, M. A., Goodman, L., Engel, L., Belamaric, R., & Murphy, M. (2004). Ethnic differences in battered women's formal help-seeking strategies: A focus on health, mental health, and spirituality. *Cultural Diversity and Ethnic Minority Psychology, 10*(4), 383–393.

Embrey, L., & Fox, J. (1997). Gender differences in the investment decision-making process. *Financial Counseling and Planning, 8*(2), 33–40.

Eurostat. (2013). Housing statistics: Statistics explained. Retrieved January 19, 2013, from http://epp.eurostat.ec.europa.eu/statistics_explained/index.php/Housing_statistics#Main_tables

Farley, M. (2008). *Just love: A framework for Christian sexual ethics.* New York: Continuum.

Farr, K. A. (2002). Battered women who were "being killed and survived it": Straight talk from survivors. *Violence and Victims, 17*(3), 267–281.

Faver, C. A., & Strand, E. B. (2003). To leave or to stay? Battered women's concern for vulnerable pets. *Journal of Interpersonal Violence, 18*(12), 1367–1377.

FBI. (2011). Crime in the United States 2010: Uniform crime reports. Retrieved February 1, 2012, from http://www.fbi.gov/about-us/cjis/ucr/crime-in-the-u.s/2010/crime-in-the-u.s.-2010/persons-arrested

Feder, L., & Henning, K. (2005). A comparison of male and female dually arrested domestic violence offenders. *Violence and Victims, 20*(2), 153–171. doi: 10.1891/0886-6708.2005.20.2.153

Feder, L., & Wilson, D. B. (2005). A meta-analytic review of court-mandated batterer intervention programs: Can courts affect abusers' behavior? *Journal of Experimental Criminology, 1*(2), 239–262. doi: 10.1007/s11292-005-1179-0

Felson, R. B., & Messner, S. F. (2000). The control motive in intimate partner violence. *Social Psychology Quarterly, 63*(1), 86–94.

Fields, J. (2003). *Children's living arrangements and characteristics: March 2002.* Washington, D.C.: U.S. Census Bureau.

Finkelhor, D., Ormrod, R., Turner, H., & Hamby, S. (2011). School, police, and medical authority involvement with children who have experienced victimization. *Archives of Pediatric and Adolescent Medicine, 165*(1), 9–15. doi: 10.1001/archpediatrics.2010.240

Finkelhor, D., Turner, H., Ormrod, R., & Hamby, S. (2009). Violence, abuse and crime exposure in a national sample of children and youth. *Pediatrics, 124*, 1411–1423.

Finn, M. A., & Bettis, P. (2006). Punitive action or gentle persuasion. *Violence Against Women, 12*(3), 268–287. doi: 10.1177/1077801206286218

Flynn, C. P. (2000). Woman's best friend: Pet abuse and the role of companion animals in the lives of battered women. *Violence Against Women, 6*(2), 162–177.

Folkman, S., & Lazarus, R. S. (1991). Coping and emotion. In A. Monat & R. Lazarus (Eds.), *Stress and Coping: An anthology* (3rd ed., pp. 208–227). New York: Columbia University Press.

Follingstad, D. R., Hause, E. S., Rutledge, L. L., & Polek, D. S. (1992). Effects of battered women's early responses on later abuse patterns. *Violence and Victims, 7*(2), 109–128.

Follingstad, D. R., Rutledge, L. L., Berg, B. J., Hause, E. S., & Polek, D. S. (1990). The role of emotional abuse in physically abusive relationships. *Journal of Family Violence, 5*(2), 107–120. doi: 10.1007/bf00978514

Follingstad, D. R., Wright, S., Lloyd, S., & Sebastian, J. A. (1991). Sex differences in motivations and effects in dating violence. *Family Relations, 40*, 51–57.

Fomby, P., & Sennott, C. (2009). Family structure instability and residential and school mobility: The consequences for adolescents' behavior. Bowling Green, OH: National Center for Family & Marriage Research, Bowling Green State University.

Forte, T., Cohen, M., Du Mont, J., Hyman, I., & Romans, S. (2005). Psychological and physical sequelae of intimate partner violence among women with limitations in their activities of daily living. *Archives of Women's Mental Health, 8*, 248–256.

Foshee, V., Bauman, K. E., Helms, R. W., Koch, G. G., & Linder, G. F. (1998). An evaluation of Safe Dates, an adolescent dating violence prevention program. *American Journal of Public Health, 88*, 45–50.

Fowler, D. N., Faulkner, M., Learman, J., & Runnels, R. (2011). The influence of spirituality on service utilization and satisfaction for women residing in a domestic violence shelter. *Violence Against Women, 17*(10), 1244–1259. doi: 10.1177/1077801211424480

Fox, J., & Zawitz, M. W. (2010). Homicide trends in the U.S.: Intimate homicide. Retrieved March 11, 2012, from http://www.ojp.usdoj.gov/bjs/homicide/intimates.htm

Foynes, M. M., & Freyd, J. J. (2011). The impact of skills training on responses to the disclosure of mistreatment. *Psychology of Violence, 1*(1), 66–77. doi: 10.1037/a0022021

Friedmann, E., Thomas, S. A., & Son, H. (2011). Pets, depression and long-term survival in community living patients following myocardial infarction. *Anthrozoos: A Multidisciplinary Journal of The Interactions of People & Animals, 24*(3), 273–285. doi: 10.2752/175303711x13045914865268

Frye, V., Haviland, M., & Rajah, V. (2007). Dual arrest and other unintended consequences of mandatory arrest in New York City: A brief report. *Journal of Family Violence, 22*, 397–405.

Garfield, G. (2005). *Knowing what we know: African American women's experience of violence and violation.* Piscataway, NJ: Rutgers University Press.

Gayford, J. J. (1976). Ten types of battered wives. *Welfare Officer, 25*, 5–9.

Geoffroy, M.-C., Côté, S., Parent, S., & Séguin, J. R. (2006). Daycare attendance, stress, and mental health. *The Canadian Journal of Psychiatry 51*, 607–615.

Gillioz, L., De Puy, J., & Ducret, V. (1997). *Domination et violence envers la femme dans le couple*. Lausanne, Switzerland: Editions Payot Lausanne.

Gillum, T., Sullivan, C., & Bybee, D. (2006). The importance of spirituality in the lives of domestic violence survivors. *Violence Against Women, 12*(3), 240–250.

Glass, N., Eden, K. B., Bloom, T., & Perrin, N. (2010). Computerized aid improves safety decision process for survivors of intimate partner violence. *Journal of Interpersonal Violence, 25*(11), 1947–1964. doi: 10.1177/0886260509354508

Goetting, A. (1999). *Getting out: Life stories of women who left abusive men*. New York: Columbia University Press.

Goffman, E. (1963). *Stigma: Notes on the management of a spoiled identity*. Englewood Cliffs, NJ: Prentice Hall.

Goldfarb, S. F. (2008). Reconceiving civil protection orders for domestic violence: Can law help end the abuse without ending the relationship. *Cardozo Law Review, 29*(4), 1487–1551.

Gomes, C. F. S., Nunes, K. R. A., Helena Xavier, L., Cardoso, R., & Valle, R. (2008). Multicriteria decision making applied to waste recycling in Brazil. *Omega, 36*(3), 395–404. doi: 10.1016/j.omega.2006.07.009

Gondolf, E. W. (2011). The weak evidence for batterer program alternatives. *Aggression and Violent Behavior, 16*(4), 347–353. doi: 10.1016/j.avb.2011.04.011

Gondolf, E. W. (2012). *The future of batterer programs: Reassessing evidence-based practice*. Boston, MA: Northeastern University Press.

Gondolf, E. W., & Fisher, E. (1988). *Battered women as survivors: An alternative to treating learned helplessness*. Lexington, MA: D.C. Heath.

Goodman, L., Dutton, M. A., Weinfurt, K., & Cook, S. (2003). The Intimate Partner Violence Strategies Index. *Violence Against Women, 9*(2), 163–186. doi: 10.1177/1077801202239004

Goodman, L., & Epstein, D. (2008). *Listening to battered women: A survivor-centered approach to advocacy, mental health, and justice*. Washington, D.C.: American Psychological Association.

Goodman, L., Smyth, K. F., Borges, A. M., & Singer, R. (2009). When crises collide: How intimate partner violence and poverty intersect to shape women's mental health and coping. *Trauma, Violence, & Abuse, 10*(4), 306–329. doi: 10.1177/1524838009339754

Goodmark, L. (2012). *A troubled marriage: Domestic violence and the legal system*. New York: New York University Press.

Graham, D. L. R., Rawlings, E. I., & Rigsby, R. K. (1994). *Loving to survive: Sexual terror, men's violence, and women's lives*. New York: New York University Press.

Grinstein-Weiss, M., Hun Yeo, Y., Zhan, M., & Charles, P. (2008). Asset holding and net worth among households with children: Differences by household type. *Children and Youth Services Review, 30*(1), 62–78. doi: 10.1016/j.childyouth.2007.06.005

Hage, S. M. (2006). Profiles of women survivors: The development of agency in abusive relationships. *Journal of Counseling and Development, 84*(1), 83–94.

Haight, W., Shim, W., Linn, L., & Swinford, L. (2007). Mothers' strategies for protecting children from batterers: The perspectives of battered women involved in child protective services. *Child Welfare, 86*(4), 41–62.

Hajkowicz, S. (2008). Rethinking the economist's evaluation toolkit in light of sustainability policy. *Sustainability: Science, Practice, & Policy, 4*(1), 17–24.

Hamby, S. (2000). The importance of community in a feminist analysis of domestic violence among American Indians. *American Journal of Community Psychology, 28*(5), 649–669.

Hamby, S. (2004). Sexual victimization in Indian country: Barriers and resources for native women seeking help. Retrieved October 5, 2005, from http://www.vawnet.org/SexualViolence/Research/VAWnetDocuments/AR_SVIndianCountry.pdf

Hamby, S. (2005). Measuring gender differences in partner violence: Implications from research on other forms of violent and socially undesirable behavior. *Sex Roles-Special Issue: Understanding Gender and Intimate Partner Violence, 52*(11/12), 725–742.

Hamby, S. (2006). The who, what, when, where, and how of partner violence prevention research. *Journal of Aggression, Maltreatment, & Trauma, 13*(3/4), 179–201.

Hamby, S. (2008). The path of helpseeking: Perceptions of law enforcement among American Indian victims of sexual assault. *Journal of Prevention and Intervention in the Community, 36*(1-2), 89–104.

Hamby, S. (2009a). The gender debate on intimate partner violence: Solutions and dead ends. *Psychological Trauma, 1*(1), 24–34.

Hamby, S. (2009b). Walking with American Indian victims of sexual assault: A review of legal obstacles and legal resources affecting crime victims in Indian Country. *Family & Intimate Partner Violence Quarterly, 1*(4), 293–305.

Hamby, S. (2011). The second wave of violence scholarship: Integrating and broadening theories of violence. *Psychology of Violence, 1*(3), 163–165.

Hamby, S. (2012). Introducing an invited panel to identify the best biolence research of 2011. *Psychology of Violence, 2*(3), 227–228.

Hamby, S. (2013a, March). *The Partner Cyberabuse Questionnaire: Preliminary psychometrics of technology-based intimate partner violence.* Paper presented at the Southeastern Psychological Association Conference, Atlanta, GA.

Hamby, S. (2013b). *The VIGOR studies: Pilot tests of the Victim Inventory of Goals, Options, and Risks.* Sewanee, TN: Life Paths Research Program.

Hamby, S., & Clark, S. (2011). *Beyond rope ladders & padlocks: A new approach to safety planning.* Paper presented at the Ending Domestic & Sexual Violence: Innovations in Practice & Research Conference, Portsmouth, NH.

Hamby, S., Clark, S., Dashiell, C., Ferrell, E., Lambert, C., Logan, L., ... Rolfe, M. (2011). *Sewanee Cyberbullying Survey--Intimate Partner Version.* The University of the South. Sewanee, TN.

Hamby, S., & Cook, S. (2011). Assessing violence against women in practice settings: Processes and tools practitioners can use. In J. Edleson, C. Renzetti & R. Bergen (Eds.), *Sourcebook on violence against women* (pp. 49–71). Thousand Oaks, CA: Sage.

Hamby, S., Finkelhor, D., & Turner, H. (in press). Perpetrator & victim gender patterns for 21 forms of youth victimization in the National Survey of Children's Exposure to Violence. *Violence & Victims.*

Hamby, S., Finkelhor, D., Turner, H., & Ormrod, R. (2010). The overlap of witnessing partner violence with child maltreatment and other victimizations in a nationally representative survey of youth. *Child Abuse and Neglect, 34,* 734–741.

Hamby, S., Finkelhor, D., Turner, H., & Ormrod, R. (2011). *Children's exposure to intimate partner violence and other family violence (NCJ232272).* Washington, D.C.: U.S. Department of Justice.

Hamby, S., & Gray-Little, B. (1997). Responses to partner violence: Moving away from deficit models. *Journal of Family Psychology, 11,* 339–350.

Hamby, S., & Gray-Little, B. (2000). Labeling partner violence: When do victims differentiate among acts? *Violence and Victims, 15*(2), 173–186.

Hamby, S., & Gray-Little, B. (2007). Can battered women cope? A critical analysis of research on women's responses to violence. In K. Kendall-Tackett & S. Giacomoni (Eds.), *Intimate partner violence* (pp. 1–19). Kingston, NJ: Civic Research Institute.

Hamby, S., & Grych, J. (2013). *The web of violence: Exploring connections among forms of interpersonal violence and abuse* Dordrecht, The Netherlands: Springer.

Hamby, S., Nix, K., De Puy, J., & Monnier, S. (2012). Adapting dating violence prevention to Francophone Switzerland: A story of intra-Western cultural differences. *Violence and Victims, 27*(1), 33–42. doi: 10.1891/0886-6708.27.1.33

Hamby, S., & Turner, H. (in press). Measuring teen dating violence in males and females: Insights from NatSCEV, the National Survey of Children's Exposure to Violence. *Psychology of Violence.*

Hanson, T. L., McLanahan, S. S., & Thomson, E. (1998). Windows on divorce: Before and after. *Social Science Research, 27*(3), 329–349. doi: 10.1006/ssre.1998.0625

Hardesty, J. L., & Chung, G. H. (2006). Intimate partner violence, parental divorce, and child custody: Directions for intervention and future research. *Family Relations, 55*(2), 200–210. doi: 10.1111/j.1741-3729.2006.00370.x

Harned, M. (2001). Abused women or abused men? An examination of the context and outcomes of dating violence. *Violence and Victims, 16*(3), 269–285.

Hart, B. (1990). Assessing whether batterers will kill. *Barbara J. Hart's collected writings.* Retrieved May 13, 2009, from http://www.mincava.umn.edu/documents/hart/hart.html#id2376223

Hart, B., & Stuehling, J. (1992). *Personalized safety plan.* Reading, PA: Pennsylvania Coalition Against Domestic Violence.

Hartsock, S. (1998). *The feminist standpoint revisited and other essays.* Boulder, CO: Westview Press.

Hassouneh-Phillips, D. (2001). "Marriage is half of faith and the rest is fear Allah": Marriage and spousal abuse among American Muslims. *Violence against Women, 7*(8), 927–946.

Hassouneh-Phillips, D. (2003). Strength and vulnerability: Spirituality in abused American Muslim women's lives. *Issues in Mental Health Nursing, 24,* 681–694.

Haynes, L., Service, O., Goldacre, B., & Torgerson, D. (2012). *Test, learn, adapt: Developing public policy with randomised controlled trials.* London, UK: Cabinet Office.

Hemenway, D., Shinoda-Tagawa, T., & Miller, M. (2002). Firearm availability and female homicide victimization rates among 25 populous high-income countries. *Journal of American Medical Women's Association, 57,* 100–104.

Herek, G., & Capitanio, J. (1996). "Some of my best friends": Intergroup contact, concealable stigma, and heterosexual's attitudes towards gay men and lesbians. *Personality and Social Psychology Bulletin, 22*(4), 412–424.

Hill Collins, P. (1998a). It's all in the family: Intersections of gender, race, and nation. *Hypatia, 13*(3), 62–82. doi: 10.2307/3810699

Hill Collins, P. (1998b). The tie that binds: Race, gender and US violence. *Ethnic and Racial Studies, 21*(5), 917–938. doi: 10.1080/014198798329720

Hirschel, D., & Buzawa, E. (2002). Understanding the context of dual arrest with directions for future research. *Violence Against Women, 8*(12), 1449–1473.

Holden, L. (2008). *Hindu divorce: A legal anthropology.* Hampshire, England: Ashgate Publishing House.

Holt, V., Kernic, M., Lumley, T., Wolf, M., & Rivara, F. (2002). Civil protection orders and risk of subsequent police-reported violence. *JAMA: The Journal of the American Medical Association, 288*(5), 589–594. doi: 10.1001/jama.288.5.589

Holt, V., Kernic, M., Wolf, M., & Rivara, F. (2003). Do protection orders affect the likelihood of future partner violence and injury? *American Journal of Preventive Medicine*, 24(1), 16–21. doi: 10.1016/s0749-3797(02)00576-7

Holtzworth-Munroe, A., Waltz, J., Jacobson, N. S., & Monaco, V. (1992). Recruiting nonviolent men as control subjects for research on marital violence: How easily can it be done? *Violence & Victims*, 7(1), 79–88.

Hornosty, J., & Doherty, D. (2002). *Responding to wife abuse in farm and rural communities: Searching for solutions that work.* Regina, Saskatchewan: Saskatchewan Institute of Public Policy.

hooks, b. (1984/2000). *Feminist theory: From margin to center.* Cambridge, MA: South End Press.

Ishida, J. (2003). The role of social norms in a model of marriage and divorce. *Journal of Economic Behavior & Organization*, 51(1), 131–142. doi: 10.1016/s0167-2681(02)00135-x

Jasinski, J. L. (2001). Physical violence among Anglo, African American, and Hispanic couples: Ethnic differences in persistence and cessation. *Violence Vict*, 16(5), 479–490.

Javdani, S., Allen, N. E., Todd, N. R., & Anderson, C. J. (2011). Examining systems change in the response to domestic violence: Innovative applications of multilevel modeling. *Violence Against Women*, 17(3), 359–375. doi: 10.1177/1077801211398621

Jelleyman, T., & Spencer, N. (2008). Residential mobility in childhood and health outcomes: A systematic review. *Journal of Epidemiology and Community Health*, 62(7), 584–592. doi: 10.1136/jech.2007.060103

Jewish Orthodox Feminist Alliance. (2005). *Guide to Jewish divorce and the Beit Din system.* New York: Author.

Jiang, P., & Haimes, Y. Y. (2004). Risk management for Leontief-based interdependent systems. *Risk Analysis*, 24(5), 1215–1229. doi: 10.1111/j.0272-4332.2004.00520.x

Johnson, D. M., & Zlotnick, C. (2007). Utilization of mental health treatment and other services by battered women in shelters. *Psychiatric Services*, 58(12), 1595–1597. doi: 10.1176/appi.ps.58.12.1595

Johnson, H., Ollus, N., & Nevala, S. (2008). *Violence against women: An international perspective.* Dordrecht, The Netherlands: Springer.

Justice & Courage Oversight Panel. (2008). *Safety for all: Identifying and closing the gaps in San Francisco's domestic violence criminal justice response.* San Francisco: Department on the Status of Women, City and County of San Francisco.

Kakavas, Y. (2010). Creepy. Retrieved, June 22, 2013, from http://ilektrojohn.github.com/creepy/

Kalichman, S. C., DiMarco, M., Austin, J., Luke, W., & DiFonzo, K. (2003). Stress, social support, and HIV-status disclosure to family and friends among HIV-positive men and women. *Journal of Behavioral Medicine*, 26(4), 315–332. doi: 10.1023/a:1024252926930

Kalmuss, D., & Straus, M. A. (1990). Wife's marital dependency and wife abuse. In M. A. Straus & R. Gelles (Eds.), *Physical violence in American families* (pp. 369–382). New Brunswick, NJ: Transaction.

Katz, J., Tirone, V., & Schukrafft, M. (2012). Breaking up is hard to do: Psychological entrapment and women's commitment to violent dating relationships. *Violence and Victims*, 27(4), 455–469. doi: 10.1891/0886-6708.27.4.455

Kaufman Kantor, G., & Straus, M. A. (1990). Response of victims and the police to assaults on wives. In M. Straus & R. Gelles (Eds.), *Physical violence in American families: Risk factors and adaptations to violence in 8145 families* (pp. 473–487). New Brunswick, NJ: Transaction.

Kazdin, A. E., & Blase, S. (2011). Rebooting psychotherapy research and practice to reduce the burden of mental illness. *Perspectives on Psychological Science, 6,* 21–37.

Killias, M., Simonin, M., & De Puy, J. (2005). *Violence experienced by women in Switzerland over their lifespan: Results of the International Violence against Women Survey (IVAWS).* Bern, Switzerland: Stämpfli.

Kim, J., & Gray, K. A. (2008). Leave or stay? Battered women's decision after intimate partner violence. *Journal of Interpersonal Violence, 23*(10), 1465–1482. doi: 10.1177/0886260508314307

Kimmel, J. (2008). *How do we spend our time? Recent evidence from the American Time Survey.* Kalamazoo, MI: Upjohn Institute for Employment Research.

Kitzmann, K. M., Gaylord, N., Holt, A., & Kenny, E. (2003). Child witnesses to domestic violence: A meta-analytic review. *Journal of Consulting and Clinical Psychology, 71*(2), 339–352.

Koepsell, J. K., Kernic, M. A., & Holt, V. L. (2006). Factors that influence battered women to leave their abusive relationships. *Violence and Victims, 21*(2), 131–147. doi: 10.1891/088667006780644299

Kopel, D. B., Gallant, P., & Eisen, J. D. (2008). The human right of self-defense. *BYU Journal of Public Law, 22,* 43–178.

Krishnan, S., Hilbert, J., & VanLeeuwen, D. (2001). Domestic violence and help-seeking behaviors among rural women: Results from a shelter-based study. *Family & Community Health, 24*(1), 28–38.

Kropp, P. R., Hart, S. D., Webster, C. D., & Eaves, D. (1995). *Manual for the Spousal Assault Risk Assessment Guide (2nd ed.).* Vancouver, British Columbia: British Columbia Institute on Family Violence.

Kulkarni, S., Bell, H., & Wylie, L. (2010). Why don't they follow through?: Intimate partner survivors' challenges in accessing health and social services. *Family & Community Health, 33*(2), 94–105 110.1097/FCH.1090b1013e3181d59316.

Lacey, K. (2010). When is it enough for me to leave?: Black and Hispanic women's response to violent relationships. *Journal of Family Violence, 25*(7), 669–677. doi: 10.1007/s10896-010-9326-4

Laing, L. (2004). *Risk assessment in domestic violence.* Sydney, Australia: Australian Domestic and Family Violence Clearinghouse.

Lanier, C., & Maume, M. O. (2009). Intimate partner violence and social isolation across the rural/urban divide. *Violence Against Women, 15*(11), 1311–1330. doi: 10.1177/1077801209346711

Lapierre, S. (2010). Striving to be 'good' mothers: Abused women's experiences of mothering. *Child Abuse Review, 19*(5), 342–357. doi: 10.1002/car.1113

Lehmann, P., & Simmons, C. (Eds.). (2009). *Strengths-based batterer intervention: A new paradigm in ending family violence.* New York: Springer.

Leisenring, A. (2011). "Whoa! They could've arrested me!": Unsuccessful identity claims of women during police response to intimate partner violence. *Qualitative Sociology, 34*(2), 353–370. doi: 10.1007/s11133-011-9190-4

Lindhorst, T., & Edleson, J. (2012). *Battered women, their children, and international law: The unintended consequences of the Hague Child Abduction Convention.* Boston, MA: Northeastern University Press.

Lindhorst, T., Macy, R. J., & Nurius, P. (2005). Contextualized assessment with battered women: Strategic safety planning to cope with multiple harms. *Journal of Social Work Education, 41*(2), 331–352.

Lloyd, S. (1997). The effects of domestic violence on women's unemployment. *Law & Policy, 19*(2), 139–167.

Logan, T. K., Stevenson, E., Evans, L., & Leukefeld, C. (2004). Rural and urban women's perceptions of barriers to health, mental health, and criminal justice services: Implications for victim services. *Violence and Victims, 19*(1), 37–62.

LogSat Software LLC. (2011). Family Tracker. Retrieved, June 22, 2013, from http://itunes.apple.com/us/app/family-tracker/id349880412?mt=8

Lonnstrom, D. (2007). *First woman president survey*. Loudonville, NY: Siena Research Institute, Siena College.

Lynn Snow-Turek, A., Norris, M. P., & Tan, G. (1996). Active and passive coping strategies in chronic pain patients. *Pain, 64*(3), 455–462. doi: 10.1016/0304-3959(95)00190-5

Maass, P., & Rajagopalan, M. (2012, July 13). That's no phone. That's my tracker. *New York Times*. Retrieved, June 22, 2013, from http://www.nytimes.com/2012/07/15/sunday-review/thats-not-my-phone-its-my-tracker.html

MacEachen, J. (2003). The community context of domestic violence: The association of pecking order violence with domestic violence. *The Indian Health Service Primary Care Provider, 28*(6), 125–129.

MacKinnon, C. (2005). *Women's lives, men's laws*. Cambridge, MA: Belknap Press.

Macy, R., Nurius, P., & Norris, J. (2006). Responding in their best interests - Contextualizing women's coping with acquaintance sexual aggression. *Violence against Women, 12*(5), 478–500. doi: Doi 10.1177/1077801206288104

Magen, R. H., Conroy, K., Hess, P. M., Panciera, A., & Simon, B. L. (2001). Identifying domestic violence during child abuse and neglect investigations. *Journal of Interpersonal Violence, 16*(6), 580–601.

Mahoney, M. (1991). Legal images of battered women: Redefining the issue of separation. *Michigan Law Review, 90*, 1–94.

Marmot, M. (2005). Social determinants of health inequalities. *The Lancet, 365*, 1099–1104. doi: 10.1016/s0140-6736(05)71146-6

Martin, M. E. (1997). Double your trouble: Dual arrest in family violence. *Journal of Family Violence, 12*(2), 139–157.

Mashhour, A. (2005). Islamic law and gender equality: Could there be a common ground?: A study of divorce and polygamy in Sharia law and contemporary legislation in Tunisia and Egypt. *Human Rights Quarterly, 27*(2), 562–596.

Mathews, B., & Kenny, M. C. (2008). Mandatory reporting legislation in the United States, Canada, and Australia: A cross-jurisdictional review of key features, differences, and issues. *Child Maltreatment, 13*(1), 50–63. doi: 10.1177/1077559507310613

McCloskey, L., Treviso, M., Scionti, T., & dal Pozzo, G. (2002). A comparative study of battered women and their children in Italy and the United States. *Journal of Family Violence, 17*(1), 53–74.

McCollum, E. E. (2012). A different set of choices: Comment on Deboer, Rowe, Frousakis, Dimidjian, and Christensen. *Psychology of Violence, 2*(1), 40–41. doi: 10.1037/a0026571

McDowell, M., Fryar, C., Ogden, C., & Flegal, K. (2008). Anthropometric reference data for children and adults: United States, 2003-2006 (NHSR No 10) *National Health Statistics Reports*. Hyattsville, MD: National Center for Health Statistics.

McFarlane, J., Malecha, A., Gist, J., Watson, K., Batten, E., Hall, I., & Smith, S. (2002). An intervention to increase safety behviaors of abused women: Results of a randomized clinical trial. *Nursing Research, 51*(6), 347–354.

McFarlane, J., Malecha, A., Gist, J., Watson, K., Batten, E., Hall, I., & Smith, S. (2004). Protection orders and intimate partner violence: An 18-Month study of 150 Black, Hispanic, and White Women. *American Journal of Public Health, 94*(4), 613–618.

McIntosh, S. C. (2004). The links between animal abuse and family violence, as reported by women entering shelters in Calgary communities. Retrieved October 12, 2005, from http://www.ucalgary.ca/resolve/files/PETABU.pdf

McLennan, S. (2010). *Jesus was a liberal: Reclaiming Christianity for all.* Hampshire, England: Palgrave MacMillan.

McNulty, J., & Fincham, F. (2012). Beyond positive psychology? Toward a contextual view of psychological processes and well-being. *American Psychologist, 67*(2), 101–110. doi: 10.1037/a0024572

Mendes, E. (2012). *More Americans uninsured in 2011.* Washington, D.C.: Gallup.

Menec, V. H., & Perry, R. P. (1995). Reactions to stigmas. *Journal of Aging and Health, 7*(3), 365–383. doi: 10.1177/089826439500700302

Merritt-Gray, M., & Wuest, J. (1995). Counteracting abuse and breaking free: The process of leaving revealed through women's voices. *Health Care for Women International, 16*(5), 399–412.

Meyer, S. (2010). Seeking help to protect the children?: The influence of children on women's decisions to seek help when experiencing intimate partner violence. *Journal of Family Violence, 25*(8), 713–725. doi: 10.1007/s10896-010-9329-1

Miles, A. (n.d.-a). Qualities of a healthy Christian marriage: A sermon on domestic violence awareness. Retrieved, December 6, 2006, from http://www.teenchallenge.com/socal/index.cfm?domesticviolenceID=1&doc_id=333

Miles, A. (n.d.-b). Qualities of a healthy Christian marriage: A sermon on domestic violence awareness. Retrieved December 6, 2006, from http://www.teenchallenge.com/socal/index.cfm?domesticviolenceID=1&doc_id=333

Miller, C., & Kaiser, C. (2001). A theoretical perspective on coping with stigma. *Journal of Social Issues, 57*(1), 73–92.

Miller, L., Wickramaratne, P., Gameroff, M., Sage, M., Tenke, C., & Weissman, M. (2012). Religiosity and major depression in adults at high risk: A ten-year prospective study. *American Journal of Psychiatry, 169,* 89–94.

Mills, L. (2003). *Insult to injury: Rethinking our responses to intimate abuse.* Princeton, NJ: Princeton University Press.

Mills, T. (1985). The assault on the self: Stages in coping with battering husbands. *Qualitative Sociology, 8*(2), 103–123.

Mitchell, M. D., Hargrove, G. L., Collins, M. H., Thompson, M. P., Reddick, T. L., & Kaslow, N. J. (2006). Coping variables that mediate the relation between intimate partner violence and mental health outcomes among low-income, African American women. *Journal of Clinical Psychology, 62*(12), 1503–1520. doi: 10.1002/jclp.20305

Moffitt, T. E. (1993). Adolescence-limited and life-course-persistent antisocial behavior: A developmental taxonomy. *Psychological Review, 100*(4), 674–701.

Murphy, C. M., Meyer, S., & O'Leary, K. D. (1993). Family of origin violence and MCMI-II psychopathology among partner assaultive men. *Violence and Victims, 8,* 165–176.

Nash, S. T., & Hesterberg, L. (2009). Biblical framings of and responses to spousal violence in the narratives of abused Christian women. *Violence Against Women, 15*(3), 340–361. doi: 10.1177/1077801208330437

National Network to End Domestic Violence. (2012). *Domestic violence counts 2011: A 24-hour census of domestic violence shelters and services.* Washington, D.C.: Author.

Nelson, H., Bougatsos, C., & Blazina, I. (2012). Screening women for intimate partner violence: A systematic review to update the 2004 U.S. Preventive Services Task Force Recommendation. *Annals of Internal Medicine, 156*(11), 1–13.

Noll, J. G., & Grych, J. (2011). Read-React-Respond: An integrative model for understanding sexual revictimization. *Psychology of Violence, 1*(3), 202–215.

Norris, J., Nurius, P., & Dimeff, L. A. (1996). Through her eyes: Factors affecting women's perception of and resistance to acquaintance sexual aggression threat. *Psychology of Women Quarterly, 20*(1), 123–145.

North Carolina Council for Women. (2007). Statistical Bulletin 2006-2007. Retrieved, June 22, 2013, from http://www.doa.state.nc.us/cfw/stats.htm

Novac, S., Brown, J., & Bourbonnais, C. (2009). Transitional housing models in Canada: Options and outcomes. In J. D. Hulchanski, P. Campsie, S. Chau, S. Hwang & E. Paradis (Eds.) (pp. 1–25), *Finding Home: Policy Options for Addressing Homelessness in Canada.* Toronto: University of Toronto.

Nugent-Borakove, M. E., Fanflik, P., Troutman, D., Johnson, N., Burgess, A., & O'Connor, A. (2006). Testing the efficacy of SANE/SART programs: Do they make a difference in sexual assault arrest & prosecution outcomes? (NCJRS No. 214252). Washington, D.C.: National Institutes of Justice.

Nurius, P., Macy, R. J., Nwabuzor, I., & Holt, V. (2011). Intimate partner survivors' help-seeking and protection efforts: A person-oriented analysis. *Journal of Interpersonal Violence, 26*(3), 539–566. doi: 10.1177/0886260510363422

O'Campo, P., McDonnell, K., Gielen, A., Burke, J., & Chen, Y. (2002). Surviving physical and sexual abuse: What helps low-income women? *Science Direct, 46*(3), 205–212.

O'Leary, K. D., Heyman, R. E., & Neidig, P. H. (1999). Treatment of wife abuse: A comparison of gender-specific and conjoint approaches. *Behavior Therapy, 30*(3), 475–505. doi: 10.1016/s0005-7894(99)80021-5

Olds, D. (2006). The Nurse–Family Partnership: An evidence-based preventive intervention. *Infant Mental Health Journal, 27*, 5–25.

Ozawa, M. N., & Lee, Y. (2006). The net worth of female-headed households: A comparison to other types of households. *Family Relations, 55*(1), 132–145. doi: 10.1111/j.1741-3729.2006.00362.x

Paymar, M. (2000). *Violent no more: Helping men end domestic abuse.* Alameda, CA: Hunter House.

Pearson, J., Thoennes, N., & Griswold, E. (1999). Child support and domestic violence: The victims speak out. *Violence Against Women, 5*(4), 427–448.

Pence, E., & Paymar, M. (1993). *Education groups for men who batter: The Duluth model.* New York: Springer.

Perilla, J. L. (1999). Domestic violence as a human rights issue: The case of immigrant Latinos. *Hispanic Journal of Behavioral Sciences, 21*(2), 107–133. doi: 10.1177/0739986399212001

Pew Research Center. (2007). *Fewer mothers prefer full-time work.* Washington, D.C.: Author.

Pew Research Center. (2012). *The global religious landscape: A report on the size and distribution of the world's major religious groups as of 2010.* Washington, D.C.: Author.

Pierce, C. A. (1996). Body height and romantic attraction: A meta-analytic test of the male-taller norm. *Social Behavior and Personality, 24*(2), 143–150.

Planty, M. (2002). *Third-party involvement in violent crime, 1993-1999.* Washington, D.C.: U.S. Department of Justice.

Podolefsky, A., & Dubow, F. (1981). *Strategies for community crime prevention: Collective responses to crime in urban America.* Springfield, IL: Charles C. Thomas.

Postmus, J. (2010). Economic empowerment of domestic violence survivors. Retrieved April 4, 2012, from http://www.vawnet.org

Postmus, J., Plummer, S.-B., McMahon, S., Murshid, N. S., & Kim, M. S. (2012). Understanding economic abuse in the lives of survivors. *Journal of Interpersonal Violence, 27*(3), 411–430. doi: 10.1177/0886260511421669

Potter, H. (2006). An argument for Black feminist criminology: Understanding African American women's experiences with intimate partner abuse using an integrated approach. *Feminist Criminology, 1*(2), 106–124. doi: 10.1177/1557085106286547

Potter, H. (2007). Battered Black women's use of religious services and spirituality for assistance in leaving abusive relationships. *Violence Against Women, 13*(3), 262–284. doi: 10.1177/1077801206297438

Powers, S. K., & Howley, E. T. (1997). *Exercise physiology: Theory and application to fitness and performance* (3rd ed.). Dubuque, IA: Brown & Benchmark.

Prochaska, J., & DiClemente, C. (1983). Stages and processes of self-change of smoking: Toward an integrative model of change. *Journal of Consulting and Clinical Psychology, 51,* 390–395.

Quillian, L. (2010). Blueprint for disaster: The unraveling of Chicago public housing. *Contemporary Sociology: A Journal of Reviews, 39*(4), 456–457. doi: 10.1177/0094306110373238y

Rabenhorst, M. M., Thomsen, C. J., Milner, J. S., Foster, R. E., Linkh, D. J., & Copeland, C. W. (2012). Spouse abuse and combat-related deployments in active duty Air Force couples. *Psychology of Violence, 2*(3), 273–284. doi: 10.1037/a0027094

Radford, L., & Hester, M. (2006). *Mothering through domestic violence.* London: Jessica Kingsley Publishers.

Randall, M. (2004). Domestic violence and the construction of "ideal victims": Assaulted women's "image problems" in law. *St. Louis University Public Law Review, 23,* 107–186.

Rennison, C. M., & Welchans, S. (2000). *Intimate partner violence.* Washington, D.C.: Bureau of Justice Statistics.

Renzetti, C. (1992). *Violent betrayal: Partner abuse in lesbian relationships.* Newbury Park, CA: Sage.

Renzetti, C. (2009). *Economic stress and domestic violence.* Harrisburg, PA: VAWnet: National Online Resource Center on Domestic Violence.

Retina Software Private Limited. (2006). ePhone Tracker: Stealth phone spy software. Retrieved, June 22, 2013, from http://spousespysoftware.com/

Rhatigan, D. L., Street, A. E., & Axsom, D. K. (2006). A critical review of theories to explain violent relationship termination: Implications for research and intervention. *Clinical Psychology Review, 26*(3), 321–345. doi: http://dx.doi.org/10.1016/j.cpr.2005.09.002

Rhodes, K., Drum, M., Anliker, E., Frankel, R., Howes, D., & Levinson, W. (2006). Lowering the threshold for discussions of domestic violence: A randomized controlled trial of computer screening. *Archives of Internal Medicine, 166*(10), 1107–1114. doi: 10.1001/archinte.166.10.1107

Richie, B. (1996). *Compelled to crime: The gender entrapment of battered Black women.* New York: Routledge.

Riemsma, R. P., Pattenden, J., Bridle, C., Sowden, A. J., Mather, L., Watt, I. S., & Walker, A. (2003). Systematic review of the effectiveness of stage-based interventions to promote smoking cessation. *BMJ, 326,* 1175–1177.

Ritchie, A. J. (2006). Law enforcement violence against women of color. In Incite! Women of Color Against Violence (Ed.), *Color of violence: The Incite! anthology* (pp. 138–156). Cambridge, MA: South End Press.

Roberts, J. C., Wolfer, L., & Mele, M. (2008). Why victims of intimate partner violence withdraw protection orders. *Journal of Family Violence, 23*, 369–375.

Rodriguez, E., Lasch, K. E., Chandra, P., & Lee, J. (2001). Family violence, employment status, welfare benefits, and alcohol in the United States: What is the relation? *Journal Epidemiology & Community Health, 55*, 172–178.

Roehl, J., & Guertin, K. (2000). Intimate partner violence: The current use of risk assessments in sentencing offenders. *The Justice System Journal, 21*(2), 171–197.

Rosenstiel, A. K., & Keefe, F. J. (1983). The use of coping strategies in chronic low back pain patients: Relationship to patient characteristics and current adjustment. *Pain, 17*, 33–44.

Rounsaville, B. J. (1978). Theories in marital violence: Evidence from a study of battered women. *Victimology, 3*, 11–31.

Rusbult, C. E., & Martz, J. M. (1995). Remaining in an abusive relationship: An investment model analysis of nonvoluntary dependence. *Personality and Social Psychology Bulletin, 21*(6), 558–571.

Sacks, S., & Ries, R. (2005). Substance abuse treatment for persons with co-occurring disorders (SMA 05-3922). Rockville, MD: Substance Abuse and Mental Health Services Administration.

Salmivalli, C., & Nieminen, E. (2002). Proactive and reactive aggression among school bullies, victims, and bully-victims. *Aggressive Behavior, 28*(1), 30–44.

Sanders, C. K. (2010). Savings outcomes of an IDA program for survivors of domestic violence. St. Louis, MO: Center for Social Development, Washington University in St. Louis.

Sanders, C. K., Weaver, T. L., & Schnabel, M. (2007). Economic education for battered women. *Affilia, 22*(3), 240–254. doi: 10.1177/0886109907302261

Saunders, D. G. (1986). When battered women use violence: Husband abuse or self-defense? *Violence and Victims, 1*(1), 47–60.

Saunders, D. G. (1994). Posttraumatic stress symptom profiles of battered women: A comparison of survivors in two settings. *Violence and Victims, 9*(1), 31–44.

Schechter, S., & Edleson, J. L. (1999). *Effective intervention in domestic violence and child maltreatment: Guidelines for policy and practice.* Reno, NV: National Council of Juvenile and Family Court Judges.

Senturia, K., Sullivan, M., Cixke, S., & Shiu-Thorton, S. (2000, November 15). Cultural issues affecting domestic violence service utilization in ethnic and hard to reach populations. Retrieved February 15, 2004, from http://www.ncjrs.org/pdffiles1/nij/grants/185357.pdf

Shannon, L., Logan, T., & Cole, J. (2007). Intimate partner violence, relationship status, and protective orders. *Journal of Interpersonal Violence, 22*(9), 1114–1129. doi: 10.1177/0886260507302880

Shepard, M. F., & Pence, E. L. (Eds.). (1999). *Coordinating community responses to domestic violence: Lessons from Duluth and beyond.* Thousand Oaks, CA: Sage.

Shorey, R. C., Meltzer, C., & Cornelius, T. L. (2010). Motivations for self-defensive aggression in dating relationships. *Violence and Victims, 25*(5), 662–676. doi: 10.1891/0886-6708.25.5.662

Simpson, L. E., Doss, B. D., Wheeler, J., & Christensen, A. (2007). Relationship violence among couples seeking therapy: Common couple violence or battering? *Journal of Marital and Family Therapy, 33*(2), 270–283. doi: 10.1111/j.1752-0606.2007.00021.x

Sirotkin, J. N., & Fecko, C. M. (2008). A case study in post-*Nicholson* litigation. *American Bar Association Commission on Domestic Violence eNewsletter, 12*(Fall).

Smyth, K. F., Goodman, L., & Glenn, C. (2006). The full-frame approach: A new response to marginalized women left behind by specialized services. *American Journal of Orthopsychiatry, 76*(4), 489–502. doi: 10.1037/0002-9432.76.4.489

Sorenson, S. B., & Wiebe, D. J. (2004). Weapons in the lives of battered women. *American Journal of Public Health, 94*(8), 1412–1417.

Stein, A. (2012). Engendered self-states: Dissociated affect, social discourse, and the forfeiture of agency in battered women. *Psychoanalytic Psychology, 29*(1), 34–58. doi: 10.1037/a0024880

Stith, S., & McCollum, E. E. (2011). Conjoint treatment of couples who have experienced intimate partner violence. *Aggression and Violent Behavior, 16*(4), 312–318. doi: 10.1016/j.avb.2011.04.012

Stith, S., Rosen, K. H., McCollum, E. E., & Thomsen, C. J. (2004). Treating intimate partner violence within intact couple relationships: Outcomes of multi-couple versus individual couple therapy. *Journal of Marital and Family Therapy, 30*(3), 305–318.

Straus, M. A., & Gelles, R. J. (1990). *Physical violence in American families: Risk factors and adaptations to violence in 8,145 families.* New Brunswick, NJ: Transaction Publishers.

Straus, M. A., Hamby, S., Boney-McCoy, S., & Sugarman, D. (1996). The Revised Conflict Tactics Scales (CTS2): Development and preliminary psychometric data. *Journal of Family Issues, 17*(3), 283–316.

Strube, M. J., & Barbour, L. S. (1983). The decision to leave an abusive relationship: Economic dependence and psychological commitment. *Journal of Marriage and the Family, 45*(4), 785–793.

Strube, M. J., & Barbour, L. S. (1984). Factors related to the decision to leave an abusive relationship. *Journal of Marriage and the Family, 46*, 837–844.

Stuart, G. L., Moore, T. M., Hellmuth, J. C., Ramsey, S. E., & Kahler, C. W. (2006). Reasons for intimate partner violence perpetration among arrested women. *Violence Against Women, 12*(7), 609–621. doi: 10.1177/1077801206290173

Sue, D. W., Capodilupo, C. M., Torino, G. C., Bucceri, J. M., Holder, A. M. B., Nadal, K. L., & Esquilin, M. (2007). Racial microaggressions in everyday life: Implications for clinical practice. *American Psychologist, 62*(4), 271–286. doi: 10.1037/0003-066X.62.4.271

Sullivan, T. P., Schroeder, J. A., Dudley, D. N., & Dixon, J. M. (2010). Do differing types of victimization and coping strategies influence the type of social reactions experienced by current victims of intimate partner violence? *Violence Against Women, 16*(6), 638–657. doi: 10.1177/1077801210370027

Sutton, S. (2001). Back to the drawing board? A review of applications of the transtheoretical model of substance use. *Addictions, 96*, 175–186.

Swanberg, J. E., Macke, C., & Logan, T. K. (2006). Intimate partner violence, women, and work: Coping on the job. *Violence and Victims, 21*(5), 561–578. doi: 10.1891/0886-6708.21.5.561

Taft, C. T., Resick, P. A., Panuzio, J., Vogt, D. S., & Mechanic, M. B. (2007). Examining the correlates of engagement and disengagement coping among help-seeking battered women. *Violence & Victims, 22*(1), 3–17.

Taylor, B., Stein, N., Woods, D., & Mumford, E. (2011). *Shifting boundaries: Final report on an experimental evaluation of a youth dating violence prevention program in New York City middle schools (No 236175)*. Washington, D.C.: U.S. Department of Justice.

The ESEMeD MHEDEA investigators, Alonso, J., Angermeyer, M. C., Bernert, S., Bruffaerts, R., Brugha, T. S.,... Vollebergh, W. A. M. (2004). Use of mental health services in Europe: Results from the European Study of the Epidemiology of Mental Disorders (ESEMeD) project. *Acta Psychiatrica Scandinavica, 109*, 47–54. doi: 10.1111/j.1600-0047.2004.00330.x

Thornton, R. S. (2009). *Inclusive Christianity: A progressive look at faith*. Pasadena, CA: Hope Publishing House.

Tiwari, A., Fong, D. Y. T., Wong, J. Y. H., Yuen, K.-h., Yuk, H., Pang, P.,... Bullock, L. (2012). Safety-promoting behaviors of community-dwelling abused Chinese women after an advocacy intervention: A randomized controlled trial. *International Journal of Nursing Studies, 49*(6), 645–655. doi: http://dx.doi.org/10.1016/j.ijnurstu.2011.12.005

Tjaden, P., & Thoennes, N. (1998). *Prevalence, incidence, and consequences of violence against women: Findings from the National Violence Against Women Survey* (pp. 1–15). Washington, D.C.: U.S. Department of Justice.

Tjaden, P., & Thoennes, N. (2000a). *Extent, nature, and consequences of intimate partner violence: Findings from the National Violence Against Women Survey*. Washington, D.C.: National Institutes of Justice.

Tjaden, P., & Thoennes, N. (2000b). Prevalence and consequences of male-to-female and female-to-male intimate partner violence as measured by the National Violence Against Women Survey. *Violence Against Women, 6*(2), 142–161.

Tjaden, P., & Thoennes, N. (2006). *Extent, nature, and consequences of rape victimization: Findings from the National Violence Against Women Survey*. Washington, D.C.: National Institutes of Justice.

Trotter, J. L., & Allen, N. E. (2009). The good, the bad, and the ugly: Domestic violence survivors' experiences with their informal social networks. *American Journal of Community Psychology, 43*, 221–231.

Truman, J. (2011). *Criminal victimization, 2010*. Washington, D.C.: U.S. Department of Justice.

Turner, H., Finkelhor, D., Ormrod, R., Hamby, S., Leeb, R., Mercy, J., & Holt, M. (2012). Family context, victimization, and child trauma symptoms: Variations in safe stable and nurturing relationships during early and middle childhood. *American Journal of Orthopsychiatry, 82*(2), 209–219.

Tutu, D. (1999). *No future without forgiveness*. New York, NY: Doubleday.

U.S. Census Bureau. (2012). American Housing Survey: 2011 detailed tables. Retrieved January 19, 2013, from http://www.census.gov/newsroom/releases/archives/housing/cb12-tps75.html

Vandell, D. L., Belsky, J., Burchinal, M., Steinberg, L., Vandergrift, N., & Network, N. E. C. C. R. (2010). Do effects of early child care extend to age 15 years? Results from the NICHD study of early child care and youth development. *Child Development, 81*(3), 737–756. doi: 10.1111/j.1467-8624.2010.01431.x

Villalon, R. (2010). *Violence against Latina immigrants: Citizenship, inequality, and community*. New York: NYU Press.

Viner, R. M., & Taylor, B. (2005). Adult health and social outcomes of children who have been in public care: Population-based study. *Pediatrics, 115*(4), 894–899. doi: 10.1542/peds.2004-1311

Walby, S., & Allen, J. (2004). *Domestic violence, sexual assault and stalking: Findings from the British Crime Survey*. London: Home Office Research, Development and Statistics Directorate.

Walker, L. E. (1979). *The battered woman*. New York: Harper & Row.

Walker, L. E. (1984). *The battered woman syndrome*. New York: Springer.

Walker, L. E. (1993). The battered woman syndrome is a psychological consequence of abuse. In R. Gelles & D. Loseke (Eds.), *Current controversies on family violence* (pp. 133–153). Newbury Park, CA: Sage Publications.

Waller, M., & Patterson, S. (2002). Natural helping and resilience in a Diné (Navajo) community. *Families in Society, 83*(1), 73–84.

Wang, C. (1992). Culture, meaning, and disability: Injury prevention campaigns and the production of stigma. *Social Science & Medicine, 5*(9), 1093–1102.

Wang, C. (1998). Portraying stigmatized conditions: Disabling images in public health. *Journal of Health Communication, 3*(2), 149–159.

Wang, P., Lane, M., Olfson, M., Pincus, H. A., Wells, K. B., & Kessler, R. C. (2005). Twelve-month use of mental health services in the United States: Results from the national comorbidity survey replication. *Archives of General Psychiatry, 62*(6), 629–640. doi: 10.1001/archpsyc.62.6.629

Websdale, N. (2000). Lethality assessment tools: A critical analysis. Retrieved May 14, 2009, from http://www.vawnet.org/Assoc_Files_VAWnet/AR_lethality.pdf

Weintraub, S. R., & Goodman, L. (2010). Working with and for: Student advocates' experience of relationship-centered advocacy with low-income women. *American Journal of Orthopsychiatry, 80*(1), 46–60. doi: 10.1111/j.1939-0025.2010.01006.x

Werner-Wilson, R. J., Zimmerman, T. S., & Whalen, D. (2000). Resilient response to battering. *Contemporary Family Therapy, 22*(2), 161–188.

West, R. (2005). Time for a change: Putting the Transtheoretical (Stages of Change) Model to rest. *Addictions, 100,* 1036–1039.

Widom, C., Czaja, S., & Dutton, M. A. (2008). Childhood victimization and lifetime revictimization. *Child Abuse and Neglect, 32,* 785–796.

Wittebrood, K., & Nieuwbeerta, P. (2000). Criminal victimization during one's life course: The effects of previous victimization and patterns of routine activities. *Journal of Research in Crime and Delinquency, 37*(1), 91–122.

WomensLaw.org. (2011). Know the laws: Tennessee state gun laws. Retrieved July 18, 2012, from http://www.womenslaw.org/laws_state_type.php?id=301&state_code=TN&open_id=750#content-5424

Wright, C. V., & Johnson, D. M. (2009). Correlates for legal help-seeking: Contextual factors for battered women in shelter. *Violence & Victims, 24*(6), 771–785. doi: 10.1891/0886-6708.24.6.771

Yick, A. (2008). A metasynthesis of qualitative findings on the role of spirituality and religiosity among culturally diverse domestic violence survivors. *Qualitative Health Research, 18*(9), 1289–1306.

Yoshihama, M. (2002). Battered women's coping strategies and psychological distress: Differences by immigration status. *American Journal of Community Psychology, 30*(3), 429–452.

Yount, K. (2011). Women's conformity as resistance to intimate partner violence in Assiut, Egypt. *Sex Roles, 64*(1), 43–58. doi: 10.1007/s11199-010-9884-1

Zanville, H., & Cattaneo, L. (2012). The nature of risk and its relationship to coping among survivors of intimate partner violence. *Psychology of Violence, 2*(4), 355–367.